THE NICOLSON INSTITUTE

THE HISTORY OF AN ISLAND SCHOOL

by Iain Smith
with Joan Forrest

THE NICOLSON INSTITUTE

THE HISTORY OF AN ISLAND SCHOOL

by Iain Smith
with Joan Forrest

Edited by Dr Frances Murray

"As a former pupil I welcome this history of a school that means so much to many. It is an informative and meticulously researched history of an island school that has been the springboard for the many islanders who went on to make their mark on the world. In addition, the book also reflects the increasing involvement of the school in the wider life of its community, especially in the development of Gaelic Medium Education. A fitting tribute to the Nicolson Institute as it celebrates its 150th anniversary."
Professor Matthew Maciver, former Chief Executive of the General Teaching Council

"The Nicolson Institute has played an important role in my life from the time I went there at age 12. After university I returned as a teacher and from there went to work in the Education Department, where interaction with the Nicolson, as our largest school, was a key part of my work. I feel very privileged to have had the opportunity to be part of it in all these roles and to have made lifelong friends along the way. I feel a deep sense of gratitude to Iain Smith for having devoted so much time and effort to bringing us this tremendous work. It will have a very appreciative and interested readership that will enjoy having memories refreshed as well as having background information as to how the school developed and how it responded positively to changing educational and community requirements."
Catherine Dunn, former teacher of Gaelic and English and
former Director of Education, Comhairle nan Eilean Siar

"From the Gibsons, from their eminent position in the town and the island, that sense of opportunity is never neglected... I cannot think of any such insight as is presented here into the conversation between Highland parents and their adult child still within Scotland."
Professor Lindsay Paterson, University of Edinburgh

"Honestly, I have not read very many histories of particular schools, or even parts of such histories, but I have never found myself reading one that was as good as this. It gets off to an interesting start which I imagine quite a few do, and then it keeps on being interesting right up to the present day."
Professor Tom Bone, former Principal, Jordanhill College and
former Deputy Principal, University of Strathclyde

"Hugely impressive research into a fascinating piece of educational history."
Graham Donaldson, former HMSCI and Honorary Professor, University of Glasgow

Contents

Introduction 7

Acknowledgements 8

Notes on Style 11

Chapter 1. How It All Began 13

Chapter 2. The Nicolson Family Legacy 25

Chapter 3. The Nicolson Institution 37

Chapter 4. Developing Secondary Education 52

Chapter 5. Under the Guidance of W.J. Gibson 61

Chapter 6. Into the 20th Century 73

Chapter 7. The Great War Years 91

Chapter 8. The Final Gibson Years 102

Chapter 9. Into the 1930s 129

Chapter 10. The Nicolson, World War II and its Aftermath 147

Chapter 11. Post-war Nicolson, 1945-1968 159

Chapter 12. Into the 1970s and the School's Centenary 179

Chapter 13. The Last Decade of the 20th Century 229

Chapter 14. Into the 21st Century 242

Appendices

   1. Rectors and Head Teachers of The Nicolson Institute 285

   2. Duxes of The Nicolson Institute 285

   3. School Captains of The Nicolson Institute 288

   4. A History of the Hostels 290

   5. Junior Comprehensive Schools, 1972 293

   6. The Original Pupils of The Nicolson Institute, 27th February 1873 294

   7. Vignettes 297

Endnotes 300

Introduction

Some years ago, when I was doing a modest book promotion in Glasgow, I was approached by Malcolm Nicolson, a professor at the University of Glasgow. He explained that his father Angus, when a teacher in The Nicolson Institute in the early 1970s had, with help from school students, produced a draft history of the school which he had hoped might be published in 1973 to celebrate the Centenary of the school. That hope had not been realised, but he had retained his late father's manuscript. What should he do with it?

After some investigation, my recommendation to Malcolm was unambiguous: if you want it to be placed somewhere which is secure but has public access, put it in Tasglann nan Eilean (the Archive of the Isles). He did so and from there a draft typescript was produced.

Tasglann nan Eilean was a suitable place for other important reasons; for one, it held multiple copies of the 50th anniversary history of The Nicolson Institute, written by the then Rector W.J. Gibson in 1924 and drawn on by Angus in his draft centenary history.

Further, Tasglann nan Eilean was also the home of the correspondence between Gibson (who was Head and then Rector of The Nicolson Institute from 1894 to 1925), his wife and their daughter Jane, who was a student at the University of Aberdeen. They corresponded regularly between 1916 and 1925. Their letters, and those to Gibson from former Nicolson students at war, paint a picture of the impact of the Great War on individuals and on the school; of illnesses and epidemics; and of social changes in the town of Stornoway and rural Lewis, most notably poverty and consequent migration in the early 1920s.

These three sources- Angus Nicolson's manuscript, the 1924 history, and the Gibson correspondence- combined to form the foundations of a history of the school, marking its 150th Anniversary in 2023.

Angus Nicolson's history (compiled with the help of his team of school student researchers) was never fully published. Now their story can be told at last.

Our grateful thanks to Professor Malcolm Nicolson for putting his father's work in the public domain.

All royalties from the book will go to The Nicolson Institute Trust.

Iain Smith
Glasgow, 2023

Acknowledgements

The following are thanked for their contributions (variously, sourcing, transcribing, scanning, critiquing, writing and editing) to the resulting book: Kate Adams, Jan Bissett, John Brown, Ceitidh Chalmers, Tom Clark, Dr Graham Connelly, Maggie Cunningham, George Cuthill, Bronagh Dallat, Professor Sir Tom Devine, Lorna Dougall, Catriona Dunn, Sherry Ferdman, Joan Forrest, Richard Fraser, Ken Galloway, Janice Hithell, Anne Hughes, Cara Loughran, the late Professor Jim McCall, Dawn Macdonald, Seonaid McDonald, Professor Matthew Maciver, Margaret Maciver, Dr Ruairidh Maciver, the late Ian Maclennan, Murdo MacLennan, Annie MacSween, Margaret Martin, Sandy Matheson, Ann Mennie, Ian Minty, Dr Frances Murray, Professor Malcolm Nicolson, Vivienne Parish, Professor Lindsay Paterson, Margaret Robertson, Professor Alasdair Smith, Iain Smith, Jonathan Smith and Malcolm Smith. The contributions of the late Angus Nicolson and Edward Young are gratefully acknowledged.

Special thanks must go to Ken Galloway of the Stornoway Historical Society, to Tom Clark and to Seonaid McDonald *(Seònaid NicDhòmhnaill) (Archivist/Tasglannaiche)* for their steadfast helpfulness.

Other Acknowledgements

    Faculty of Humanities and Social Sciences, University of Strathclyde
    Glasgow University archivists
    Aberdeen University archivists
    Mitchell Library archivists
    Museum nan Eilean/Tasglann nan Eilean archives
    Stornoway Historical Society

Material Sources

The book includes extracts from the following material sources, woven together to produce a living account of the emergence and development of The Nicolson Institute, with resultant varying styles and views. The material sources are indicated throughout:

The Nicolson Institute school magazines, notably those of 1973 and 1999
Logbooks of The Nicolson Institute, courtesy of Tasglann nan Eilean

The unpublished manuscript by Angus Nicolson and school students*
(see, in particular, Chapters 1-6; 9-11)

Edited chapters of Saints and Sinners by Iain Smith with Joan Forrest

History of The Nicolson Institute by W.J. Gibson (1924)**

Commissioned original contributions *(acknowledged as appropriate in the text)*

Materials retrieved from the archives of The Stornoway Gazette and Back in the Day

Materials from the Stornoway Historical Society and Tasglann nan Eilean *(see Chapters 7 and 8 for the Gibson correspondence)*

Minutes of the Stornoway Parish School Board, courtesy of Western Isles Libraries, Stornoway and Tasglann nan Eilean

The Publisher is grateful to the following for providing funding towards the costs of the book:

    Roinn an Fhoghlaim, Comhairle nan Eilean Siar
    Sgioba na Gàidhlig, Comhairle nan Eilean Siar
    Horshader Community Development Trust
    The McCaig Trust
    The Nicolson Institute
    Point and Sandwick Trust
    Urras Oighreachd Ghabhsainn

The Publisher is grateful to the following for permission to use photographs:

    Leila Angus
    John Mackinnon
    Malcolm Macleod
    Malcolm Smith
    Multi-media Unit, Comhairle nan Eilean Siar
    Scottish Daily Express
    Scottish Field
    Stornoway Historical Society
    Tasglann nan Eilean
    The Nicolson Institute

---

* *Tasglann nan Eilean archive Ref No GB3002 GD061/1 Manuscript history of The Nicolson Institute by Angus Nicolson and groups of school students*

** *Museum nan Eilean Ref No 1992.50.6 Gibson, W.J. (1925). The Nicolson Institute, Stornoway: a record of the school, 1873-1924. Stornoway*

Notes on Style

Dates are written as follows: 21st March 1920.

Numbers under 21 are written in full.

The designation 'head teacher' is written as two words and capitalised when referring to a specific person. 'Trustee' and 'Inspector' are similarly capitalised when referring to a particular person.

Designations of school year groups differ according to era: Class VI in 1930; S6 in 2020.

Extracts are reproduced as in the original unless clarity demands otherwise.

Footnotes are referenced using cardinal numerals and endnotes are referenced using roman numerals.

Common acronyms appear unpunctuated (e.g. HRH, LLB, MA, MP, SNP, USA, YMCA)

Educational acronyms which appear in the text (also unpunctuated):

CfE: Curriculum for Excellence

EIS: The Educational Institute of Scotland

GME/GM: Gaelic Medium Education/Gaelic Medium

HMI (HMIE): Her/His Majesty's Inspectorate (of Education)

HORSA: Hutting Operation for the Raising of the School-leaving Age

IDL: Inter-Disciplinary Learning

SED: Scottish Education Department

SQA: Scottish Qualifications Authority

RME: Religious and Moral Education

ROSLA: Raising of the School-leaving Age

TVEI: Technical and Vocational Education Initiative

YPI: Youth and Philanthropy Initiative

Chapter 1:
How It All Began

February 2023 marked the 150th anniversary of the founding of a new school in Stornoway: the Nicolson Public School. Although it was not named as an Institute until 1901, The Nicolson Institute, as it is now called, can stretch its roots back as far as 1865, when a young businessman died in Shanghai, bequeathing a considerable sum of money to a charity school in his native town of Stornoway.

An image of the school, circa 1900 (courtesy Tasglann nan Eilean)

The Nicolson Institute in the present day

'An Institution is the lengthened shadow of one man'[i]

Alexander Morison Nicolson was born in 1832, the fifth child in a family of seven sons, to Roderick Nicolson, a fish curer of Bayhead Street in Stornoway.

Alexander Morison Nicolson

On completing his apprenticeship in shipbuilding, he had made his way to the Far East where he flourished and, in due course, acquired the joint partnership of a substantial foundry and shipbuilding business in Shanghai. In 1865, at the age of 33, he was tragically killed in a boiler explosion on board one of his own vessels.

Nicolson's papers contained requests for the disposal of his estate of £5,672, one third of which was to be donated:

> *to the most approved charitable institution in my native town for the education and rearing of destitute children in the hope that I may be the indirect means of rendering some assistance to the children of some of my oldest acquaintance.*

The bequest amounted to £1,898 (about £250,000 at current prices), and his brothers Roderick and Angus were left to decide on the best use to which this sum should be put. Stornoway, at that time, had four schools.

By 1870, Roderick and Angus had determined that Mackay's School (see page 20) qualified as *'the most approved charitable Institution'* and paid into its bank the sum of £1,898. The school building, however, was deemed to be unsuitable and it was agreed that a new school and teacher's house should be erected out of the available funds. Sir James Matheson[1] gave a site for the new school on Sandwick Road and an endowment in perpetuity of £35 per annum (just over £4000 per annum at current prices) to supplement the teacher's salary.

*Painting of James Matheson by Sir Daniel Macnee
(Museum & Tasglann nan Eilean Collections)*

In 1905, the two surviving Nicolson Brothers, Roderick and Kenneth, installed a clock and chimes in the school tower, a memorial to their brother Alexander. To mark the occasion the brothers wrote this letter to the then Chairman of the Stornoway School Board, highlighting the school's achievements so far and their vision for the future:

> *… your very prosperity as an educational institution would seem to threaten you with serious embarrassment… you have increased your classrooms; you have enlarged your buildings and playgrounds to receive the incoming flow and still the cry is 'more room'.*

---

1   A benefactor of extraordinary wealth of the most dubious origins.

Your teaching staff is now not inferior to that of the great educational establishments in the land. It now numbers over a score of carefully selected and highly efficient teachers, by whom every branch of a high class education is taught, enabling your pupils [to go] direct into the classrooms of the great universities of England and Scotland, and even into their professional staff; and the whole of this work is supervised by your admirable Rector, Mr Gibson, to whose wisdom and energy are very much due the very high standing of your Institute in the education world; and as an inevitable result your pupils are daily spreading out into the world before them to push their fortune in more favoured lands.

They are... to be found... not only in the home kingdom but in all the distant colonies and dependencies of the Empire, where we are assured many of them, very many of them, hold positions of trust and honour, and most of whom we may assume in the absence of training at your Institute would now in all likelihood be found leisurely resting at their native homes and contentedly engaged in the humble pursuits of their fathers....

Hitherto, Stornoway... may be still better known as the great centre for the higher education[2] of the Western Isles.

... how much more than amply have the hopes of its youthful founder been fulfilled as he modestly but nobly expressed them – 'In the hope that I may thus benefit the children of some of my early school companions.'

Angus Nicolson (no relation), some 70 years later in researching the first hundred years of history of The Nicolson Institute, commented:

The letter sums up, perhaps more than anything else, the spirit and dedication of many who had seen the school through its years of crisis and trial, through the threat of closure in its early beginnings. A tradition was born whose flame burned more brightly as the years passed. The close-knit friendship which had been engendered among those who had laboured to keep this flame alight bred a fellowship among those who became associated with it.

---

2   A familiar term then for what we would now call secondary education.

This heritage is reflected in the regard in which it is held, not only in Stornoway but throughout Lewis; not only in educational and other circles throughout the British Isles but even in wider spheres through the ties it wrought among its former pupils who followed in the path of the Nicolson brothers to seek greater opportunities in far-flung and widely separated countries... When they foregather, thoughts of home and school form a bond of kinship brought about by another exile in Shanghai so many years before.

Plaques on the clock tower commemorating the contribution of Alexander Nicolson

Education in Lewis, Prior to 1873

The credit for the large and wide-scale advancement of education, especially leading up to the early and middle 19th century, must go mainly to church authorities; notably for Lewis via the Edinburgh Society for the Support of Gaelic Schools (founded 1811), Christian societies and private individuals.

In 1824, the Church of Scotland set up a permanent Education Committee. In the next forty years there were 200 'Assembly Schools.' After the Disruption of 1843, a major religious fissure resulting in the creation of the Free Church of Scotland, the only schoolmaster to remain in the Established Church of Scotland in Lewis was the Master of the Stornoway Parish Church School. The newly created Free Church made a great effort to place education within the reach of all the children within its denomination. Their number of schools increased in Lewis until there were twelve in 1867.[ii]

After a period of comparative prosperity, extreme poverty was experienced in Lewis following the failure of the potato harvests in the 1840s and 1850s after Sir James Nicolas Sutherland Matheson had bought the island in 1844 for £190,000 (£22m at current prices).[iii] He took on himself the task of relieving the widespread starvation by providing work, supplying meal and potatoes, and helping over 2000 islanders to find a better life by emigrating to Canada.[iv] He also promoted various schemes: peat reclamation, road building, brick works, the building of a slipway, a pier, gas works, chemical works, and educational facilities for poor and needy children, at a cost of nearly £12,000 (approximately £1.5m at current prices) for the latter by subsidising schools and augmenting teachers' salaries.

Both the General Assembly School and the Free Church School were well conducted and employed certificated masters. The church schools placed great emphasis on religious instruction, some insisting that two afternoons a week be devoted to it; and church attendance on Sunday was compulsory. Censors and informants were used to enforce discipline. Those considered guilty of gross misdemeanour were excluded as a lesson to the others. This over-emphasis on religion was gradually relaxed. The Parish Church School became empty of scholars and the building was sold to Sir James Matheson. It lay within the Parish Church grounds opposite where the Stornoway Drill Hall still stands. (Initially it was the only school falling under the jurisdiction of the School Board which came into existence with the Education (Scotland) Act 1872.)

In 1847, Lady Jane Matheson, wife of Sir James Matheson, founded the Female Industrial School at the corner of Keith Street and Scotland Street at a cost of more than £2,000 (about £200,000 at current prices). It was attended *'by girls of the poorer classes'* who received not only tuition in the elementary branches of learning, but also instruction in millinery, needlecraft, and laundry work.

Word of the Female Industrial School spread far and wide, even making the pages of the Sydney Morning Herald on 1st July 1857, albeit in a somewhat condescending tone:

> And now to conclude with a very different matter, Sir James Matheson's doings in his Hebridean domain. The education of the female aborigines of the Lewis goes on prosperously. Instead of forty or fifty little ragged semi-savages attending occasionally at their own pleasure, there are now 120 regular scholars; clean and neatly clothed girls, of quite refined appearance, and much school-industry. This reform in externals, which has been accomplished by Lady Matheson, assisted by some ladies of Stornoway and the neighbourhood, has given a new tone to peasant society in the Ultima Thule; and cleanliness, neatness, and tidiness are the order of the day.—*Chambers.*

The Sydney Morning Herald, *1st July 1857 (National Library of Australia)*

The site of Lady Matheson's Seminary

However, as Lady Matheson began to take an increasing interest in its welfare, with one or more weekly visits by the pupils to the Lews Castle, it became an educational establishment for the more genteel young ladies of the town, where they learned social graces as well as the fundamental essentials of learning. It remained open until 1906 when its closure placed a heavy burden on The Nicolson Institute, already suffering from a lack of accommodation. The building has recently been restored by the Hebridean Housing Partnership.

The other school founded by the Mathesons was 'Mackay's School,' eventually located in a building owned by Sir James on the corner of Keith Street and James Street.

John Mackay, who had been born in Smith's Lane (now New Street), was the best known and probably the most gifted headmaster in Stornoway at this time. Not only did he teach the subjects common to such schools at the time, but he became best remembered for his teaching on Nautical subjects, whose terms were precisely learned by rote. The rules governing conduct, nautical custom and ship routine in all its many forms, whether in calm, fog or storm, were rigidly taught. Sea-love became second nature to his pupils from his vast store of nautical knowledge. During the winter evenings he taught, sometimes in Gaelic, a class in seamanship. A small man, stooped with downcast eyes as if in constant thought, and seldom seen without his huge book on navigation, he inspired such a great deal of loyalty amongst his pupils that several years after his death his former scholars and friends collected a considerable sum of money and erected a handsome granite tombstone over his grave where he lies with the rest of his kinsfolk. The inscription sums up the regard in which he was held:

> *In Memory of John Mackay who died 4th Jany (sic) 1879, aged 70. A Christian patriot, forty years a zealous loving and devoted teacher in Stornoway, educating many gratuitously in the chief branches of useful knowledge, especially in the Science of Navigation.*

His grave is near the Nicolson family burial place, overlooking Sandwick beach where he took his pupils, many of whom were later to become sea-captains, to learn the use of the sextant and how to take bearings. Many came to see him after long sea voyages. Annie Macaulay Jamieson, the wife of a sea captain, wrote of him with deep feeling and affection:

Headstone to John Mackay in Sandwick Cemetery

This Good man's step was slow, never hasty. There was never lack of footsteps on threshold of the little schoolhouse with its air of unaffected repose when these lads of the sea came home from distant journeyings their hearts would turn to the gentle little man who knew so much. With feeling hearts, they marked his last resting place. They talked still of their old friend and the old days and long past years with the depth of interest and affection that proves at least their hearts have undergone no change. His work had not been in vain.

The balance from the money raised for his tombstone, which amounted to £10 from the money collected, was handed over to the School Board to provide a medal for Science which would include Mathematics and, if possible, Navigation. Among the prize winners of this medal were three who were to devote almost a lifetime of teaching in the service of The Nicolson Institute: Mr John Macrae, who was to succeed Mr Gibson as Rector; Mr Roderick Macrae, who became Principal Teacher of Science; and Miss Maggie Stewart, who for many years was First Lady Assistant. It was also won by Miss Jane Gibson, daughter of the first Nicolson Institute Rector.[3] Many years later the prize was renewed by a Mr John Mackay Shaw of Florida at the express wish of his late mother, a niece of John Mackay, as a prize for excellence in Mathematics.

In the 1860s, a Royal Commission of Inquiry investigated educational provision in Scotland. One of the areas studied was Lewis, under a Sheriff Nicolson, a Gaelic speaker, and a man of diverse talents. His account of the conditions of educational facilities in Lewis was issued in 1865. Of the 3,332 children on the school rolls only 2,647 attended. A further 2,500 were not even enrolled at any school. Some of the schools were comparatively satisfactory, but others were in a lamentable condition and could only be classified as hovels. The range of subjects taught was narrow and inadequate, although a surprising amount of advanced learning was given. Several recommendations were made by the Commission, the most important of which were that a central authority should be set up, and a well-organised educational system established, with the building of many schools and teachers' dwellings and with the use of certificated teachers, adequately paid and qualifying for pensions.

The Commission also recommended that 'High Schools,' which would bring pupils to university entrance standard, should be set up in the more densely populated areas.

However, that took many years to happen.

The Education Act of 1872

With the introduction of the Education (Scotland) Act 1872, education was seen to be a matter of great national concern which could no longer be left largely to various voluntary authorities, often with conflicting views. But many of these authorities resented handing over the schools under their control to the secular authorities and the charging of fees was an issue.

---

[3] The medal now lodged with Tasglann nan Eilean.

This, however, they found eventually inevitable due to financial difficulties. By and large, only Roman Catholic and (most) 'endowed' schools stayed outside the new system.

The school boards, set up under the 1872 Act, were given extensive powers under a central body to enforce the Act's provisions. Members were appointed by the local parish ratepayers on a three-yearly term, which was a much more democratic approach to school management than pre-1872. The boards qualified for government grants and could borrow money for capital expenditure, making them much more independent and (generally) free of financial embarrassment. Only certificated teachers could be employed as head teachers.

The School Board of Stornoway was established in 1873. Prior to 1872, parishes could establish schools, but they were not obliged to do so. Both the Gaelic Society of Scotland and the Society in Scotland for Propagating Christian Knowledge were active in the Western Isles, setting up temporary or travelling schools.

From 1872, the state assumed responsibility for education. The Stornoway School Board was established, answerable to the UK-wide Board of Education and later (from 1885) to the Scotch (sic) Education Department. The following schools fell under Stornoway Parish School Board: Aird, Back, Bayble, Knock, Laxdale, Nicolson Institution[4]/Nicolson Public School/The Nicolson Institute, Sandwickhill, Tolsta and Tong.

The Board consisted of elected members and was responsible for providing education for all children in the area, funded by a parliamentary grant and local rates. School attendance was compulsory up to the age of thirteen, except in cases of illness or where the school was more than three miles from home. Fees were payable, but, if the parents were unable to pay, the Stornoway Parochial Board or Parish Council met the cost from poor relief; elementary school fees were abolished in 1890. The Board was also responsible for the medical inspection of children.

With the coming of (largely) free, universal and compulsory education, there was a vast improvement in the school buildings, school equipment, and in the range of the curriculum, but there was also a loss. The schools were no longer identified with the life of the community; they came from outside as it were, instead of springing up from within. Over a long period of years thereafter they tended to absorb more and more urban ideas, to be increasingly narrowly academic and aggressively English.

---

4   Years of controversy, however, passed before the Stornoway School Board eventually took over control of The Nicolson Institution.

The 1872 Act made no provision for Gaelic-Medium Education. One of the authors of this volume went to school in 1952 in an overwhelmingly Gaelic-speaking community. One of his infant classmates was bilingual. All the others were monolingual Gaelic speakers. In Primary 1, they were taught exclusively in English. Seventy years later, this has moved on.

This century of educational development also saw many changes in the social life of the people and in their economic progress. This was the case despite the fact that changes calculated to contribute to the educational improvement of the people were sometimes resisted in the quiet, passive way that was most difficult to overcome.

Many of the older people shrewdly foresaw that the educational advantages being presented to their children meant the break-up of their homes and the loss of their sons and daughters. Previously, many had known the wrench of their children leaving them as a result of the exercise of arbitrary power, callously employed. Now, once again, their forebodings were confirmed by the event. The price had to be paid. The individuals concerned nearly always gained; the community lost.

Thus, paradoxically, education could be spoken of along with economics as a contributory factor in the depopulation of the island. The fact remained that education provided a means of escape from a thoroughly dire economic situation.

In summary, the two great landmarks that benefited educational provision in Lewis, as in the rest of Scotland, were the Disruption of 1843 and the Education Act of 1872. The scene was set for Alexander Nicolson's bequest to make its mark on educational provision in the island.

Chapter 2:
The Nicolson Family Legacy

Sons of an affluent Stornoway merchant, the six Nicolson brothers contributed, in varying degrees, across more than a quarter of a century, to the foundation and growth of the school that became The Nicolson Institute.

Alexander Morison Nicolson

As we have seen, Alexander Morison Nicolson was the fifth son of a family of seven sons (one of whom, Donald, died in infancy). He was born in Stornoway in 1832. Like all the brothers, he received his early education in the Parish School of Stornoway. From there he went to the High School of Glasgow. Angus Nicolson (see Chapter 1) speculated whether:

> *... it was this early enforced separation from home to further his education, a privilege granted only to the few, invariably the sons of wealthy parents, or the scenes of extreme poverty which he must have so often seen, that put in his mind at the early age of thirty the desire to provide better educational facilities for destitute children, especially the sons of the companions of his youth. Throughout his short exile thoughts and memories of his native town must have remained strong and permanent.*

The Nicolson family home in Bayhead, Stornoway

After completing an apprenticeship, he went abroad, as many others had done, to find greater opportunities. Showing the initiative and drive which seems to have characterised all the family, he was soon to acquire a large business, including a foundry and shipbuilding yard, in a partnership in the city of Shanghai. For several years earlier he had been employed in the service of the Chinese government with the members of which he remained on extremely friendly terms. While actively engaged in building up a prosperous career, his life was tragically cut short in 1865 at the age of thirty-three.

When his private papers were gone through after his death, a will was found in his own handwriting, signed but unwitnessed. This document appointed two trustees[5] and tasked them with transmitting his 'entire property' to the 'properly authorised authorities in the town of my nativity' in conjunction with his father and brothers, Angus and Roderick. Their instruction was to 'distribute the entire fortune in the following order':

> *...for the education and rearing of destitute children even... may be the indirect means of rendering some assistance to the children of some of my oldest acquaintances.*

It seems strange that, while still a vigorous and active young man, with a prosperous and rewarding career ahead, the thought of an early death should occur to him, especially as he had named his father, then in his seventy-first year, as an executor. One wonders if some other fatal accident in these early days of steamship building, perhaps more hazardous in foreign ports, caused the impulse to draft this remarkable document. Though unwitnessed three years later at the time of his death, its validity was never challenged.

When all the formalities were completed, it was found that total assets amounted to £5,672. As their father had died, it was now left to the two brothers, Angus and Roderick, to decide the best use to which this third part of their brother's assets, calculated at £1,898, should be put. Most of this task, often involved and beset with legal problems, was to devolve on the Reverend Roderick Nicolson.

---

5   They refused this task.

Angus Nicolson

ANGUS NICOLSON
BORN AT STORNOWAY JULY 7TH 1824
DIED AT SKIPTON MAY 31ST 1896

Angus Nicolson, who had been named by his brother Alexander to supervise with Roderick the charitable distribution of Alexander's bequest, was born in 1824, the eldest son of the family. He went, as all the brothers did, to the Parish School and at the age of thirteen left home to receive higher (secondary) education at Torbreck Academy, a well-known private educational establishment near Inverness, where he remained for four years. He spent his annual holidays chiefly on his father's farm at Coll where he took a great delight in shooting of all kinds.

Angus was then articled to James Thomson who at that time was the leading civil engineer in Glasgow. Along with Mr. Thomson, Angus was engaged in the building of various railways, particularly in the North of England. When the rush of railway construction ceased, he accepted the position as land steward on the Yorkshire estates which had belonged to Sir Richard Tafton. He built a large cotton and woollen factory employing more than a thousand hands. He died in Skipton in 1896 and was buried in the local cemetery. The mill was carried on, with the aid of a manager, by the two remaining brothers, Roderick and Kenneth. In his will, Angus gifted a sum of £500 (about £65,000 at current prices) to the school which his brother had founded. His tombstone bears the epitaph: 'Here lies a true man.'

Colin John Nicolson

COLIN JOHN NICOLSON
Born at Stornoway Sep. 10th 1825
Died at New Orleans 1877

Colin John, the second son (born 1825), in his early years followed closely in the footsteps of his elder brother. He spent some time in business with his father but, being extremely interested in various aspects of finance and commerce, he took up an appointment in the City of Glasgow Bank in Glasgow. Having resided in Glasgow for many years, he crossed the Atlantic to become a partner in the firm of John Hardy and Company, cotton factors and exporters, in the city of New Orleans. Colin John's plantations appear to have been in Hinds and Copiah counties in Mississippi, areas where there were very high levels of slave ownership; if his ownership of these plantations dated to the years prior to the Civil War, it is likely that Colin John was a slaveowner. Business flourished until the Civil War broke out, which caused a sharp decline in the cotton trade. He took up arms almost immediately *'in defence of the great institution which he believed was that best suited for the country.'* When the Southern States were defeated, he was imprisoned for nearly six months. On his release, Colin John returned to his business in New Orleans, but his hostility to the North was as strong as ever and often led him into personal trouble. His health, impaired by imprisonment and the hardships of war, was now severely affected. At some point, he gave a large part of his estate to his youngest brother, Kenneth Donald, who moved to Mississippi to help run the plantations. Colin John retired to one of his cotton plantations, where he died in 1877. He was buried in New Orleans.

Peter Hay Nicolson

PETER. HAY. NICOLSON
BORN AT STORNOWAY DEC. 20TH 1826.
DIED AT ALBANY WEST AUSTRALIA AUG. 28TH 1897.

Peter was the third son of the family, born in Stornoway in 1826. From an early age he was never happier than spending his free time, like many other local boys before and since, in the various activities about the harbour. He found great pleasure in sailing small boats and in climbing the riggings of the many brigs and other ships which spent the winter months at the piers of Stornoway. The arrival and departure of his father's ships must have stirred longings for far-distant places, the names of which he must have often heard, for his father's home was a frequent haunt for the many sea captains which the little town had produced. After several years he acquired a large three-masted vessel which he commanded for over twenty years, plying chiefly in eastern waters between India, China and Australia.

His parents having died and all the other members of his family having by this time left Lewis, Peter settled in Australia, first in Melbourne and later in Albany, Western Australia, where he became a well-known and respected citizen, commonly known as the 'Honest Sailor.' Although enjoying a happy retirement, it was not to last long. He died suddenly in 1897. Having no children, he bequeathed a sum of £7,000 (almost £1m at current prices) to his surviving brothers, Roderick and Kenneth. As they understood that it was his intention to help the school founded by his brother during his lifetime, they later handed over this bequest by deed of gift to the Stornoway School Board when all the formalities were completed, and his widow's claims met.

Roderick Nicolson

RODERICK NICOLSON
BORN AT STORNOWAY.
JULY 10TH 1829.

The fourth brother, Roderick, was born in 1829. Having received his early education in the same school as his brothers, he became a pupil in the High School of Glasgow as his brother Alexander was to do after him. He became a student at Glasgow University with a view to entering the ministry. After being ordained, he was inducted into the parish of Applecross where he remained for several years until he was appointed by the War Office as a chaplain to the Brigade of Guards in London, where he soon became a well-known figure in Scottish circles.[i] When he gave up this service, he retired permanently to his large property, 'Ravenswood', on the Kyles of Bute. Before doing so he had erected, at his own expense, a memorial tablet, which was incorporated in the structure of the original Nicolson building in honour of his brother:

Alexander Morison Nicolson, Engineer, Shanghai who founded this Institution in his native town - 'In the hope that I may thus benefit the children of some of my early school companions' - This token is placed here in affectionate remembrance by his brother, Roderick, late Chaplain of the Brigade of Guards, London.

He endowed The Nicolson Institute with his share of the £7,000, inherited from his brother Peter, to provide bursaries to enable promising pupils to enter university. When Roderick learned that secondary education had been introduced, his interest was immediately revived and continued to grow until his death. Not only by this increasing participation in the school's affairs, but also by his personal example and persuasion, he influenced the surviving brothers to follow the fortunes of the school and, with their co-operation, managed to help it during its critical years and place it on a sound financial basis. He died at 'Ravenswood', on the night of Saturday 4th May 1907, and was buried at his own request in the family burial ground in Sandwick Cemetery.

When the School Board and managers met in their official capacity, the chairman paid tribute to the part played by the Reverend Roderick Nicolson. As part of his address, he said that he was sure that the others shared the feeling that the unique burial place in Sandwick Cemetery gave the impression of a lasting memorial, but they too would also feel that the most lasting memorial of the family would be found not in the piece of solid masonry at Sandwick but in the lives of the many pupils trained in The Nicolson Institute.

Roderick, more than any of the other brothers, deserves the greatest credit in carrying out the wishes of the founder but, as he and Angus were the only ones to remain in Britain, and latterly resident in Scotland, he was closer to the actual events and, therefore, developed a closer personal interest.

Alexander Morison Nicolson of Australia, a nephew of the founder, and son of the Rev Roderick Nicolson and the sole third generation member of the family, made an influential intervention in the 1930s (see Chapter 9).

Kenneth Donald Nicolson

Kenneth Donald was the youngest of the family. Born in 1839, he received his early education in the parish school and later in Easter Ross. He was sent to Dumfriesshire to learn farming. He migrated to South Africa, where he took up sheep farming. After successful years of farming, at his brother Colin's request, Kenneth moved to Drygrove, Mississippi, where he was given a substantial interest in his brother's estates. Kenneth found little time for travel because of the incessant demands inherent in the organisation of large cotton plantations. While chattel slavery in North America had been abolished in 1865, this was an industry in which former slaves and their descendants continued to work under restrictive and often highly oppressive conditions. Distance and protracted communication made active participation in the progress of the school in its early years virtually impossible. Few family links remained with his native town. More than twenty years after Colin's death, endowed with more wealth and leisure, his visits to Roderick's 'Ravenswood' became more frequent and prolonged. As the only surviving members of what had been a close-knit family, companionship and the bond of brotherhood drew Roderick and Kenneth Donald closer in their declining years. This relationship between the brothers was to have a profound effect on the future history of the school. In the last few years of their lives, interest in fostering its progress seems to have become the main motivating force. With the moral and financial support of both brothers, The Nicolson Rector's task, still beset with problems caused by an ever-increasing roll, would appear less harassing, and the achievement of secondary education for gifted pupils easier.

Continuing Support of Roderick and Kenneth

The close relationship between Roderick and Kenneth seems to have stemmed from the legacy which they had inherited from their brother, Peter. When he died in Albany, Western Australia, in August 1897, under a will drawn up eleven years before, he bequeathed the rights to his Australian estate *'to be equally divided among surviving brothers.'* This estate consisted of various properties in Western Australia, Victoria and New South Wales. When assessed for legal purposes, Peter's estate was valued at £15,500 (about £2m at current prices). His widow, dissatisfied with the terms, challenged the will. She was awarded one-third of the heritable estate and a life interest in the remainder.

When the Reverend Roderick Nicolson informed the School Board that a sum of £7,000 would ultimately come to The Nicolson Institution from this estate, he explained the reasons why he and Kenneth were handing over their rights to the balance of the revenue to the school. As Peter and all the brothers who had predeceased him had left no issue, they (Roderick and Kenneth) were the only beneficiaries. As their brother had expressed the desire to help the school during his lifetime, Roderick explained that he wished to carry this out. He quoted the paragraph in Alexander Morison Nicolson's will, in which he had expressed the desire to further the education even of destitute children and those of his oldest acquaintances, they and their late brother, who had been unable to do so during his lifetime, desired to follow this example. He suggested that the money in part should be used to give bursaries to promising boys of working men who through poverty, or other reason, might not be able to continue their studies in the secondary department to qualify for university bursaries.

He also informed the School Board that he was forwarding a deed of gift which had been drafted by his lawyers in November 1898 for this purpose.

Kenneth made changes in his American will. He left instructions to his executors that the sum which he had inherited from his brother, Peter, of Albany, Australia, should go to what is now The Nicolson Institute, Stornoway. The residue of his estate should be invested for the benefit of the poor boys and girls of his native town.

These endowments by both brothers, in their wish to follow the example of the founder, were initially intended to benefit the children of Stornoway, but, as the organisation of the school had vastly changed since its early years, these were widened in scope to provide secondary education for Lewis children.

Each of these two surviving brothers was presented with an illuminated scroll by the Provost, magistrates and councillors of Stornoway on their own behalf and that of the community at large.

Illuminated scroll from Stornoway Burgh Council

These were duly framed and presented to The Nicolson Institute. Peter Hay Nicolson's widow survived the brothers by six years. On her death in 1913, the estate was wound up and the School Board informed.

In June 1900, Kenneth visited Stornoway, the town which he had left so many years before. In some ways, it would have been a sad return. The family home, probably occupied by a family friend, would have brought back memories of happier times. Many changes had taken place, and much had gone. The harbour scenes were much less colourful than in the days of his youth. Although sailing smacks, or wherries as they were known locally, were still numerous, the great days of sail were over.[6] He renewed acquaintance with the companions of his youth, but the school where he and his brothers had received their early education was no longer in existence. He met local dignitaries and, on 22nd June, visited the school which his brother had founded. Reality probably exceeded expectation. The original school had been extended, a small timber and iron building housed the infants and the Francis Street building, which incorporated the Free Church School, had opened two years before. The school roll exceeded 500 and 84 of them were following a secondary course which had already brought some to Higher Leaving Certificate standard.

As a result of this visit, his interest in the welfare of the school and its continuing progress greatly increased. In his conversations with Mr Gibson, Kenneth must have been impressed by the young Headmaster's ambition to provide educational facilities comparable to those of other recognised and long-established secondary schools on the mainland. In the few years since his arrival, Mr Gibson had come to know the island and its problems, especially the drift to Scottish industrial centres and overseas. In these early years, at the time of Kenneth's visits, Gibson's main aim was to provide opportunities, hitherto denied, to a better way of life for those of talent through the benefits of university education. In Roderick and Kenneth Nicolson, bound by family sentiment to the school, he found generous benefactors with similar ideals and kindred ambitions.

This remarkable family, although they had severed their ties with their native town and had risen to positions of eminence in various callings, never lost their deep regard for Stornoway. One feels that no matter what distances separated them, or oceans divided, a strong link of love and brotherhood bound them into a tightly knit family with strong home ties which fostered an innate bond with the small town in which they had spent their youthful days. Perhaps nothing brings out more clearly this bond of kinship than the inscriptions the two surviving brothers Roderick and Kenneth added to the family memorial stone, which lies in the centre of the walled burial ground, urn-crowned on one side, in the south-east corner of the old cemetery at Sandwick. On the northern end of the polished granite

---

6 As consequently were, more or less, the great days of herring fishing from Stornoway.

plinth which lies on two sandstone bases probably inserted at the time, is carved the simple inscription: *'The Nicolson Family.'* This is continued on the other side by the words: 'Some whom rest here and others in various parts of the world.' On the other side of this stone are the names of their father and mother flanked by those of the grandfather and his wife with the word 'Sons' interposed. Beneath are the names of the seven sons in order of birth. On the upper part of the sandstone base are carved the inscriptions:

> *This stone is placed here in loving and lasting memory by the remaining sons, Roderick and Kenneth (1905)* and underneath:
> *All true men and prosperous in their various callings of life.*

The Nicolson family lair in Sandwick Cemetery

In monetary terms alone this family had bequeathed to The Nicolson Institute almost £23,000, a considerable sum (perhaps £3m) in modern times. This, however, said Angus Nicolson:

> *pales into insignificance when one considers the fruits reaped, the traditions wrought and the benefits which it conferred on all those who passed through its corridors.*

Chapter 3:
The Nicolson Institution

Mackay's School was the school first chosen to benefit from The Nicolson legacy. It was decided that it should be placed on a more permanent footing under a public trust with certain conditions laid down as regards its management. The main ones, proposed by Sir James Matheson, stipulated that all those on the Board of Trustees should be of the Protestant faith,[7] that the proposed school should be known as The Nicolson Institution and that it be a non-denominational institution for the poor or working classes of Stornoway without any reference to sect or creed.

After further deliberation, however, it was decided that the Mackay's School building (proposed to be The Nicolson Institution) was not suitable, because of age and structural defects, as a permanent institution and that the greater part of the available funds should be expended on the building of a new school and a schoolmaster's house. To this Sir James Matheson contributed by donating a free site and an annual grant of £35 in perpetuity by way of supplementing the schoolmaster's salary.

Apart from The Nicolson family, a major benefactor - and Trustee - of The Nicolson Institution (as it was called at its foundation) was Sir James Matheson (1796-1878).[i][ii] Sir James was one of Britain's biggest landowners, purchasing the island of Lewis in 1844 and building the Lews Castle. To this day a memorial to Sir James, erected by his widow, stands within the Castle Grounds.

Of mainland Highland origin (born in Lairg), Matheson had accrued his considerable wealth initially in trading in tea through the East India Company but then essentially by working with his partner Jardine, a fellow Scot, in smuggling opium into China.

---

[7] This is what became a major bone of contention when the Trustees tried to hand over The Nicolson Institution to the Parish Board of Stornoway.

Today, Jardine Matheson describes the firm's origins thus:

> *Jardine, Matheson & Co (JM & Co) was founded in Canton in July 1832 by Scots William Jardine and James Matheson.*
>
> *Following the end of the East India Company's trading monopoly with China, Jardine Matheson sent its first private shipments of tea to England in 1834.*
>
> *JM & Co saw the development potential of Hong Kong as a trading base and moved its operations temporarily from Macao to Hong Kong in 1839.*
>
> *In 1841, JM & Co purchased the first plots of land at East Point for £565. The Firm's Chinese name 'Ewo' – 'the state of happy harmony' – was adopted the following year.*
>
> *Hong Kong was officially declared a British colony under the Treaty of Nanking in 1843.*[8]
>
> *JM & Co completed the move of its main office to Hong Kong and opened its office in Shanghai when it purchased Lot No. 1 in 1844. More offices were subsequently opened in Canton, Amoy and Foochow.*
>
> *Offices were later opened in Kobe, Nagasaki and other ports.*

Other historians are less coy. One of them quotes the view of the Hong Kong vice consul of the 1840s (not, one would have thought, a person of necessarily radical views):

> *By the sale of this pernicious drug Great Britain's sons gain gold; and create opprobrium for dealing destruction around them, bringing into derision the name of a Christian country, by enabling the Chinese to violate the laws of their own nation, in obtaining the accursed and prohibited poison; the use of which entails destruction, mentally and bodily, on its infatuated devotees.*[iii]

---

8   At the conclusion of the First Opium War.

Equally unfavourable views of Matheson can be seen elsewhere.[iv]

Thanks to Matheson's involvement, the site chosen for the new school building was the western portion of the field at the corner of Sandwick Road and Matheson Road. The building was to consist of what Mr. Gibson was later to describe as *'one schoolroom and a small classroom'* with the schoolmaster's house attached. The accommodation provided by both the new school building and the schoolhouse was extremely limited in size. It was only many years later, when several buildings providing greater accommodation to cope with a vastly increased roll had been added, that a new schoolhouse was built in keeping with the school's academic reputation.

Financial considerations in the 1870s, however, limited any thought of more grandiose plans to match the outward splendour of other, better-endowed schools.

Shortly after the decision to build a new school was taken, the necessary plans and specifications were issued for tenders. What the new school might lack in appearance and size was more than compensated for in the quality of the materials with which it was built.

The main walls were to consist of Isle Martin stone hewn from the quarry of the small island at the entrance to Loch Broom. The Torridonian sandstone, evidence of desert conditions millions of years earlier, had a warmth of reddish-brown colour which contrasted vividly with that of the still older, cold, grey Lewisian gneiss. The stones had all to be perfectly cut and free from defects, bound with the best mortar and built on a sound and secure foundation. All freestone dressings, more easily cut and shaped, were to be taken from Glasgow and only set in position after approval by the architect. The main roofing timbers, joists and window frames were to be of the best Swedish redwood, and the doors and other woodwork of the best American yellow pine. All the slate work, both roof and main corridor, was to consist of the finest quality Caithness slate.

The school cost almost £1,500 and had to be finished by the 1st of August 1872. That original Nicolson school building was demolished in 1972. On its demolition Angus Nicolson reflected:

> *When one sees such a building demolished in a matter of days with little regard for the preservation of memorial plaques, one wonders if there is not a place in a modern society for the retention of such a building and some use found for it, especially because of its historic interest especially in Lewis and the regard with which it is held by those who taught and others who sat, maybe unwillingly at the time, to absorb the educational requirements of their day.*

The main plaque to which he referred was marble and placed in a prominent position inside the building with the following inscription:

> *This Institution has been erected and endowed under the Will of Alexander Morison Nicolson, son of the deceased Roderick Nicolson, shipowner, Stornoway. Born in Stornoway 1832, died at Shanghai 1865 and further endowed by Sir James Matheson, Bart., Proprietor of the Lewis and Lord Lieutenant of Ross-shire, with a free site and playgrounds and an annual grant in perpetuity - 1871.*[9]

A New School

When the newly founded school opened its doors to scholars in February 1873, a number of trustees had been appointed to the Board of Management. These were men of authority from various walks of life. After the appointment, key decisions were taken by the two main Trustees, Sir James Matheson and the Rev. Roderick Nicolson. The balance of funds, after the cost of building the school had been met, and Sir James Matheson's annual grant were to form a permanent endowment. All alterations and new plans concerning the school had to be submitted to Sir James Matheson for approval. The number of children to be admitted, the courses to be followed, and the number of scholars to be educated free were to be given priority. The Trustees had the power to exempt some pupils from the payment of fees, but they were not bound to comply with this mandate (which seems rather strange because it ran counter to the wishes and purpose implicit in the original endowment).

The Trustees were to be the sole judges of the merit and appointment of head teachers and have the power of dismissal with the three months' notice, with no obligation to give the reason, but two-thirds of the committee had to be present. They were also to fix the salary of the head teacher who had to live in the schoolhouse and vacate it on resignation or dismissal. The head teacher, however, had the power to appoint pupil teachers[10] or assistants.

The first meeting of the Trustees was held on 29th January 1873 and their first decision was to uplift the balance of money left, amounting to £457, to pay advances made by Sir James Matheson. A letter from John Sutherland offering his services as Head Teacher was postponed for further

---

9   This represents the year when the decision to build was taken. As this was also inscribed outside, it has led to some confusion as to the actual year when it became an educational establishment.
10 See page 43 for an explanation of what 'pupil teachers' were.

consideration, but his appointment was later formally confirmed on 4th February 1873 at a salary of £82 annually: consisting of Sir James Matheson's £35, £20 from the Trustees' endowment, and the £27 granted to certificated teachers. The schoolhouse was rent free, and a garden would be provided later. It was decided to admit twenty children as non-fee-paying pupils and notices were printed to ensure, if it was possible, that these should be children of parents who had been acquainted with the founder.

John Sutherland

The keys of the building were handed over to the newly selected headmaster, Mr. John Sutherland, the former master of the General Assembly School. With him came all his pupils, numbering 105 (see Appendix 6), to be duly registered as occupants of the new building. The General Assembly School lay to the west of the Parish Church; when its master and pupils moved in a body to The Nicolson Institution it reopened but was forced to close three years later.[11]

At noon on Thursday 27th February 1873, in the presence of the Trustees, local dignitaries and parents, the school was formally opened with due ceremony.

---

11   This was an era of considerable school closures across Scotland, notably of church schools.

After the formal opening, the newly founded school settled down to the normal routine of instruction and learning. In the first few years, the main holiday period was announced after the annual visit by HM Inspector of Schools. In his report the Inspector made allowance for the disruption caused by moving from one school building to another and the short time the school had been in existence, but most subjects, although fairly good, needed improvement.

Mr. Sutherland was referred to *'as a young man of great vigour and earnestness.'* The staff consisted of the Headmaster, two pupil teachers and the sewing mistress.

Performance rapidly improved. Three years on, it was reported that the school was being taught with energy, firm and kindly discipline, and that a pleasant tone prevailed. The following year there were still further improvements: excellent order prevailed, and the results were very good. Latin, English Literature, and Mathematics had been added to the subjects taught. By August 1879, Mr. John Sutherland was raised to Certificate, 1st Class, the highest teacher qualification prevailing under the School Code.

Despite the improvement in performance, the new institution was soon beset by troubles. The school was plagued by a rather loud and persistent echo. One Inspector of Schools found it particularly annoying. Despite the inspectors insisting on its removal on three occasions, the echo remained.

Her Majesty's Inspectors of Schools appeared to have considerable influence and power under the regulations of the Scotch Code, but they were also men (always men until 1902)[v] highly dedicated to their profession. In the first few years they acted with due gentlemanly decorum, announcing in advance the date of their annual inspection. The school's ordinary timetable was departed from in preparation for the forthcoming visit and intensive tuition given in the subjects to be examined. This was duly entered in the logbook. To the annoyance of many headmasters, probably harassed by other problems, there was a sudden departure from this normal practice. The inspectors would now appear unheralded on a visit.

Two years later (1880), J.L. Robertson, who was to play a decisive role in the history of the school, was appointed to Her Majesty's Inspectorate. He joined two other Inspectors in looking after the affairs of the Northern Area.

The Influence of John Lindsay Robertson

J.L. Robertson

John Lindsay Robertson, a person of talent and drive who became one of the top civil servants in Scotland, was born in Stornoway in 1854. He was educated at the local General Assembly School in Stornoway, i.e. one of the church schools that preceded both the 1872 elementary school reforms in Scotland and the 1873 foundation of The Nicolson Institution in Stornoway.

According to the 1871 census, he was still living at home, aged seventeen, but was a 'pupil teacher.'[12] This concept generally indicated a student staying on at school beyond the usual leaving age of twelve or thirteen and possibly intending to become a certificated, non-graduate teacher via a course in a teacher training college. Some school students, always males, used the pupil teacher scheme to enable university entrance; and this was what Robertson did.[13]

Robertson attended the University of Edinburgh and graduated with distinction in Arts (MA) and then in Law (LLB). Aged 26, he became one of Her Majesty's Inspectors of Schools. We know from Professor T.R. Bone's classic study of the Scottish School Inspectorate[vi] that inspectors at the time were recruited because of academic distinction rather than because

---

12 Some authors use the style 'pupil-teacher'.
13 There is an account of Robertson that claims he went to a mainland secondary school; but the evidence, e.g. the 1871 Stornoway census, suggests otherwise.

of experience in school teaching. Much to the disgust of the main teacher union, then as now the Educational Institute of Scotland, some school inspectors of that era had no school teaching experience at all. Whether Robertson himself had briefly been a teacher after graduation is uncertain; but he had at least some years of experience as an apprentice pupil teacher.

As acting Chief Inspector of Schools (HMCI) in 1888, a position he later held on a permanent basis, he oversaw thirteen - essentially insolvent - Highland school boards.

As Professor Bone describes it:

> *Robertson was a Stornoway man who, though quite young as an inspector, was admirably suited by background, temperament and energy for the responsibilities now entrusted to him... by an unusual combination of tactfulness and audacity he brought them to accept the Department's policy. The attendance figures were raised sharply, and though strict economy was practised, educational advances were made in the schools by the broadening and brightening of the curriculum... it was generally admitted that he was just and sincere, and within a few years the position was becoming satisfactory again, with the return of the boards to a position of solvency.*

By 1890, the three previously insolvent Lewis school boards were indeed balancing their books and the others followed at various stages. School fees in elementary (primary) board schools were abolished in 1890. Thereafter they relied, as their state school successors largely do to this day, on a combination of government grant and local rates.

The fact that Robertson's home was near the school must have added to the general concern of managers and Headmaster alike. Having reported unfavourably on the lack of cleanliness of the *'offices'* during his official inspection the same year as he was appointed, he returned three months later unexpectedly on another visit. He had found that Mr. Sutherland had been compelled to close these premises because of lack of water. Robertson insisted that a supply of water should receive the utmost priority. Once again, the appropriate entry had to be made in the logbook, duly signed by the Inspector, and the entry reported to the Managers. This was followed by the threat, the first in the history of the school, that if the same conditions existed on his next visit of inspection, a serious reduction in the annual grant might occur.

Yet there were no threats issued of reducing the grant because of serious over-crowding of classrooms. Although the number of pupils on the register was large, this was not matched by attendance. For this there were several reasons. No compulsion to attend was exercised. Truancy was a natural way of life for many pupils. In this policy of voluntary attendance lay the seeds of future financial embarrassment.

Poverty Affects Attendance

As fees had to be paid for each subject taught, poverty on the part of many families was often an influential factor. During the summer fishing season, many younger and especially older boys did not attend. Often the mother also had, through necessity, to find work in curing herring, so older girls were kept from school to do the housework and tend the younger children. During the late spring and early autumn, peat-working was essential and the services of the young often required, especially if the father had to follow the various herring fishing seasons: many local boats went to the east coast, starting at Lerwick and finishing at Yarmouth late in the year.[vii]

The desire for education for their children on the part of the parents did not go deep. An effort might be made for a son who showed exceptional talent, but girls were placed in a different category. They, it was hoped, would eventually marry. Lady Matheson's Seminary for Girls, more charitable in outlook, could provide the basic requirements of domestic training.

Of the original 105 pupils of The Nicolson Institution, 85 were boys and twenty were girls (see Appendix 6). It was also significant that these twenty girls came from the wealthier section of the community. During visits of inspection, some attempt must have been made to coerce pupils to attend school. On these occasions the attendance was usually more than 80. When the school reassembled after the holidays granted after the first inspection, only 43 pupils attended.

The school was inspected again in May 1880, with 94 boys and sixteen girls present, but only 40 pupils took the trouble to attend following the inspection. One can reasonably assume that, for most of the school year, the attendance by pupils fell far below what would now be regarded as an acceptable level.

The fact that the school was empowered to charge fees caused hardship among the poorer members of the community and, for the next twenty years, at each of the Stornoway Parish School Board meetings, hardship appeared to account for their children's absence from school.

As school grants depended on the level of attendance, there were attempts at rigorous enforcement; but fines and imprisonment aggravated rather than provided a solution when extreme poverty was the cause. There was also the fear held for many years by many Lewis parents that if their children were educated, they would leave home and settle permanently elsewhere. It was only later, when social conditions had improved and secondary education introduced, that attitudes changed. If free education had been introduced with the 1872 Act, much bitterness would have been avoided. The deep-felt sympathy which had prompted Alexander Morison Nicolson to benefit destitute children would have found real expression.

In January 1875, the Trustees recognised that, as the funds at the command of The Nicolson Institution Trustees were inadequate for the proper management of the school and the buildings, these should be transferred to the Stornoway School Board. This began the thirteen-year period of - often involved - negotiations. It was necessary to consult Sir James Matheson and the Rev. Roderick Nicolson because of the gravity of the decision which had to be taken. The Rev. Nicolson was also asked to attend the meeting if it was at all possible. Sir James Matheson, although initially against handing the school over, agreed, provided that twenty children be given free education under the original condition which could be met from his annual contribution to the Endowment Fund. Rev. Nicolson also agreed:

> *provided that the Institution should retain its original name, that the funds and Sir James Matheson's annuity remain in the hands of the Trustees for paying the above fees and the teacher's salary to be paid by the School Board, and finally that the Trust should continue as it was then constituted to supervise the choice of, and payment for, the twenty children.*

On two occasions, meetings were held to obtain unanimity but the Rev. J. Greenfield, Free Church Minister of Stornoway, dissented each time, unless all the managers, as previously decided, were of the Protestant faith, and that this should be brought to the notice of the Board of Education. In reply, the Board of Education outlined various ways in which the school could be transferred to the School Board. They could transfer the school under one article of the Code of the Education Act if agreed to by the Court of Session, under a Deed of Gift, provided there was a two-thirds majority and there were no conditions laid down which the School Board could not accept.

One of the conditions which the School Board had refused to accept was the one on which Rev. Greenfield insisted. Under the Trust Acts, by which the original document had been drawn up, the Trustees had no power to sell or gift; but probably no objection would be raised, according to the Board of Education, if it was gifted as an educational establishment, because one endowed school had already been accepted under this condition. In their view the name of the school was no obstacle. The condition of entry of twenty non-fee-paying pupils and visits by the trustees to check on this, they considered inadmissible, but this might be covered by their right of disposal of the Trust Fund. Also, from the deed, one trustee could dissent and effectively oppose transference. The Scotch (sic) Education Department had concluded that the only way in which any progress could be made was by the dissenting Trustee reconsidering his decision in the light of what had been stated and *as the clause to which he had taken exception was unlikely to be materially affected for many years to come.*

The School Board, which had also been in touch with the Scotch Education Department, received the same answer. When Counsel's opinion was sought, the Dean of the Faculty of Advocates maintained that under the Trust Deeds Act it could not become a public or state-aided school. However, as there had been a precedent, the Board of Education would probably have accepted it if there had been unanimity among the Trustees.[14]

During this prolonged legal wrangle, low levels of attendance continued to be noted in the school logbooks, with the beginning of the fishing season, peat-cutting, and inclement weather noted as reasons for this.

This general apathy towards education on the part of the economically poorer section of the community continued into the early years of the 20th century, despite energetic measures taken by the School Board.[15] Directives were issued to warn parents of their responsibilities. Yet, over a period of many years, at each successive meeting of the School Board, many parents appeared on summons to account for the prolonged absence of their children from school. At every meeting, some parents were remitted to the Sheriff Court for trial, and fines or short terms of imprisonment were imposed; despite this, the attitude towards school attendance on the part of the poorer section of the community showed little change, even when fee-paying had long ceased (as it did in 1890). Probably over-dependence on the charity provided under the punitive Poor Law Acts to obtain even adequate clothing and footwear brought the threat of harsh penalties, or even the separation of families. The fear of the 'Poor House' was a much greater mortifying force than compliance with any educational obligations: one brought ignominy and shame; the other a minor inconvenience to an inherent way of life in which learning had not been regarded as essential.

Yet the Trustees of The Nicolson Institution made little effort to deal with the problem. It continued its rather haphazard way, typical of many schools at that time.

---

14 Quite a few 'endowed' schools became parish board schools after the 1872 Act.
15 A problem in many schools of the time.

A New Head Teacher

Mr. Forbes

In 1882, Mr. Sutherland was appointed to the post of Headmaster of Anderson's Institution, Forres. The Trustees expressed regret at his departure and highly praised the service which he had rendered, not only to the school but also to the community. He was succeeded by Mr. John Forbes of Laxdale School; the school remained under his charge for the next twelve years and during this time his wife joined the staff.

In the first flush of enthusiasm over his new appointment, as if to impress the Trustees, Forbes complained bitterly of the state of the school, especially of *'its lack of cleanliness and the wretched lack of repair to much of its equipment.'* As a result, the school was closed for a week to bring it into a fit state of repair. Even harsher criticism was levelled at the educational standards prevailing: the pupils were very backward in Arithmetic and some classes knew nothing of grammar. However, Forbes, too, was shortly to incur the displeasure of Her Majesty's Inspectorate of Schools.

The school session was longer than at present. Recognised holiday dates during this period in the school's history were those of the Harvest Thanksgiving Services and the Market Day *(Latha na Dròbha)*. The latter, by custom held on the first Tuesday in July, had developed over the years an atmosphere usually associated with that of the fairground rather than that of the sale of livestock. Local delicacies sold in gaily bedecked stalls; the itinerant fraternity peddling trinkets, games of skill or chance; or the occasional visits of small travelling circuses attracted both the old and the young alike.

In 1880, however, the main holiday period of the year, announced after the annual inspection, was brought forward and extended from late May to mid-July. As the Market Day fell within these dates, its place in the school calendar was taken for many years by another colourful event, the Volunteers' Inspection. Each year into the town came Royal Navy and Army reservists for training with local contingents in gunnery, rifle practice, signalling, drill and other exercises.[16] When this course of intensive training was completed, the various branches of each service were drawn up in serried ranks to be inspected by a high-ranking officer at the Battery Park. Gun salutes rang out, flags flew, bugles sounded the various calls and, as the various commands were given, every section came to attention to be inspected. This display was watched each year by a vast gathering of admiring spectators.

Other occasions of national or local importance, once meriting the granting of a day's freedom from lessons but now meaningless to most, are highlighted in the logbook with due patriotic fervour: the visit of HRH Duke of Edinburgh in 1882; Queen Victoria's Diamond Jubilee; the Relief of Mafeking (in 1900 in the Boer War); Coronations (1902 and 1911); and the visit of King Edward VII and Queen Alexandra (the former being the first reigning monarch to visit Stornoway and being greeted with even greater pomp and ceremony than the 1956 visit of the late Queen Elizabeth and her Duke of Edinburgh). In 1882, these occasions of royal patronage or national rejoicing, however, lay mostly in the future.

Shortly after his appointment as Headmaster, Mr. Forbes, under pressure from certain parents and probably from personal ambition, began to bring some older pupils to a more advanced stage in some subjects. This did not escape the notice of the Scotch Education Department's Inspector, who in his annual report on the school, stated that the general performance was excellent in many ways and the zeal and vigour of the teaching showed creditable success. Yet the attempt to do too much was very apparent.

---

16 In a moderately flourishing (but still cash-poor) island in the late 19th century, this was a good way to earn cash. Come 1914, some reservists paid a heavy price by being mobilised into armed services.

The next year's report brought greater censure and once again the threat of reduction in the grant to the school was forcibly stated:

Too much was still being attempted, a state of affairs which had been called to the Managers' attention the previous year - resulting in a marked decline in the work of the lower classes.

The Trustees compromised. They informed Mr. Forbes that these advanced stages in subjects could be taught to pupils whose parents desired it, provided it was only done for one hour daily and did not encroach on the ordinary work of the school.

This placed Forbes in rather an unenviable position. Although the report on the school was much more favourable the following year, Mrs. Forbes's absence from school due to tuberculosis had become prolonged. This caused serious overcrowding of the classrooms. The problem had become even more acute because of a steadily increasing roll.

But, again during the fishing season especially, there was a marked decline in attendance. Absence from school for this reason, or when working at peats was required, was regarded as a matter of right by the pupils and largely ignored by the Trustees; although Mr. Forbes complained that many older and even some younger pupils took advantage of this seeming privilege to leave school without permission. Mrs. Forbes continued to teach, despite her long illness, until a week before her death. It seems rather fitting, after such a supreme effort, that the school should receive its greatest praise yet. HM Inspector of Schools had issued an excellent report and at the annual presentation of prizes the Trustees had expressed their gratification at the high place taken by the school in the Inspector's opinion.

With such high praise recorded from both Her Majesty's Inspectorate and the Trustees, the events of the next six years (1888-1894), although veiled in secrecy and conjecture, questioned the level of teaching at the school for its large number of pupils. By this time, Mr. Forbes had been raised to the highest status under the prevailing Scotch Code of Education and was later to become a Fellow of the Educational Institute of Scotland. Prospects of a successful career must have seemed bright, but the future was only to bring disagreement, bitter disillusionment, and eventual dismissal.

The desire by some parents for more advanced education for their children, despite its partial discouragement earlier, was still strong enough to bring pressure on the Trustees. This is clearly implied in the School Inspector's Report submitted to the Trustees just months before management was handed over to the School Board of the Parish of Stornoway in 1888:

> *The work [is] fair, but excellent in some departments. The work done as far as the staff is concerned and the amount of work attempted in the upper station is beyond the powers of a single teacher. It is most desirable in the Circumstances of the Case that this amount of work should not be lessened but rather increased and to accomplish this it is necessary that further assistance should be given to the headmaster.*
>
> *While My Lords are prepared to recognise the school as 'centre' for the purposes of Article 21(a)[17] the higher grant cannot be paid as conditions with respect to staff are not satisfied.*

The School Board, with several schools under their management, were more educationally orientated than the Trustees of one endowed school. Radical changes in policy were inevitable. It seems rather ironic that the desire for a more advanced level of education (which Mr. Forbes had been censured for introducing) should set in motion a train of events which would lead to his displacement. The School Board of the Parish of Stornoway was itself to suffer censure, undergo criticism and incur the displeasure of the Scotch Education Department.

Although Mr. Forbes and his wife were the only certificated teachers on the staff and had only a young female assistant to help them, the roll steadily increased. While there was a certain amount of criticism by various inspectors, and even the threat to withdraw the grant, this was more often directed against the overcrowding.

His wife's death, circa 1894, from tuberculosis, left Mr. Forbes an embittered man. As Professor R.M. Maciver stated in his autobiography, *As a Tale That is Told*, he presented:

> *a figure deteriorating with the years, morose and often indifferent. He was rather warm-hearted except in his blacker moods, a man who must have been lonely. He did not seem to have friends.*[viii]

John Forbes remained as Head Teacher until 1894. The Stornoway School Board in 1888 appointed additional teachers and sought to develop secondary education at The Nicolson.

---

17   i.e. as a school providing some secondary-level education.

Chapter 4:
Developing Secondary Education

The years following the Education (Scotland) Act 1872 saw elementary (i.e., primary) schooling reasonably well established across Scotland, certainly once it became free in 1890. Problems of truancy, initially high, were largely solved.

Attention from about 1885 onwards increasingly came to focus on what we now call 'secondary education'.[18] This was, in part, fuelled by the Scotch Education Department (SED)'s foundation in 1888 of the Higher Leaving Certificate, which quickly became, as it largely remains today, the major benchmark for university entrance.

In 1892, the first state grants for secondary education appeared (ten years earlier than in England) and were used to build up schools in smaller towns as well as to strengthen existing ones. They formed an effective national network able to prepare both for the universities and for business careers.[i] There was considerable agreement that post-elementary 'higher' education should be expanded, especially for bright but poor students, but there was great controversy about how to do this.[ii]

In a complex and ongoing debate, the central choice was between the School Boards developing their own 'higher grade' with a government grant; and the existing secondary provision of fee-charging 'endowed schools' and 'higher schools' - e.g., Kelvinside Academy, the Royal High School of Edinburgh, Inverness Royal Academy, Perth Academy, which were mostly independent of the Boards – receiving an S.E.D. grant to expand their provision.[iii]

Some school boards, for example Govan and Glasgow, were particularly active in creating new secondary ('higher grade') schools, and evidence of this can still be seen emblazoned on surviving 19th and early 20th century buildings. On the other hand, as noted above, hitherto independent 'higher' (or 'endowed') schools also received an SED grant to expand their provision; some of them are today simply part of the state-funded system.

While both things happened and the debate in some senses dragged on as far as the 1970s, the boards and their successors essentially won (except arguably in Edinburgh). But even Govan encountered opposition because of nearby 'higher' or 'endowed' schools (e.g., Kelvinside Academy and Glasgow Academy) and, where areas had several or many pre-existing 'higher schools', e.g., in Edinburgh, progress was slower and mired in controversy.

---

18   Confusingly (for us of the 21st century) it was often called 'higher' education until well into the 20th century.

In the Isle of Lewis, matters were clearer cut, for it had no 'higher' schools. And its sole 'endowed' school wanted to become a Board School.

When the Stornoway School Board took over the management of the newly named Nicolson Public School in 1888, Mr. Forbes was retained as Headmaster on the same conditions of service. His salary was to be £150 annually, but, if future circumstances merited further increases, this sum would be reviewed. Also included in the letter of appointment were instructions that the School Board was to receive the income from grants, fees and other sources. A copy of fees levied for each subject was to be hung in a prominent position in the main schoolroom. As the school roll now exceeded 130, the difficulty of maintaining a reasonable standard of efficient teaching and discipline seems formidable for a staff of two qualified teachers. Several months later, however, a Mr. Fowler was appointed as Assistant Master. Despite this, the various Inspectors' Reports were extremely favourable about the teaching achievements; the censure, however, was levied at the School Board for the gross overcrowding, which was raised now for the first time.

The school pre 1900

Thus, in 1890, the Isle of Lewis was an island with only elementary or primary schools (one of which was The Nicolson Public School) and from where university could normally only be accessed by going to mainland schools such as Inverness Royal Academy and Aberdeen Grammar School.

By 1910, Lewis was an island with a renowned secondary school (The Nicolson Institute) and rural feeder schools, allowing Government reports to extol what had happened as a prime example of what could be achieved more generally in Scotland.

How did this transformation happen?

One feels a certain compulsion to record the various events of the next five years in some detail, because of the sudden change in outlook by the School Board towards the introduction of higher (secondary) education. As Mr. Gibson was to remark many years later, a seed was to be sown, *'a seed which was to grow into a goodly tree.'* Much of the credit for this rebirth of higher education in his native town must additionally go to J.L. Robertson, HM Inspector of Schools.

Although steps were now being taken to deal with truancy by the appointment of a Compulsory Attendance Officer, the School Board soon found that this only brought further problems. In the first annual report after having taken over control, in 1889, the School Board was duly informed of the chaotic conditions prevailing and the steps which were necessary to rectify them:

> *The school has risen in efficiency and is in good condition. Results are generally satisfactory. There is a lack of desks, in fact very insufficient. Discipline is kindly, effective and a good tone prevails the school. Because of the overcrowding an addition is very desirable. The junior room designed to accommodate 31 has had an average during the year of 43 pupils. As many as 57 names have been on the register. This is to be brought to the attention of the Managers.*

The following year's report of 1890 by Her Majesty's Inspector was even more specific regarding the measures which should be taken to remedy the overcrowding:

> *In the circumstances the school has passed well. An extension to furnish two classrooms is strongly recommended, especially one for the junior classes. In view of the steadily increasing*

> *importance of the School the superficial space is barely adequate for proper management and is hoped an extension will be set about this year.*

By modern standards, the comment regarding the available space seems a gross understatement in view of the continuous increase in the number of pupils attending the school. The nearby Free Church School was also well-attended, and the girls' (Lady Matheson's) Seminary on Keith Street was catering for the basic elements of education for many of the older girls.

By 1891, the Nicolson roll had risen to almost 180 pupils. This must have made conditions for adequate teaching seem at times almost impossible and is reflected in the tone expressed in that year's report:

> *The long-contemplated extension and the very great enlargement of the premises has yet not been effected. Conditions are unfavourable because of the crowded state of the benches. The discipline is good and work creditable.*

Also included in the report was the threat that, unless conditions improved within a very short period, the grant to the school would not be renewed. This report, with its inherent threat of closure, was immediately brought to the notice of the managers.

The overcrowding must have been all too evident to the members of the School Board. Periodic visits were made to the school by individual members, but the only hint of any awareness of the problem was the rather laconic remark by one member on his two visits: *'56 present in the junior classroom.'* One cannot but feel that drastic measures were taken at times to impart knowledge to rows of pupils sitting closely packed on benches. These hard, long and comparatively narrow *'forms,'* and the equally inadequate desks, were hardly conducive to the pursuit of learning.

To ease the task of the two teachers on the staff, the service of several others, some of whom were university graduates, was used for short periods. On Mr. Fowler's departure in June 1891, Mr. Younie was appointed to the post, the first graduate to take up full-time employment in the school. He was soon to be joined by others holding university degrees.

Under the threat of the withdrawal of the annual grant, the School Board borrowed £1,200 with the sanction of the Scotch Education Department to build an extension to the original building. Work began in the opening months of 1892. In July, J.L. Robertson was asked to attend the next meeting of the School Board to advise the members on the number of teachers needed for the enlarged school. He forcefully advocated the introduction of higher education. In this he was successful, having failed in the late 1880s with a previous Board.[iv] It was common in many parts of Scotland, notably Glasgow, for boards to be divided on the respective merits of expanding school education versus the attractions of keeping rates low.[v]

Robertson's continued involvement with the decision-making in respect of the 'Nicolson School' was recorded in the minutes of the Stornoway School Board:

> **September 5**
> *It was agreed that Mr JL Robertson H.M. Inspector of Schools should be asked to be present at one of the meetings of the Board in order that the Board may conver [sic] with him and get his advice as to the staffing of this School.* [vi]

and:

> **October 3**
> *Having conferred with Mr Robertson H.M. Inspector of Schools with regard to the establishment of a department in the School for Higher Instruction unanimously resolved to advertise for an assistant master (who must be a graduate in Arts) at a salary at the rate of One hundred pounds per annum; and also for a Lady Assistant (with University qualification) for Modern Languages, advanced Music, Drawing and needlework at Ninety pounds per annum.*

This had been one of the conditions put forward by The Nicolson Institution Trustees when the control of the school was transferred to the School Board. The meetings of the School Board were usually held in the Volunteers' Drill Hall. The next six meetings of the School Board were held in the Coffee House (now the Star Inn). Here matters of vital importance concerning the future trend of education in Lewis were decided. By October 1892, the decision to introduce much more advanced courses of learning was reached.

The School Board received a letter in December from J.L. Robertson HMI confirming *'the proposed establishment of a Department for Higher Instruction.'*[vii] Mr. John Macleod, MA, was appointed as Senior Male Assistant, and began duties in the Senior Department in the same month.[viii]

The New Senior Department

In January 1893, Mr. Forbes was placed in charge of the new Senior Department, which was to introduce the teaching of Latin, Greek, Mathematics, Geography, History, English, French, German, Drawing, Music, Domestic Economy and Advanced Needlework. The range seems very extensive for the limited number of teachers available. A Junior Department was also to be formed where Mr. Forbes and Mr. Younie were to introduce a commercial course, including Book-keeping and allied subjects, in addition to the previous elementary duties. The Infant Department was to be the responsibility of Miss Riddoch who had come to the school in the same year as Mr. Forbes. Miss Agnes Galbraith was appointed from three applicants to the other post. Mr. Younie, who also had university qualifications, felt some degree of grievance, and applied for an increase in salary. It was only in March of the following year that his salary was raised to £100 per annum and Miss Riddoch's to £55.

The Scotch Education Department approved the introduction of secondary education. Its letter to the School Board agreed to recognise the school as a secondary department centre, provided the necessary facilities were introduced. In view of the inevitable increase in the school roll, the School Board applied for a grant of £1200 for extension purposes. Two graduate assistants were appointed to supplement the staff: one a male assistant; the other a lady assistant qualified to teach Modern Languages, and, if required, Advanced Music, Drawing and Needlework, as per the recommendation of the School Board minute above.

HM Chief Inspector Robertson submitted his recommendations for the reorganisation of The Nicolson Public School in view of the impending introduction of higher education. In the Higher Department, Mr. Macleod was to be responsible for the teaching of Latin, Greek, Mathematics (Geometry, Algebra and Higher Arithmetic), Geography, History and English; and Miss Galbraith for French, German, Drawing, Music, advanced Needlework and Domestic Economy. Mr. Forbes and Mr. Younie were to share in the teaching of Scientific and Commercial subjects (including Book-keeping) in the Junior Department. Navigation and Agriculture had been introduced shortly after Mr. Younie's arrival. Mr. Forbes would supervise the work of all the departments.

On 13th January 1893, the new extension to the school was formally opened. The occasion was marked by the presence of members of the School Board, the local Science and Art Committee, and members of the general public by invitation. The Chairman of the School Board expressed the satisfaction of its members with the able and successful way the school had been conducted for many years under the staff; words which Mr. Forbes might recall the following year with bitter anger.

On 10th April 1893, there was a special meeting of the Board with J.L. Robertson present. Robertson, on an inspection of The Nicolson School, had discovered a second garden and a byre, both being run by Forbes, the resident Headteacher. The Board took the J.L. Robertson view, i.e., the byre was a health hazard to pupils; and the area of it and of the second garden was intended to be a pupil playground, not an adjunct to Forbes's garden.

The HMI Report, as recorded in logbook of May 2, was critical:

> *I venture to suggest tentatively that the Assistant now in charge of the fourth and fifth standards should devote at least half his time to the secondary department and a large part of the remainder to the sixth standard. The recommendation on the last point is very urgent in view of the lamentable deficiency shown in the Composition, and particularly the Arithmetic, of this the highest standard, and the passport to the secondary department of the school.*
>
> *... the proper development of the institution needs very close supervision indeed.*

This report was probably written by Robertson. It would certainly have required his approval, for he was by now, as the archives confirm, acting Chief HMI for the district.

A new annual grant of £60,000 had been allocated nationally within Scotland to promote secondary education.[ix] (That is over £7m per year at current prices.) After much debate, it had been agreed that it should be administered, at least in rural areas, by County Committees on which Board members, county councillors and H.M. Inspectorate served.

In July 1893, the School Board resolved:

> *to apply to the Ross and Cromarty County Committee [for Secondary Education] for a grant of two hundred pounds for Nicolson Public School... [and] to explain in doing so that the School is the largest and most advanced in the island... as a superior centre of Higher Education it will likely soon to have to solve the needs in this direction of a population of thirty thousand.*[x]

In addition, they made the point that the school was available to scholars from 'outlying districts,' of whom there were ten at that point, so that the Nicolson Public School was already, albeit on a small scale, acting as a secondary school beyond the town of Stornoway. Their case was further supported by highlighting that they had appointed two staff and opened new premises; but they needed more staff and more equipment. All this was explained to the Board by J.L. Robertson, *'acting Chief HM Inspector and Chair of Ross and Cromarty County Committee.'*

In December, the Board received £150 from Ross and Cromarty County Committee for Secondary Education.

Permission was given to erect an extension to the original building in January 1893. These developments were now officially recognised by the County Committee on Secondary Education which recommended that the other Lewis Parish Boards should be informed of the status of the school and the conditions of entry. A further grant was requested, as The Nicolson Public School was now the largest and most advanced centre of education in the island, and it would have to serve an area with a population of nearly 30,000. Additional staff would soon be required. For this purpose, a sum of £600 (about £73,000 at current prices) would be needed in addition to the former grant.

Having received £150 from the Secondary Education Committee, it was decided to appoint an assistant in the Secondary Department, especially to teach Advanced Science, at an annual salary of £130. When Mr. John Don intimated that he was unable to take up this post because he had been offered a more lucrative post in Cambridge, Mr. W.J. Gibson was appointed.

In March 1894, the Board noted that Mr. W.J. Gibson, MA, of Rothesay Academy had been appointed Science Master. He was additionally put in charge of Standards V and VI (what today we would call Primary 6 and Primary 7) and of the Secondary Department.

Gibson immediately asked for, and was given, a mandate to reorganise the Secondary Department in all its branches with the proviso that he should have regard to successful procedures in similar departments in other centres of higher education. He was also commissioned to consider the possibilities of having Navigation included, either during the day or as an evening school activity.[19]

The report on secondary education which Mr. Gibson soon produced was fully endorsed by the School Board.

Around the same time, Mr. John Ross, Clerk to the School Board received notice about the Leaving Certificate, founded in 1888 but only opened to Board schools in 1892:[xi]

> *Sir... I am to state that my Lords are prepared to recognize (sic) the above named school as adequately equipped for the purposes of Article 70(e) of the Code.*
>
> *H. Craik*[xii] *Scotch Education Dept.*

This was formal permission to enter pupils for the newly founded Leaving Certificate, something for which explicit SED authority was required, not least because such students attracted a higher level of grant.

The HMI Report of May 21st, which was transcribed into the school logbook, mentioned the imminent reorganisation which would reinforce the Secondary Department, and described development delightfully as, *'promising but very gradual indeed.'*

Again, this was almost certainly written by Robertson.

Forbes was asked by the Board to tender his resignation as Head Teacher. The only minuted discussion was about whether he should be *'asked'* or *'instructed.'*

By July 1894, Forbes had resigned. The historical documentation on this is limited. The main Nicolson Log records neither the departure of Forbes nor the promotion of Gibson. That decision would have been that of Gibson himself: school logs were written by head teachers. In October it was reported that, *'Mr. Forbes (had) gone away to take up another appointment.'*

This entry - in a supplementary secondary department log - glosses over what one finds in the Stornoway School Board minutes: Forbes had been dismissed.

---

19 Evening school activities across Scotland then and for many years to come were the way of delivering what we would now call further education.

Chapter 5:
Under the Guidance of W.J. Gibson

Within four months of his appointment as a Science Master, W.J. Gibson was perhaps the obvious choice as Head Teacher of the Nicolson Public School, following the (sudden) departure of John Forbes. His appointment - in charge of what we would now call the Primary and Secondary Departments - was confirmed at an annual salary of £150 (about £18,000 per annum at current prices).

Mr. Gibson

Gibson had attended school in Greenock and studied at Glasgow University and was for a short time Assistant Master at Douglas Academy before paying a visit to the USA. He was for a year on the staff of the Boys' Latin School in Boston (established 1635), the oldest and (many would say) the best organised school in America. He then returned to Scotland for a further spell of study in Glasgow and was three years on the staff of Rothesay Burgh School before coming to The Nicolson Public School (as the school had been renamed under Stornoway Board).

As the new Science teacher, as we have seen in the previous chapter, Gibson had also been given charge of Standards V and VI (now P6 and

P7) and the Secondary Department. He had already started reorganising secondary education at the school and the Stornoway School Board were impressed by his plans for secondary education. The Nicolson had just been recognised to enter pupils for the new National Leaving Certificate (see Chapter 4).

We shall see in subsequent archival material the opinion of J.L. Robertson of the effect of this transition with the 1894 appointment of Gibson. But there is also on record, albeit written some 70 years after the event, the opinion of Robert M. Maciver, Nicolson school student at the time, winner of the Medal for English in 1896 and a future Dux:

> *There was nothing at school to arouse any incentive. During these years the school had been descending from bad to worse. Our Nicolson Institute had been the leading school in the outer islands and had acquired a fine reputation over the north of Scotland.[20] But it was under a headteacher who had been gradually deteriorating.*

Until:

> *the school had been placed under a new administration. When I went to school on Monday the old headmaster had disappeared. There was a new head and there had been a general shakeup… he certainly knew his job, and once he had reformed the system everything went smoothly enough. We all came to respect him, although he did not evoke any feeling of warmth.[i]*

Maciver's testimony to the effect of a new Head Teacher some 130 years ago is worth quoting today, for it would stand up rather well to what is written currently about how schools achieve excellence:

> *The changeover was a turning point in my life. There was now something to strive for. Paths were opening to the future. When I heard there were to be prizes for excellence, I felt it was a call to me, and I was eager to respond. The new discipline was an uncomfortable shock to our school habits. Our listlessness met with sharp reprimands. Punctuality was insisted upon. Homework, negligible before, was imposed, although not excessively. But once the initiation stage was over schooling*

---

20   This sentence is suspect. Maciver is probably confusing the pre-1894 school with its subsequent reputation.

became meaningful to most of us. Something had been missing from my life, and now I knew what it was. I owe a great debt to this headteacher - W.J. Gibson - and in retrospect I realise that I never properly acknowledged it. In youth we take so many gifts as if they had dropped from the sky.[ii]

In December, the Board accepted a £160 county grant from Ross and Cromarty County Committee on Secondary Education (Chair: J.L. Robertson)[21] and a proposal from them that £50 of it be devoted to five scholarships for students who lived at least three miles from The Nicolson School. The importance of these bursaries, each worth about £1,200 per year at current prices, for rural access to The Nicolson, was emphasised by Macdonald.[iii]

By May 1895, the next HMI Report,[iv] transcribed into the school log, commented positively on the school's reorganisation of its Secondary Department:

Since last inspection this important school has been very thoroughly organised, and the staff in the higher department has been greatly reinforced by the appointment of well qualified assistants. The school is now established and equipped as a centre for secondary education for the whole island of Lewis and in this respect it is specially subsidised by the County Committee on Secondary Education and by the Trust for Education in the Highlands and Islands. The main aim is presentation for the Leaving Certificate.[v]

The declared function of the school as the chief secondary centre for the island was gradually being realised, with an influx of selected pupils from rural schools into the Secondary Department as evidence of the school's standing outside the immediate area. It was also noted that the school had ten staff, four of them pupil teachers.

The same minute recorded that Donaldina Macleod was the first Dux of the school.[vi] She subsequently qualified as 'Lady Literate in Arts.'[22]

There is a list of pupils having achieved Leaving Certificate passes, the first from the school in August 1895. The names include: Donaldina Macleod (Lower English; Lower Mathematics); Robert M. Maciver (Higher

---

21   Professor Bone has stated that HMIs of this era often took direct managerial actions in a way not found today.
22   A sub-degree, but a respectable qualification invented by the University of St Andrews at a time when, across Scotland, women were denied access to degrees. See more in footnote 26.

Arithmetic; Lower French); Alexander Macdonald (Lower Arithmetic).[vii] The first two were school Duxes - in 1895 and 1898 respectively; the last was possibly Alexander Macdonald of Swordale, one of the last pupils to go to university via a combination of The Nicolson School and Aberdeen Grammar School.

Several pupils received a Merit Certificate (awarded for high performance to pupils over the age of 13): one of whom was D. Mackenzie.[viii] This was the Donald Mackenzie of Aird who was to be Nicolson Dux in 1900 and subsequently a professor in the 1930s at Princeton Theological Seminary. Unlike Maclean (Dux 1897) and Maciver (Dux 1898), Mackenzie came from no merchant class background. Son of a single mother, his uncles and aunts were mostly crofting and fishing folk. He probably did rely greatly on the £10 bursary.

The Secondary Department transferred to the (newly acquired) Free Church School Building in March 1896.[ix] The school now had fourteen staff and the HMI Report of May 11th spoke of good progress, a number and variety of subjects being taught successfully, and very satisfactory general discipline.[x]

In April 1897, J.L. Robertson inspected the specific subjects and reported *'most encouraging'* general results, *'methodical work'* and *'loyal cooperation'* on the part of the staff. The construction of an expensive and modern building for the *'accommodation of the secondary pupils'* was also noted.[xi]

By June, the Leaving Certificate was being undertaken in several subjects, notably Maths, with 26 Lower, five Higher and one Honours candidates, English (22, thirteen and four) and French (twenty, six and two).

The Leaving Certificate had been introduced in 1888 and its accessibility was extended greatly in 1892. 'Highers' were quickly accepted by universities and 'Lowers' by certain professions, e.g., as an entry to banking. The category of 'Higher' lasts to this day, largely unchanged, and was a brilliant advance. The category of 'Lower' was abandoned in 1962, to be transformed into Ordinary Grade (a considerable success story), then into Standard Grade, and now into National Qualifications.[xii] The category of 'Honours' was abandoned very early in the 20th century. An intended 1888 function had been like the 1998 one for the 'Advanced Higher', to give accelerated or 'fast track' entry to specialist university study. That intent of the late 19th century was as unrealised as that of the late 20th century.

In July 1897, the Dux Medal was awarded to Donald Maclean from Bragar. Coming from fifteen miles outside the Parish of Stornoway, Maclean lived in Stornoway from Mondays to Fridays and probably on at least some weekends,[23] showing that by now the school was indeed serving as a secondary school for the wider island. Maclean was probably too early to have benefited much, if at all, from the £10 scholarships designed for such rural pupils;[xiii] but census data show that his father was a village merchant living in a substantial Bragar house.

New Beginnings

On August 29th, 1898, the new premises on Francis Street, built and furnished at a cost of over £3,000, were formally opened. This is the only pre-20th century Nicolson Institute building which survives to this day, although now operating as *e-Sgoil*, a centre for electronic learning for schools both in the Western Isles and further afield.

The new Secondary School building on Francis St, opened in 1898

Under the direction of Mr. Gibson, the new scheme of secondary education thrived. A bursary scheme, initiated on the advice of Chief Inspector Robertson, was arranged for bringing into the school the best pupils from the rural areas. As the SED had opened the Leaving Certificate examinations to state-aided schools from 1892, the examinations being

---

23 See Maciver's autobiography which refers to Stornoway weekend activities involving Maclean.

taken in individual subjects only, tentative arrangements were made from 1894 onwards to take advantage of this by the presentation of some of the older pupils in Lower English and Arithmetic. Pupils and teachers threw themselves into the effort and, although there was much leeway to make up, the first results were regarded as encouraging.

Four years' work had brought The Nicolson School to the point where sending pupils directly[24] to the universities was feasible. To give parents confidence that the course of education being provided was a suitable preparation for the universities, it was necessary that some pupils should have enough trust in their own abilities to start the new tradition. Two of the boys due to finish their school course in 1898 elected to set the new fashion: Donald Maclean of Bragar, winner of the Medal for Gaelic, and Robert M. Maciver, the Dux; Maclean with a bursary of £30 per annum for four years; Maciver with one of £25 for three years[xiv] (respectively about £3,700 and £3,000 per annum at current prices).[25] Robertson noted that several Nicolson candidates took 'a high place' in the bursary competition of the Trust for Education in the Highlands and Islands in that year.

Donald Maclean entered the University of Aberdeen and graduated four years later in Arts with First Class Honours in English. He was afterwards to become Principal Teacher of English and later Rector of Boroughmuir High School, Edinburgh, from which he retired in December 1943.[xv] Robert M. Maciver of Stornoway, went to Edinburgh University where he graduated with First Class Honours in Classics, and afterwards at Oxford University took a First Class in Moderations and First Class in Greats. He was to become Professor of Sociology and Political Theory at Barnard College and Columbia University, both in New York, and came to be regarded as one of the leading authorities in sociology in his time.

The success of these school students made it clear to parents that pioneer work had been done; and it became standard practice for school students to pass directly from The Nicolson Institute to universities.

But formidable barriers (of socio-economic status and gender) remained. Census data in Bragar and Professor Robert Maciver's autobiography show that the fathers of Maclean and Maciver were both relatively prosperous merchants;[xvi] and this almost certainly was a factor in the educational progress of their sons. And it was no accident that the 1895 predecessor of Donald Maclean and of Robert Maciver as a Nicolson Institute Dux (Dina Macleod) had to settle for a sub-degree LLA, the delightfully titled 'Lady

---

24 As opposed to going via Aberdeen Grammar School.
25 Although Maciver went on to be much better known academically than Maclean in adulthood, this, and other evidence, suggests that it was Maclean who excelled as a school student.

Literate in Arts' qualification;[26] Scottish universities began to admit women undergraduates to degree courses only in 1892, and initially the numbers were small.

Success in secondary school provision across Scotland had, however, put financial pressure on government. Elementary (primary) students progressing to secondary schooling attracted a higher per capita government grant for the School Boards, so Robertson and the SED in the 1900s insisted that thirteen- or fourteen-year-old students in rural elementary schools passed a newly established 'qualifying exam' to access the secondary education provision.

Parents also showed themselves eager to take advantage of the new facilities by leaving their children at school beyond the compulsory age (then thirteen). Several older children who had already left school returned when they heard what was being done and resumed their studies. Parents in the rural area were most anxious to have their children avail themselves of the new privileges provided. When the Carnegie Trust (see Chapter 6) gifted £100,000 (about £12m at current prices) annually to the Scottish universities to pay the fees of deserving children of Scottish birth, the way was now rather more open for even the poorest pupil to receive the benefit of higher education. Thus, the Scottish ideal of a wide democratic system of learning edged a little more towards reality.

The Centenary School Magazine of 1973 summarised Gibson's contribution:

> *It was extremely fortunate that at this period in its history The Nicolson Institution came under the guidance of Mr. Gibson, one of the greatest and most enlightened headmasters of his time in Scotland. As an educationalist he was years ahead of the conditions prevailing in almost all other schools, especially in his conception of secondary education. He maintained this position against the restrictive practices advocated even by the [Scotch] Education Department; he passionately believed in a broad based and wide-ranging education and soon became a pioneer in certain aspects of educational advancement when Scottish education was meeting its greatest challenge. He took a*

---

26 The LLA was a 'distance learning' qualification for women, introduced to allow them access to university-level education in the days before they were admitted as students to university itself. Students studied at colleges local to them, and sat examinations set by St Andrews University, at centres all over the UK and in many places throughout the world. Many thousands of women participated in the LLA scheme, which was so popular that it survived for 50 years, into the 1930s - long after women were admitted as full-time university students. *(Archives of University of St Andrews).*

great interest in all matters affecting the school. His intellectual stature was such that it ranged from a wide knowledge of English Literature and Classics to aspects of scientific study which took him on many expeditions of a geological or biological nature. With Mr Stevens, a teacher in the school, who was later to take part in Shackleton's expeditions, he studied in detail the geological structure of many parts of Lewis. (Mr Stevens was later to become Professor of Geography at Glasgow University.) Often accompanied by his wife, Mr Gibson went on many botanical expeditions which he described graphically in his farewell address on his retirement. With his many varied duties he still found time to write several pamphlets on scientific and educational topics.

Although small in stature, his energy, drive and enthusiasm for the welfare of the school was to make The Nicolson Institute one of the leading educational establishments in Scotland. He established a tradition of high class education.

In Lewis his name became a household word and his imaginative organisation of secondary education, with the many new ideas incorporated in it, made his name also well-known in educational circles in Scotland. For his contribution to education, not only in raising its standard in Lewis but also in promoting concepts which opened new horizons for his school students, he richly deserved the honour conferred on him the first schoolmaster in Scotland to receive the CBE.[xvii]

Jottings from The Nicolson Institute Annual

Some extracts from The Nicolson Institute Annual (Edition 1) of 1901 give a sense of the life of the school at the turn of the century from the perspective of the *'schoolboys and schoolgirls'* under W.J. Gibson:

> *Our magazine is out at last! We hope our contributors like their appearance in print. Will our readers please to remember that most of the magazine, as the work of schoolboys and schoolgirls, cannot be expected to be free from the marks of juvenility. We hope that such old people as read it may belong to the happy class of those that remain youthful in spirit. May such a production as this help to renew their youth during the hour at least that it whiles away.*

The seasons of the year have been rather bewildering, but May, the month beloved of Chaucer, was this year a marvel of good weather. In school this is a pleasant time, though it takes some self-control to keep one at books on a summer evening. The Leaving Certificate Examinations will soon be here. The dates of the various papers are as follows:

June 19th—Arithmetic, Geometry, Algebra.
June 20th—English, German.
June 21st—French, Greek.
June 24th—Latin, German (2nd Honours paper).
June 25th—Trigonometry and Logarithms, Dynamics.
June 26th—English (2nd Honours paper).
June 27th—French (2nd Honours paper).

The Highland Trust Examinations begin on 3rd July — 'Which subject do you profess — Gaelic or Greek?'

We are glad to see that with the returning spring something of a revival has occurred in school athletics. By next season it is hoped that each of the senior classes will be able to furnish a football team, and then we shall be able to make up for the want of outside competition by the device of inter-class matches. We are glad to see that there has been enough of esprit de corps among the girls to enable them to revive the game of targette. Will they have enthusiasm to make them rival the play of the old days?

The singing of the German songs by the School Choir at Christmas was quite a novel experiment. Even the non-musical ones among us enjoyed them, and the German airs sung by the Choir at the Headmaster's Lecture. They are said to be quite the fashion in London now. The girls used to get up very pleasant impromptu concerts on the Friday afternoons. What has become of them now?

Provost Anderson's idea of presenting each pupil of the School with a penny of the last issue of our late Queen's[27] coinage was a happy one. The pennies distributed by him fresh from the mint will form an interesting souvenir of our great Queen's reign.

The School has contributed its tiny quota to the great collections of the Glasgow Exhibition. It naturally took the form of something characteristically Hebridean. A selection of the current folklore tales of the Lewis, collected by the scholars, was made and written out, some in English, others in Gaelic; and these were forwarded as the Lewis contribution to the educational exhibit. The material is rather unusual, and this, taken with the use of the two languages in the telling of the tales, may make the exhibit of some interest to those engaged in teaching English composition.[xviii]

The Art contributions received by the editors were a pen-and-ink sketch of the Secondary School from D M, pen-and-ink sketches of the present Headmaster and his predecessor from M M'D., and a portrait of our late Queen in black and white from Miss H.

We of the present are glad to see that the old Nicolsonians at the Universities are giving a good account of themselves. Of special interest has been the success of Donald Maclean at Aberdeen, and of Robert Maciver at Edinburgh. We congratulate them and believe that their good work will be an encouragement to us to keep up the tradition.

Of our old masters, we see that Mr McKim has gone recently from the Stirling High School to be English Master in the Mackie Academy,[28] Stonehaven. Mr Taylor is still on the staff of the EC. Training College, Aberdeen.[29] He must realise by this time that there is quite a colony of Nicolsonians in the 'granite city'.

---

27   Queen Victoria had died in 1901.
28   Founded 1893; still exists.
29   Aberdeen at the time had two Church colleges for the training of teachers. But the precise meaning of 'EC' is mysterious. The 'E' may be a mistranscription of 'F'. In which case it was the Free Church Training College.

> The LLA[30] Examination has had this year at the Stornoway centre a larger number of candidates than on former occasions. As in previous years the Rev. George Macleod was in charge. The St Andrews authorities deserve our thanks for their willingness to continue these examinations at this centre, even when, as was the case on one occasion, there was only one candidate.

> It is satisfactory to know that candidates in music have had an opportunity for the first time of taking their examinations in Stornoway. The Royal Academy of Music recently allowed a candidate to take the theory paper here; and a local committee for the Trinity College Examinations was recently formed, with J. M. Morrison, Esq., as its chairman, and Miss M. A. Morrison, LRAM, as its secretary, and the Practical Examination has now been held, Mr Edwards being the examiner. It is matter for congratulation that it has been so arranged, for obviously a trip across the Minch is very bad preparation for a candidate's pianoforte practice. The examination in Theoretical Music is to be held on 22nd July.

> Our Headmaster's Lecture on the old schools of Lewis supplied us with some very curious items. We cannot but admire the heroism of our forefathers who turned up at school each morning for lessons at seven o'clock. Another fact that struck us was the eighteenth-century practice of having the scholars come to school on the Sunday afternoon to be examined on their notes of the morning's sermon.

> It is a great satisfaction to Nicolsonians, past and present, to note the continued interest taken in the School by the surviving members of The Nicolson family. The latest instance of their kindness is the offer of Messrs Roderick Nicolson, Tighnabruaich, and Kenneth D Nicolson, Mississippi, to add a tower to the buildings in Sandwick Road.[31] There can be no doubt that such an erection will greatly improve the appearance of the building.[32]

---

30   Lady Literate in Arts. See footnote 26.
31   Finished in 1904.
32   The tower has survived into the 21st century. The building it adorned has not.

How many of us are entering the competitions for the special prizes? The ones of most interest this year are those for the best collection of Lewis sedges, rushes, and grasses, and those given by a local gentleman for folklore tales in Gaelic or English. The competitors for either set of prizes should find a reward in their work, even if unsuccessful.

The competitive event of the year is of course the struggle for the Dux Medal. A keen competition is expected this year, and the question that is being most debated among us is whether it will fall to a boy or a girl? Will the steady succession of 'Macs' in the Dux List be continued, or will it meet with its first break this year? Time and the examinations alone can tell.

Chapter 6:
Into the 20th Century

On 30th March 1900, the school was inspected by J.L. Robertson[i] with the HMI subsequently reporting on May 29th:

> *As to its Secondary Department, the School is in the very first rank in the County*

and:

> *(the) Upper department is recognized... as a separate Secondary Department.*

Andrew Carnegie

If Gibson and other Scottish head teachers had played a large part in developments at secondary school level, and if Robertson, in particular, had played a big part at School Board and County levels, another Scot, one Andrew Carnegie, also made a very decisive intervention in 1901.

Andrew Carnegie

Carnegie decided he would give about $5m to Scottish universities (at current prices possibly about a quarter of a billion US dollars, although these conversions are tricky). Never himself having been near a university, he took some advice and decided it should go into a trust which might be expected to generate spending power of about £50,000 a year to pay tuition fees for poor students. £50,000 per year was about what the state then spent

annually on Scottish universities and is over £2.5m a year at current prices.
The Carnegie Trust itself today says:

> ...it should be stressed that...access to university education in Scotland has not always been free...fees were charged by the universities (originally by the professors directly) which represented a significant barrier to access, and there was no provision for subsistence. There was hot competition for the small number of available bursaries, and the award of a bursary was, within living memory, the occasion of a school holiday. It is precisely because student fees constituted such a serious barrier to entry for the 'qualified and deserving' that Carnegie was first persuaded to consider this endowment.[ii][iii]

It was hard enough for J.L. Robertson, D. Maclean and R.M. Maciver, all sons of prosperous families, to make their way to university in the 19th century. But in the early 20th century, Carnegie made a further addition to opening pathways to universities. In his draft history of The Nicolson Institute in the early 1970s, Angus Nicolson wrote:

> The debt which Scotland owes to Andrew Carnegie...is beyond measure; and the benefits which the Carnegie Trust has bestowed on students and universities alike are greater in value far beyond the riches he bestowed on his native land.

By 1904, half of all Scottish university undergraduates were benefitting from the Carnegie endowment[iv][v] and there were certainly many school students from Stornoway and the wider island who were deeply indebted. On 19th October 1900, according to the school log, Donald MacKenzie passed the Arts Preliminary Exam for the University of Aberdeen, and in 1901 was awarded a Ross-shire County Committee bursary £25 for 3 years.[vi] (At current prices that is about £2,750 per year.) In addition to this bursary, set up by J.L. Robertson, his university tuition fees were paid for by Carnegie.

Urgent Needs
Perusal of the school logs and Board minutes for the first decade of the century gives a sense of the key issues which were to dominate these years: the growing school roll and expanding staff numbers; accommodation problems; new buildings; and educational developments.

As secondary education grew in importance under the guidance of Mr. Gibson, the pressure on accommodation steadily increased - this despite the addition of the Francis Street Buildings. Even with the use of Church Halls and the Drill Hall, the facilities for the increasing range of subjects were stretched to their limits. HMI Robertson emphasised the urgent need for a further extension if the school was to meet the Department's approval.

The probable closure of Lady Matheson's Seminary for Girls,[33] with the consequent boosting of The Nicolson roll, gave further cause for anxiety. In 1898, a fruitless approach had been made to Lady Matheson for the acquisition of the Girls' Seminary as a Centre for the new Science Department, despite the urgent necessity to provide higher education of such a nature, and although Ross-shire County had allocated a considerable sum for Science and Technical Education as part of a national scheme which might prove of great benefit to the older girls.

A small wood and iron building had been built adjacent to the original school building to house the infants, but, as this was proving inadequate, Robertson recommended that a new and more modern Infant Hall should be built with a central hall and enough classrooms. This, he maintained, should receive priority over a proposal to build a technical school. This new stone building was erected in 1904 on Matheson Road, consisting of five classrooms and a central hall to cater for the growing number of infant pupils.

As the school roll steadily increased, bringing greater problems and further extensions in the range of subjects taught, it was unanimously decided to designate Mr. Gibson as Rector.[34] The title of 'Headmaster' was later (December 1905) confirmed as being changed to 'Rector.' (SSB).

Looking up Matheson Road with the Infant School in the foreground (courtesy Tasglann nan Eilean)

---

33   See photograph in Chapter 1.
34   A designation for the Head of The Nicolson Institute which, over a hundred years later, is still a matter of controversy.

A New Name

On 26th February 1901, following application to the Lords of Council and Session from the School Board, and with the Nicolson brothers' increasing interest, the name of the school was changed to The Nicolson Institute. In a letter the Rev. Roderick Nicolson expressed his feelings:

> *When I agreed to the transference of this Institute to the School Board, I did so on the express condition that it should retain its then present designation in all time…It is very pleasing to learn from you that the original designation has been reverted to.*

Thus ended a chapter, which had been extremely stormy at times, marked by conflicting opinions and dissension. Now a happier time seemed to lie ahead, one of increasing harmony and loyalty to an Institute and not a public institution. From the original 105 pupils the roll had increased to nearly 550; the number of teachers to sixteen from the original three; this progress was due almost entirely to the imaginative genius of Mr. Gibson and HMCI Robertson.

In the school log of July 1901, it is noted that Murdo Morrison from Tong was employed as a teacher at £130 per annum. His salary was just over £15,000 at current prices, as compared to the actual 2020 starting salary for a teacher in Scotland of £23,000. In September 1903, after at most two years on the staff of The Nicolson Institute, Murdo Morrison departed to a post of *'sub-inspector of schools,'* a school inspectorate post that no longer exists. He went with the Board's 'highest approbation.' He subsequently became Director of Education for Inverness-shire and lived to an age of over 100, contributing to the 1973 School Magazine.[35]

Meanwhile in 1904, Mary Crichton (Dux of 1901) returned to the school as a teacher, initially temporarily. Locally educated teachers were unusual at that time, at least in the upper parts of the school.

In July 1903, the Board addressed the issue of school pupils being in residence in Stornoway. They determined to provide *'a home for the lads in town where they would be better cared for than was the case at present.'* (SSB) There was no reference to girls although by then the school had several in the secondary department, albeit perhaps few from rural areas. The (school) bursary competition of that year had eight entries, four from Carloway.[vii]

---

35 See Chapter 12.

The Nicolson Institute staff, 1903 (courtesy Tasglann nan Eilean)

An *'epidemic of German measles'* was recorded in the school log that autumn, with an outbreak of whooping cough shutting the Infant Department for some time the following November. Such reports were a common feature of school logs of the time.

It was recorded in the school log, as of June 30th 1905, that the school had 147 infant pupils, 430 elementary pupils and 146 secondary pupils. By then, although this is not recorded in the log, 'secondary' pupils become so by passing a 'qualifying exam' about the age of twelve; those who failed had to remain in school in 'post-elementary' classes to the age of fourteen.

On December 7th, the clock and chimes for the tower[36] were handed over. A speech by J.N. Anderson (Chair of the Parish School Board) quoted extensively from a letter from the two surviving Nicolson brothers (Roderick and Kenneth)[viii] in which they referred to over 700 students, *'some from the Hebrides and from opposite shores of Ross and Inverness-shire.'* This, while strictly accurate, can lead one to overlook the fact that most of the 700 were from the town of Stornoway itself (a continuing feature of The Nicolson Institute for many years).

By 1907, the School Board had received intimation from Major Matheson that the Female Industrial Seminary proposed to close on 30th June 1906. It was therefore now necessary to find fresh accommodation for 85 pupils. The resulting school congestion was solved by school students from Battery Park going to Sandwickhill School and school students from Coulegrein going to Laxdale School. The latter part of that arrangement lasted for many years.[ix]

---

36 See photograph in Chapter 1.

The Nicolson Institute post-1905 with the clock tower (courtesy Tasglann nan Eilean)

Early in 1907, the School Board decided to build a wood and iron building to contain five classrooms. This building soon became known as the *'Tin School.'* In the same year, the two surviving Nicolson brothers, Roderick and Kenneth, proposed to present a gymnasium to the school. The school authorities readily agreed, suggesting that it should be part of the new technical school they were arranging to build. Shortly afterwards, however, the Reverend Roderick Nicolson died on 6th May. Only a few months later the last surviving brother, Kenneth, followed: they were both buried in Sandwick Cemetery.

Kenneth Nicolson

But all was not necessarily harmonious in the first decade of the 20th century. The Lewis Local Committee set up by Lord Balfour, Secretary of State for Scotland in 1903, whilst acknowledging that *'elementary education... was fairly well established in Lewis'* with The Nicolson Institute as the island's *'secondary centre,'* suggested the following next steps:

> *The Committee are unanimously of the opinion that the prominence given to Technical Education... is thoroughly justified and they regard a large well-equipped provision of Technical Education as absolutely indispensable for the island of Lewis... if... social and industrial improvement... is to be definitely assured. The Committee wished to keep especially in mind the question of female Technical Education, especially in the matter of practical training in household economy (cookery, laundry and household hygiene)... they suggested that a central institution... be founded in Stornoway... The Technical training of boys was not neglected and they proposed a scheme for the teaching of Trades, Navigation and Practical Seamanship.*

The Stornoway Gazette commented in 1972: *'this was to be implemented, but not for many years.'*

In 1909, the Educational Institute of Scotland (EIS) sent a special Commission to Lewis, specifically Barvas, Lochs and Uig, to gather evidence on rural education. The conclusions were heavily critical of the state of the school buildings; heating arrangements; staff quality; poor salaries; system of management; and low school rates.

The Commission also made observations on the peculiar position of Dr J.L. Robertson, the Chief Inspector:

> *He must take care that the receipt of special grants must not be made a cause for local ratepayers to shirk their fair share of the cost of education... He must at the same time satisfy the Treasury through the Department that not a penny more than the watchdog of the public purse thinks absolutely necessary has been expended. He must hold an even hand between school boards and teachers - in short, he must reconcile his education duties as Inspector with his financial responsibilities as Manager - and... will probably please neither party... he must encourage education... and at the same time he must exercise an economy so strict... Need it be said that he has failed to do the impossible.*

They suggested that Mr. Robertson should have been *'more educationist and less the economist.'* If this had been so, 'the children and teachers in the parishes of Barvas, Lochs and Uig would today be the gainers.'

The Secretary of State for Scotland invited comment from the school boards. They alleged that the EIS representatives were incompetent, that their visit to the island had been of a hurried nature and that consequently their investigations were unreliable. The truth lay between the two standpoints, but there is no doubt that many of the findings were genuine and sincere. There was much difficulty, for example, at this time in obtaining suitably qualified staff despite repeated advertisements in many newspapers. Hence many schools were grossly understaffed. The Commissioners of the EIS visited the Shetland Islands the following year and it is significant that they reported how much more pleasant a task it was to report on the conditions under which education was carried out there compared with the island of Lewis.

The Nicolson Institute was, at this time, accessible to the best of the pupils from outlying villages by a system of small bursaries, which were woefully inadequate in number and amount. Otherwise, the school continued to flourish under Mr. Gibson, and it at least could boast of being well-equipped and well-staffed,[x] in contrast to some of the EIS findings in the other schools.

By 1906, there were 748 on the roll and the school log makes reference to the 'Qualifying Exam' taking place. In July, there were four pupil teacher candidates from The Nicolson Institute for the 'King's Scholarship Exam'. Pupil teachers, as we have seen, were school students who did a mixture of teaching and of advanced school study and who were paid - modestly - for that. Every year they could compete for a 'King's Scholarship' or, prior to 1901, a 'Queen's Scholarship' that took them to a training college for a two-year teacher training course. In 1906, the whole system was undergoing a radical reform, including the abolition of the role of pupil teacher.[xi]

The school log records the story of Jane A. Fraser. A school student in 1889, she had become a pupil teacher in July 1900; in September 1902, she had won a 'King's Scholarship, 1st Class' which had taken her to the Church of Scotland Training College in Edinburgh (now the Moray House School of Education and Sport of the University of Edinburgh) for two years of study and then a year of study abroad (then as now needed for those who intended to teach a foreign language). She had returned to The Nicolson Institute as a certificated teacher in 1905. But by 1907 she was dead. She could not have guessed that her brief life would provide, more than 100 years later, a vivid illustration of a scheme of teacher training which was then widespread but is now almost forgotten.

A New Building

A decision was made in 1907, with a school roll of more than 800, to erect a new building in Springfield to relieve the now overcrowded Secondary Department on Francis Street. This new building was built with the aid of a £7,000 grant from the Scottish Education Department and incorporated five classrooms, a Science laboratory, Technical workshop and Art room. The new building was opened in 1910 by Lady Pentland and, adjacent to this, a gymnasium was erected, paid for by money received from the estates of the last surviving brothers of the founder, Alexander Morison Nicolson.[xii]

Lady Pentland opening the Springfield Building, August 1910

The Pentland Building and Gym, 1911. Both parts remain in use today

Inscription on the 'Old Gym'

The school log records that by 1908, there were 810 in the school, with 250 in the secondary department, of whom 80 were *'living away from home' in 'approved lodgings.'* Five students gained the full Leaving Certificate that July, with a further seven the following year. Eleven sat the King's Scholarship Exam.

The 1908 school log makes reference to 'Pryde's School.' Mr. Pryde was the 'second master' in charge of elementary (or primary) classes. It was to take another 53 years to see the establishment of the distinct Nicolson Primary and a further eight before Stornoway Primary School opened on Jamieson Drive in 1969, for The Nicolson Institute to become solely a secondary school.

Girls' first gym class, 1911 (courtesy Tasglann nan Eilean)

Murdo Murray was the school Dux in 1909. Quite a lot is known and written about Murray, the son of a Lewis shoemaker. Graduating in 1913 with an MA from Aberdeen, he went initially to teach in Paible Public Higher Grade School in North Uist. He fought in the Great War with the Gordon Highlanders and wrote well-known Gaelic war poems. Subsequently, he was Headmaster of Beauly Public School; and then, about 1930, he became an HMI, eventually in charge of the Inverness district; he inspected some Lewis schools; and, in retirement, survived until 1964. He was a chronicler of the life of John Munro, Dux in 1911.[xiii]

The school report of 1909 also records John Munro to be 'first in Class IV.' For someone who had just joined the school, migrating from being a pupil teacher at the elementary school at Knock, this was a remarkable achievement.

By April 1910, the secondary department had 23 school students from the Parish of Barvas; 29 from the Parish of Uig; 37 from the Parish of Lochs; six from Harris; two from Barra; and 55 from the 'landward' part of the Parish of Stornoway i.e., from outside the Burgh of Stornoway.[xiv]

This total of 152 represented a huge advance on the 1897 position where the equivalent total was ten. But the Burgh of Stornoway had another 150 in secondary education. Given that Stornoway at the time had perhaps one-fifth of the Lewis population, rural school students were clearly still under-represented.

Some rural schools in Lewis also did well in this 20th century regime. We have mentioned above for example the 1900s school careers of the great, if tragic, John Munro from Knock school (son of a fisherman) and the almost equally great Murdo Murray from Back school (son of a shoemaker), both examples of rural elementary school students of humble origins who accessed secondary education in The Nicolson Institute and subsequently became university graduates just before 1914.

Munro was a teenage prodigy in writing Miltonic verse in English, his second language; he was a good Gaelic poet; he was a war hero; and he was dead in France before he was 30 years old. Murray was a war poet; a schoolteacher; a school inspector and - in his elderly years in the 1950s - a chronicler in Gaelic of his deceased friend, Munro. Both almost certainly had their paths through secondary school smoothed by J.L. Robertson-instituted bursaries.

Steady Growth
To illustrate the steady growth that was taking place in the various subjects up to this point, one can look at developments in the Science department.

Even in the first year of Mr. Gibson's appointment, scientific work was undertaken. A special course of individual work was developed that could be taken, although no laboratory facilities were available. A movement for individual work in experimental science spread from a school in England to America, a practice which Mr. Gibson may have seen during his year teaching in Boston. Scottish schools were slow to adopt this method, but one of the first, even with its limited resources, was The Nicolson Institute. Photography was taught as a Science subject; original research on beekeeping was carried out in the school: a new observation hive was invented which was called after the school and a disease which was worrying beekeepers throughout Britain was first identified here.[xv]

Later, one of the rooms of the old Free Church School, which was subsequently to become the first Commercial room of The Nicolson Institute, was converted into a small laboratory. When the small wood and iron building was vacated on the completion of the new Infant Hall in 1904, it was converted to the same purpose: a much better equipped laboratory was incorporated in the Springfield building[37] - the 'Upper Lab':

> *One must salute the remarkable results achieved in these early formative years with the limited accommodation and resources available.*[xvi]

It is important to consider the structure of the curriculum and the aims that Mr. Gibson hoped to achieve through it, as outlined in the account of the history of the school given by him on its Jubilee in 1923, and later put into the more permanent form of a booklet at the request of friends.[xvii] As The Nicolson Institute was the only secondary school serving a large population, it had to make provision for a wider range of needs than was usual in a secondary school. Although great importance was attached to the preparation of pupils for university entrance, a broad-based educational scheme was needed to equip pupils for a wide variety of callings. Examinations had not been allowed to dominate the educational outlook of the school or the subjects taught. A school had to fit its pupils not only for making a living but also for life. This involved not merely preparation for work and citizenship but also for leisure. Many opportunities were denied to Lewis children because of their remoteness from centres of culture, and so the school had to try to make up for the lack of such things as lectures, concerts, museums, picture galleries and the hundred and one avenues of interest open to some city children. Gibson had a profound belief in

---

37   The building still exists as part of the school, albeit with extensive renovations.

literature as ameliorative and life-improving and at the same time in the cultural value of such practical subjects as Science and handiwork. These beliefs had coloured the scheme of work throughout.

To provide the wide range of instruction that Gibson envisaged, as distinct from a narrow academic one, Commercial Subjects, which included book-keeping, shorthand, typewriting and office routine, were introduced as early as 1899 and taught by Mr. William Grant,[38] who was later to found the *Stornoway Gazette* and to compile the 'Lewis Roll of Honour.' A room on the ground floor of the old Free Church School in Francis Street, which initially was used as a laboratory, was eventually used for the teaching of Commercial Subjects and for many generations of Nicolson school students it was known as the 'Commercial Room.'

When facilities became available, every girl received instruction in housecraft from twelve years of age onwards, and every girl who passed through the school was taught needlework. (Unsurprisingly for the time, these facilities were not made available to boys.)

The milestone of 1914 - after which everything was going to change - provides an appropriate point at which to review progress. As it happens, there is a school booklet of Session 1914-15 which gives us handles on progress in terms of staffing and attainment at this point.

The secondary school had twenty teaching staff, including the Rector Mr. Gibson, up from six in the late 1890s. The expansion over these years had been dramatic. Names which spring out of this page in the school booklet are: John Macrae, later Rector; Roderick Macrae, subsequently Science Master; Donaldina Macleod, first school Dux back in 1895; and William Grant, founding editor of the *Stornoway Gazette*. The elementary school staffing and the staffing of the Infant Department had been much more stable over these fifteen or so years.

There had now been precisely twenty school Duxes, and their qualifications and 1914 occupations were listed, examples being:

1895 Donaldina Macleod, LLA Honours, German. Nicolson Institute teacher;

1897 Donald Maclean, MA (Aberdeen) 1902, 1st Class Honours, English and History. Senior English Master, Boroughmuir School, Edinburgh;

1898 Robert M. Maciver, MA (Edinburgh) 1st class Honours, Classics 1903; 1st Class Classical Mods, 1905 Oxford; 1st Class Litt Hums, 1907 Oxford. University Lecturer, Aberdeen;

---

38   Father of James Shaw Grant.

1909 Murdo Murray, MA (Aberdeen) 1913. Assistant Master, Lairg High School;

1911 John Munro, MA (Aberdeen) 1914. Divinity student, Aberdeen.

In terms of the students of 1913, the report documents 34 passes in Higher English, nineteen in Higher Maths, nine in Higher Latin, eleven in Higher French and 23 in Higher Science.

This was a school unrecognisably different from what it had been fifteen years earlier in 1898.

In a speech in the House of Lords on 'National Training' in July 1916, Lord Haldane[xviii] said:

> *What was called The Nicolson Institute at Stornoway was turned into a secondary school and the effect upon the Hebrides has been extraordinary. The sons and daughters of crofters go there, many of them with little bursaries which they get through the County Council. They get a secondary education at The Nicolson Institute and from there go out into the world to become teachers, doctors, lawyers and ministers; the effect on the social life of the Hebrides has been remarkable. I give your Lordships that as an illustration of what reform will do if it is judiciously and simply applied.[xix]*

This was something of an over-statement. Haldane believed that school education in England in the 1910s was inferior to that in Scotland; and both were inferior to school education in Germany, a country in which, during a first degree in Edinburgh, he had been a student for some time. He may well have been right; but, in the middle of the Great War with Germany, these views cost him his political career for many years. Calling his favourite dog 'Kaiser' did not help.

The school staff, June 1912 (courtesy Tasglann nan Eilean)

A panoramic view of the school in the early 20th century

Experimental Science

(images courtesy Tasglann nan Eilean)

Students in 1912: making hives and studying bees

Laboratory work

The Nicolson apiary

Pupils at work in the laboratory in 1912

A junior class visiting the apiary in 1910

1912 students displaying apiary processes

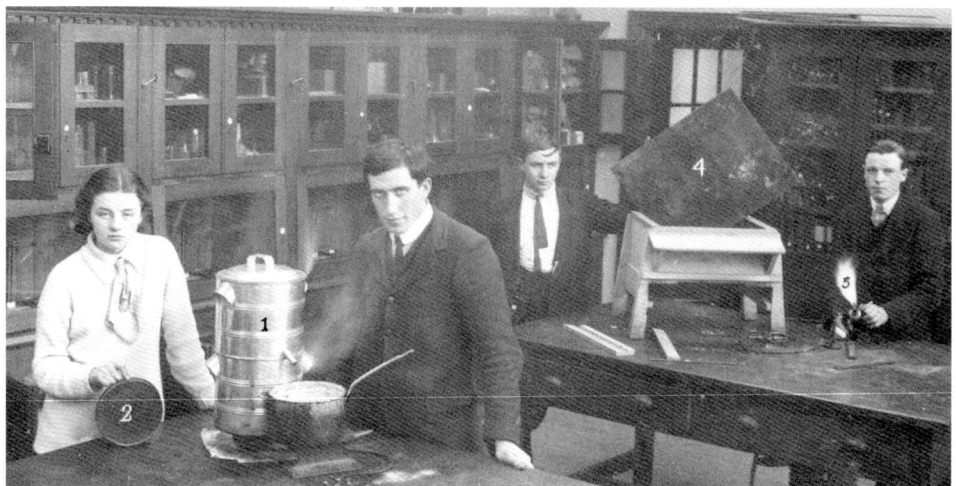
Melting old combs into wax and disinfecting hives

Counting the pollen bearers as they enter the hive

Chapter 7:
The Great War Years

W.J. Gibson, Head and then Rector of The Nicolson Institute from 1894 to 1925, and Mrs. Gibson (née Laird) had two children. One, a boy, Henry, died in infancy. The other, daughter Jane, attended The Nicolson Institute and became its Dux in 1916, the year in which she departed from home to become a student at the University of Aberdeen. Father, mother and daughter corresponded regularly with each other.ⁱ

W.J. Gibson (courtesy Tasglann nan Eilean)

In 2020, museum and archive staff busied themselves in transcribing letters from the W.J. Gibson collection.[39] This extensive archive was gifted to Museum nan Eilean in 1992 by the executor of the will of Lady Jane Urquhart (née Gibson).[40] It includes a highly intriguing series of letters that provide glimpses of both a school and a community dealing with the effects of the Great War.

---

39 Not only was W.J. Gibson a prolific writer of letters to his daughter and to former students, he wrote a huge number of articles for newspapers and academic journals. The collection now resides with Museum nan Eilean.
40 Jean Gibson was born in 1898. She was registered on her birth certificate and in formal documents as Jane Gibson, but referred to as Jean (and also Sheann) Gibson by her parents.

As Professor Lindsay Paterson of the University of Edinburgh comments:

The letters from the Gibsons to their daughter are particularly illuminating, principally, of course, of life and education at the time, but also, I suspect, of a type of family relationship that has rarely been documented. There has been much writing before... about the long-distance family correspondence with emigrants... although we often think of emigration as a matter for regret, for the emigrants it very often was their route to success. From the Gibsons, from their eminent position in the town and the island, that sense of opportunity is never neglected... I cannot think of any such insight as you have presented here into the conversation between Highland parents and their adult child still within Scotland...

If most parent-child relationships had been contained within the local community, education would never have led to opportunity for personal advancement, and the poverty and restricted horizons which Mrs Gibson, especially, notes would never have changed...

War Declared

As many of the older school students were members of the Territorial Army, 27 were mobilised[41] on September 18th, 1914, as members of the local Ross Mountain Battery. This number rose to 42 before the Battery left Bedford. After the Leaving Certificate examinations, no boys were left in Class VI and in 1917, there was only one boy in Class VI.[ii] Many former pupils, including recent graduates Murdo Murray and John Munro, the school Duxes of 1909 and 1911 respectively, enlisted directly from university as a wave of patriotism swept the country.

The regular contact maintained by them with their old school is striking. This is reflected in the numerous letters from alumni which Mr Gibson received from various theatres of war, and which appeared in the war-time magazines.[iii] These included very graphic impressions of conditions at the front. Even amidst all the horror around them, from time to time including the death of their school companions, their letters breathe forth a spirit of intimacy, camaraderie and courage.[iv]

---

41 Not called up: it was 1916 before conscription started. But those who had been in the RNR (Royal Naval Reserve) or the TA (Territorial Army) were mobilised in 1914. This UK mechanism still exists (as some TA members found with the much more recent invasion of Iraq).

A. Thomson wrote:

> My best wishes to the boys of the old School and at the present crisis I could not wish for them better than to be led by the hand which has led so many of us already. May you find comfort in the thought that those of us who have been so fortunate as to have passed through your hands still bear the stamp of the old School and try to live up to your standard of looking on life.

Murdo Murray was keen to continue with his Gaelic studies:

> I should like very much to get the Higher Gaelic papers. If you have any ones I shall feel obliged if you send me one. I heard it was much too difficult for the ordinary pupil.

And Alick Mackenzie enjoyed the *Stornoway Gazette*:

> We carry about 90 men, everyone from England but myself. I have great laughs over them trying to read the Gaelic in the 'Gazette'...I believe every Lewisman in the service look forward to its coming as it's just like paying a visit to old SY. I like that debate between D.Y.M. and Neiseach...They remind me of the old Debating Society in school...

Aeneas Mackenzie reflected fondly on what Mr. Gibson would say about boys returning:

> I hope that I may see the old school before I am sent into action. I owe it a great debt – perhaps however I am not forgotten as I remember hearing you say that when a boy came back to you made it a point to forget the quality of his Latin prose and his distaste for Browning – the latter misfortune in my case has been healed by time.

And John Munro, a writer of several letters to Mr. Gibson, summed up the feelings of many of the Old Nicolsonians:

> *Your warm interest in us reaches and moves us, Mr Gibson. I'm sure it is the same with all the boys.*

Each year, as the war progressed, the older pupils were called up. Some volunteered for the Ross Mountain Battery; others enlisted in famous Highland regiments to suffer the hardships of trench warfare and the anger of massed guns, the mud of Flanders and the horror of Passchendaele, or the mindless slaughter of battles such as Mons, Ypres and the Somme. Others served at sea in ships of all kinds from minesweepers to dreadnoughts. Women enlisted in the Women's Royal Naval Service, the Women's Army Auxiliary Corps or in one of the various branches of the Nursing Services.

This long and bloody conflict took a heavy toll of lives. The Nicolson Institute Annual of 1916 reported the extent of the losses:

> *The number of our school losses, we grieve to say, has been greatly increased during the year: those who have made the supreme sacrifice now number 53.*[v]

Later, when Mr. Gibson was asked by the editor of the 'Lewis Roll of Honour'[vi] to include an account of the contribution made by pupils of The Nicolson Institute, he numbered the dead at 101. Most had been killed in action; others had died from wounds or the hardships they had endured. In April 1932, several years after his retirement, when Mr. Gibson was asked to unveil the School War Memorial bronze plaque in the Francis Street Building[42] the number of those who had fallen had risen to 148.

Underneath the number who had given their lives he had written:

> *Their example will remain to inspire their successors in the school with something of their spirit of brave endeavour and the recognition of the high purposes for which life is given.*

He also listed the number of decorations won by former pupils - an impressive catalogue of awards for gallantry and self-sacrifice gained in all the sections of the armed forces.[vii]

---

42 Still there in 2023.

In The Nicolson, a School Training Corps had been formed in which the older pupils liable for military service received instruction in drill, signalling, stretcher-bearer practice and rifle firing. Rifle firing practice took place in the playground, but on wet days the corridors and gymnasium were used.

As the school had already contributed so much, representations were made to the Scottish Education Department that the Higher Leaving Certificate should be granted to all pupils who had enlisted before having the opportunity to sit examinations. This was agreed, provided that their previous scholastic achievement was satisfactory and that records were kept for scrutiny if required.

As the war developed a longevity which most would not have anticipated, the following extracts from the Gibsons' letters provide insight into the day to day lives of the island community and the pressures put on the Rector, staff and pupils by the frequent withdrawal of staff and senior pupils to enrol in the service of King and country. The school continued to provide high quality education and the community continued to offer a range of social, intellectual and other activities; although individuals were clearly saddened by the loss of life and injuries suffered by the men and women from Lewis, they believed in the righteousness of the cause.

In 1916, Mrs. Gibson wrote to Jean of local and national concerns:

> *Maggie[43] and Mrs. Murray the school cleaner have been busy all the week putting in peats. There is now a big stack at the back and they are not nearly finished yet. Maggie is staying on till Saturday next to see it all finished. Then she is talking of going to munitions in Glasgow.[44] Last night she and I were busy putting away the contents of two boxes of groceries...*
>
> *The prices are astonishingly high. Bread in Stornoway is to be 1/-. This week, 6d a loaf!*
>
> *The teachers have been applying to the S.B. [School Board] for an increase in salary to cover the rise in prices and make it possible to live. They have a reply refusing and giving 'a reasoned statement' but no sympathy. What will the teachers do next? We shall see.*

---

43   House servant.
44   A common occupation for women in World War I and World War II.

School War Memorial bronze plaque in the Francis Street Building (now e-sgoil)

First World War Roll of Honour (courtesy Tasglann nan Eilean)

The issue of teachers' salaries and inflation was ongoing. Inflation over the years of 1914 to 1918 averaged over 19% per annum.[viii] Unlike today, teacher pensions were not inflation-proofed.

A few months later, Gibson wrote very presciently:

> *Lord Leverhulme (Sunlight Soap) crossed the Minch at the same time as Mr. Anderson. It is being said in Stornoway that he is a possible purchaser for the Island. Have you visions of Stornoway being converted into Port Sunlight and Lewis breaking out into an eruption of garden cities?*

Bad weather hit school attendance in January 1918, as Mrs. Gibson reported:

> *Today and yesterday have been double sessions for the whole school. Today there were two infants present out of 172! Two brave boys! Both today and yesterday Rudland[45] has come before breakfast to make a way out for Papa. Today 'Lil Lizzie' did not come in the morning. She tried to make Goathill in the afternoon but had to turn at the hospital.*

The war and its privations went on, as Gibson's letter a month later mentioned:

> *Today in school I was distributing rationing application forms to pupils in lodgings. They have to apply for individual cards, and not to be put on the landlady's household form. Is that how it is to be with you? At holiday time they will get an emergency card to enable them to get supplies when at home. This refers to butter, margarine, and tea. Mamma is just now reading '34 ways of cooking potatoes,' issued by the Food Control folk.*

---

45 School janitor

In the same letter he noted an honour to a former Nicolson Institute teacher:

> *Mr. Stevens and his companions of the Antarctic have got special Polar Medals granted by the King. He is on instructional work in the S. of England, the last I heard.*

He also recorded a visit from a former school student:

> *Lt. John Munro was in seeing us on Thursday evening on his way back from leave. He had been ill with trench fever and bronchitis.*[46]

In early March 1918, the Gibsons had dramatic news for their daughter:

> *Now, to tell you about Stornoway's great misfortune. The municipal buildings were completely burned down yesterday evening. It is sad to see so much good work of many hands through many months destroyed in a few hours, and with it the result of much thought and effort over years.*[47]
>
> *Mamma and I had had tea early & were getting ready to go down to the reading-room to have our usual look at the pictures, when from one of the front windows we saw some smoke rising over the house roofs. A girl who came to the door with a parcel told us the town hall was on fire and we were just in time to see from the lavatory window the flames rush up and wrap the little clock tower. Through the flames we could see the hands still pointing to the time, then they dropped. Then the dial dropped bodily, and a minute or two afterwards the tower toppled over sideways.*

---

46   He was to die two months later in Flanders.
47   A real disaster for The Nicolson Institute which relied greatly on the Town Hall library. It took until the 1950s for it to acquire a serious school library of its own.

The war continued to occupy many of Mr. Gibson's thoughts:

> *Word has come that John Munro had been awarded the Military Cross for his work during the Somme fighting in the early part of this great offensive. The award, however, had not been intimated until three days after his death. I hear that Angus Maclean, of your class, has been wounded again and is in hospital somewhere. I haven't got the address yet.*

Mrs. Gibson intimated a picture typical of the times in October 1918:

> *The inft. sch. [infant school] is closed for three weeks for the measles. Miss Reid went home last night.*

But, in the same letter, there was a rumour of the approach of peace:

> *The Gaelic choir is being resusitated [sic] and meets for its practices in - The Cottage! Jessie Pope told me today that the Sopranos at last meeting were Mrs. Rose, Mrs. Aeneas, and Dora. They hope to have a concert to celebrate the peace - if and when as Mrs. Asquith would say.*

However, some privations persisted:

> *Got the fires started this last week. The pupils in the Francis St. Building had to bring their own firewood before we could get started.*

Post-Armistice (11th November 1918), Mr. Gibson wrote:

> *Behold! George [not known] has come; arrived on Tuesday night. I found him at the gangway and recognised him by his likeness to Joe and his father. He had had a good crossing. Was in London when the armistice was declared and got close to the balcony at Buckingham Palace when the King and Queen appeared. Was greatly impressed by the sight of London off its head with news.*
>
> *The influenza[48] has reached Story (Stornoway) now. It has been pretty bad in the country for some time now, and there have been a number of deaths. The first death in Story was that of Jo Maclennan, of which I think I told you on Sunday. To-day Dr. Murray has closed the School (including the Secondary Dept.) for three weeks.*
>
> *On Monday shortly after 11 o'clock the sirens and hooters began to blow, proclaiming the armistice. Tuesday was intimated as a Town holiday, so after the Bible lesson on Tues. morning we were off for the day. On the Monday evening there was a tea for the naval men at the hut. Mamma and I were down. Mr. Murray got me to say a few words on the occasion to the men. Then there was a sing-song and I believe they enjoyed themselves till eleven. Mamma and I came off about nine…*
>
> *We got a gift of pictures – reproductions in colour of some of the great pictures – from Lord Leverhulme,[49] some sixteen, for school decoration. They are quite good, and will prove an acquisition…Best love. Papa.*

---

[48] 'Spanish flu' as it was popularly – and erroneously – called. It was a major pandemic, which like the 2020 one almost killed a Prime Minister: Lloyd George.

[49] Who had acquired the Island of Lewis in May 1918.

Chapter 8:
The Final Gibson Years

The years between the wars were characterised by a number of recurring themes, many of which were recorded in the Gibsons' continued correspondence with their daughter, Jane. Whilst the school, which celebrated its Golden Jubilee in 1923 and continued to flourish under Gibson, and the progress of former pupils predominated, other matters were raised: housing shortages in Stornoway (with consequences for housing of staff and pupils from rural areas); illnesses in the community; poverty and emigration to Canada, and Lord Leverhulme's ownership of the island.[i]

Mr. and Mrs. Gibson

Mrs. Gibson's letters in particular provide fascinating insights into domestic matters and social change in Stornoway:

> *The* Sheila *now sails only three times weekly so we are back to the old bad arrangements again. We get our milk now from Aberdeen so for that also it is very awkward. We will see if Stornoway will stand it.*[ii] *So far I haven't heard much said…*
> *Roddie Smith*[50] *is the new provost and Norman Stewart and Hugh Macleod are the baillies. Mrs. Julia Fraser is standing for the County Council opposing Ex provost Maclean for Lochs. Hope she will go in. Aren't the women coming to the front in Lewis – at least the cheeky ones?*[51]

---

50   See Vignettes in Appendix 7.
51   Mrs. Fraser was the wife of the Sandwickhill headteacher; but a formidable politician in her own right.

The following year, Mrs. Gibson celebrated a famous moment in the history of Stornoway:

> *Have you seen in the papers that Sy. has gone dry. Doesn't it seem too good to be true? Flora Smith and I were out for several hours again on Monday on propaganda work and on the voting day all hands were there from dinner time till the poll closed at 8 o'clock. The result was announced about 10 – 720 for no licence. 149 for no change – 5 for limitation. I hear there is great indignation among the drooths!*

Mr. Gibson later updated his daughter on further temperance-related activities in which her mother was involved:

> *Mamma is out just now at a No Licence meeting. The J.P. court meets to-morrow and Rev. Rod. Morison and Mamma are to appear for the Temperance party and to speak if they are allowed. They probably won't be. What they want to prevent is the giving of restaurant licences once the ordinary licences have been refused.*[52]

The post-1918 reorganisation of education proceeded, but not without problems, as Mr. Gibson observed in June 1919:

> *There was a teachers' meeting on Saturday with a moderate turnout. They are not content with three teacher members out of 22 on the new School Management Committee for Lewis and in the meantime, pending adequate representation, refuse to nominate any. They are also opposed to a Bible Examination of the schools. This is partly in answer to the appointment of a ministerial committee by the Authority to draw up a uniform Bible syllabus for the schools of the county.*

The generalities, if not the specifics, of the above staff concerns would continue to feature in coming generations.

---

52   They failed.

Another issue which would continue to beset the school for many years was the timekeeping of the clock tower:

> *Yesterday forenoon Mr. Roderick Macrae[53] and I were busy trying to rouse our gong-clock in the Springfield building to renewed action. It had proved too much for Mr. Ewen. We did not entirely succeed but we mean to have another go at it. Later I went with Mr. Rudland[54] up the clock tower[55] to see what is the matter with the clock to make one hand so unmannerly as to contradict the other three to the extent of 15 minutes.*

Mr. Gibson wrote in the same year of the plans which were afoot to mark his 25 years in post:

> *We see from the Gazette that the former pupils of 'the Nicolson' are getting up a presentation to me on the occasion of my semi-jubilee. How do you think it feels?*

He updated his daughter later in the year as planning for the event continued:

> *Did I mention what I had asked the presentation money to go in? Enough of it to endow the Dux Medal and a Dux Prize is to be the first charge. This will take, I think, about £80. A bookcase (about £20), a typewriter (about £20), Mamma's necklet of art silver work and the balance in books. How's that?*

Mr. Gibson's Semi-jubilee

On 21st January 1920, former pupils and others interested in the school gathered in the United Free Church Hall to celebrate Mr. Gibson's semi-jubilee in The Nicolson Institute and pay tribute to the great advance which the school enjoyed under his guidance. After a congratulatory speech, Dr J.L. Robertson, HM Senior Chief Inspector of Schools for Scotland,

---

53 Science master
54 Janitor
55 Tower still in existence. See picture in Chapter 1.

presented a collection of books, a typewriter and a balance of £200 from the sum subscribed.

> The Nicolson Institute,
> Stornoway, 5th Feb., 1929
>
> Jean dear,
>
> This is my first letter on my new typewriter and as is proper it is to Sheann. It seems a very handy little machine and you'll be able to practise on it during your Easter vacation. It is arranged so that either blue or red can be used at will. That should prove very useful to you when you want to write vividly to your friends. How do you like the effect? I have been asking Mamma if she means to use it, but she says "No!" You will see from this line that two arrangements of spacing between the lines is possible.
>
> Papa.

The first letter written by Mr. Gibson on his new typewriter (Tasglann nan Eilean)

Mr. Gibson in his reply stated that it was his intention to devote this balance to endowing a Dux Medal and a suitable selection of books which would help the winner in his subsequent studies. The Dux Medal continued to be awarded in his name for the best part of the following century.

The 1973 *Centenary Magazine* paid tribute to Dr Robertson's support of Mr. Gibson and the school:

> *In his tribute to Mr. Gibson, Dr J.L. Robertson made little reference to his own vast contribution to education, especially in its organisation in the Highlands and notably the support he had given to secondary education in The Nicolson Institute during its formative years. It was a happy chance that two such great educationalists, men of vision and drive, should be contemporaries and find themselves working in close collaboration. With Dr Robertson's professional guidance, authority and support, Mr. Gibson's task in raising The Nicolson Institute to its position in Scottish education was made much easier. Although the role played by Mr. Gibson in furthering secondary education in The Nicolson Institute may have been more immediately apparent to most people (as it is to this day),*

Dr Robertson deserves at least equal credit for the part he took in those events, often behind the scene (sic)*, where his influence made its development possible and its progress more rapid.*

This 1973 judgement, some 50 years later, has stood up well to the test of time.[56] It is worth dwelling on his influence at this point.

As we have seen earlier, J.L. Robertson was originally chosen as Her Majesty's Inspectorate representative to aid School Boards in the Highlands which were encountering financial difficulties. Because of his work in furthering education, especially in the Highlands, he received the honorary degree of Doctor of Laws from Edinburgh University in 1912. Three years later he was elevated to the post of Senior Chief Inspector of Schools for Scotland.

The Nicolson Institute football team, 1923 (courtesy Tasglann nan Eilean)

---

56 Surprisingly there are some memoirs of The Nicolson Institute that make no reference to J.L. Robertson. The (rather modest) Robertson Road in Stornoway is named after him. History has not been as kind to him as it should have been.

The Nicolson Institute staff, 1922
Back row: *Mr. Rudland (Janitor), Mr. J. Macdonald, Mr. N. Macleod, Miss A. Macleod, Miss A. Macdonald, Miss C. Macarthur, Miss A. Morrison, Mr. D. Mackay, Miss G. Morrison, Miss M. Clarke, Miss C. Macleod, Miss R.E. Bassin, Miss M. Macfarlane*
Second row: *Miss A.S. Barron, Mr. C.W. Bell, Miss K. Harrold, Miss M.A. Young, Miss M. Love, Mr. R. Macrae, Miss H.A. Hart, Mr. J. Thomson, Miss B. Morrison, Miss M. Stewart, Mr. K. Macdonald*
Front row: *Miss A. MacCallum, Mr. J.M. Pryde, Miss M.S. Pope, Miss L. Macleod, Mr. W.J. Gibson (Rector), Miss D. Macleod, Miss D.C. Hutchings, Mr. J. Macrae, Mr. W.W. Ewing*

Dr J.L. Robertson's Gift

In 1925, having now retired and having been honoured with the CB (Order of the Bath), he donated £2,000 to Lewis and £3,000 to the rest of the county. The £2,000 was to be used to provide two bursaries of £25 each, tenable at Edinburgh University, to help students whose home circumstances deserved them of financial aid.[57] From a man whose maximum career salary would have been £900 per year, this was not an inconsequential sum: it is over £120,000 at current prices. Mr. Gibson, in a letter of 1924, confirmed the interesting news about Robertson's school bursaries:

> *I had a letter from him the other day. He has been endowing two bursaries for the School at Edinburgh University, but his name is not to be attached to them whilst he survives.*

---

57   One was subsequently held in the 1960s by Matthew Maciver of Portnaguran, later appointed Chief Executive of the General Teaching Council for Scotland and a little later still, like Robertson, created an Honorary Graduate of the University of Edinburgh.

The universal respect in which Robertson was held was well expressed in the remarks made by the Chairman of the Management Committee at a meeting held on 21st June 1927, a week after his death:

> *Among the many brilliant sons of Lewis who have shed lustre on their native isle, his is no second place. He was a born educationalist and the reorganisation of the education system of the country was due in no small measure to his intelligent outlook and mature genius. Lewis owes its front-rank position educationally to his splendid powers of organisation and efficient foresight. Time and thought and energy were unselfishly given to the raising of his beloved Isle to the place of usefulness it now holds in educational matters. His viewpoint was broad and enlightened as became an official of high standing and he was eminently successful in correlating educational matters in Lewis with the general system of progress.*[iii]

When he died in Inverness, six years after his retirement, his popularity was clear in the extent of the activity surrounding his funeral; when his body was returned to Lewis the flags on the island were at half-mast and all businesses were closed at noon. All schools throughout Lewis were closed and it was reported:

> *... the senior boys of Nicholson [sic] Institute headed the funeral procession, which included the Lewis Pipe Band, the Brethren of the Masonic Lodge, the Provost, Magistrates and Councillors of Stornoway and members and officials of all the other public bodies...there was a very large and representative attendance of the general public, including people from all parts of the island.*

Sir George Macdonald, the Secretary of the Scottish Education Department, extolled his virtues and said, 'Few men in our time have laid their native country under so deep an obligation as he has done.'[iv]

Headstone to Dr J.L. Robertson in Sandwick Cemetery

The Gibsons' Continued Correspondence

On a brighter note, end of term functions in the form of staff picnics to 'the links' at Broad Bay and Arnish featured in the correspondence in both 1920 and 1922:

> Staff picnic yesterday, to the links at Broad Bay.[58] Weather fine, golf (for those who cared), rounders, and the other games of childhood days. Found three birds' nests among the sand and shells, which Mamma and I were much pleased to have seen.

and:

> Friday evening from 4.30 to 11.30, Teachers' picnic to Arnish. Weather kept up, though a little cold. Presented Mr. Thomson with a clock and Miss Gina Morrison with a wristlet watch; also bade farewell to Messrs. Ewing and Barron.

58 Now Stornoway Airport

New appointments were also noted:

> *Did we mention that the School is getting a Singing Mistress – a Miss Bassin from Liverpool Holt School.*[59]

as were the post-War university and employment successes of some returned former pupils:

> *We'll be interested to hear about the rest of the English list when it comes out. We haven't seen anything of the gradn. list in History yet. John Martin was 2nd in Moral, John Macsween it was who was 1st in Zoo, and I hear (I don't know whether correctly) that another of the soldier laddies, Donald Campbell, is 1st in Logic. If so, 'The Nicolson' is showing up well. I met Henrietta Mackenzie. I think she is through in three Degree subjs. this year.*

and:

> *Had tea with Dr R. at his club; then went out to see the Macleans and to hear how the Boroughmuir appointment was getting on. By the way, we had a telegram to-night at teatime saying Donald (MacLean)*[60] *had been appointed. I am much pleased – but Boroughmuir is even to be more congratulated than D, on the Authority's action... It was quite correct that Donald was 1st in Medicine (class of about 400).*

A letter of Mrs. Gibson's in 1922 revived some local history. She mentioned that Mr. Gibson was contemplating appointing Donald Mackay to the staff of The Nicolson Institute. When Donald was at school, each week he would walk from his Barvas croft to his lodgings in Stornoway (a 24-mile round trip). He served at Gallipoli with the Ross Mountain Battery (as did many former pupils). One can find Donald Mackay of 9 Upper Barvas in the 'Loyal Lewis' Roll of Honour:[v]

---

59 She was to be a long-serving member of staff. Extant files show her photographed at a staff and F.P. reunion dinner of 1950. See photograph in Chapter 11.
60 Donald Maclean (Dux 1897), Rector of Boroughmuir School.

The Serbian gold medal was awarded by the Sovereign of that gallant little nation to Gunner Donald Mackay, 9 Upper Barvas, Ross Mountain Battery.[vi]

Donald was indeed appointed to the staff of The Nicolson Institute. Thereafter, he became Head Teacher in Lionel, Munlochy, and then Muir of Ord, retiring in 1962. He died in 1984, aged almost 90.[vii]

In 1925, Mr. Gibson reflected on the success of ex-NI students in the market for recently qualified doctors:

> *...Zadok has got a temporary post in a big mental hospital in Lancashire. Kenny Kiltie goes to London next week for an interview for a medical post in Nigeria. Most of the other boys are now fixed up, or in the way of fixing up. They have managed sooner than I had ventured to expect.*

Mrs. Gibson also passed comment on the progress of former pupils, writing in the previous year:

> *In the Aberdeen list of (graduates) we found that Jamie Munro and your old classmate, Angus Macphail, had completed their final. Duncan McLellan had distinction. I am waiting now for the Glasgow list. I expect it will have a number of our people. The prospects for women medicals seem more hopeless than ever. It will take a long time before the market assimilates the present glut.*

Years earlier, Gibson reported to his daughter:

> *In school we began our 1st Term's exam. to-day. Things look better this year. There is a very large Third Class – about a hundred – and the Sixth has 27, and of distinctly better quality than last year's. So we shall do better.*

Although accommodation for school pupils continued to cause anxiety, things got better soon. Miss Haldane, an executive of the Carnegie United Kingdom Trust, visited the island and negotiated the purchase of the Imperial Hotel from Mr. Carnegie to be a new girls' hostel.[61] It could house 50 girls and resident staff and was officially handed over by the Trust to the education authority on 24th October 1922. The Louise Carnegie Hostel was named after the wife of Andrew Carnegie. Reportedly Mrs. Carnegie gifted a piano, and the Trust created a special girls' library.[viii]

A point of interest in the founding of this hostel is that it was intended to assist in ensuring continuance of the supply of teachers to the schools of the County of Ross and Cromarty. This is shown by the following excerpt from the Deed of Disposition in 1922, which states that the trust:

> *resolved to establish a hostel in Stornoway for the accommodation of 50 female scholars and students and especially of such of said scholars and students as proposed to become teachers in the public schools in the county.*[ix]

The Elizabeth Haldane Hostel[62] (for boys) on Church Street opened in 1928.[x]

The Gibsons continued to be concerned about on-going staff turnover and salary difficulties. One example was of a teacher accepting a post in Wishaw which paid £45 more than his current salary despite no longer holding a Principal Teacher role. Both Mr. and Mrs. Gibson attended a meeting in Dingwall to defend a proposed salary increase for experienced non-graduate teachers, despite Gibson's misgivings about his wife's attendance:

> *Mamma is for facing the Minch to-night! I don't feel too easy about her attempting it, but she thinks she ought to, as an attempt is to be made by the territorial magnates – Sir Kenneth Mackenzie*[63] *& Co – to turn down the modest recommendation of the Special Committee appointed to consider teachers' salaries.*

---

61   Rather confusingly the owner of what was to become the Louise Carnegie hostel was also a Carnegie. No relation.

62   Named after the sister of Viscount Haldane: she had been a formidable champion of hostels for Highland schools and possessed a great intellect. See pp 31-33 and first set of photoplates in Campbell, J. (2020): Haldane: the Forgotten Statesman who Shaped Modern Britain. London. Largely home-educated, she wrote a 'Life of Descartes' about 1905 for which the University of St Andrews awarded her an honorary LLD. She was also a Companion of Honour and the first woman JP in Scotland.

63   Landlord.

Mrs. Gibson reported on the success in Dingwall:

> *At Dingwall there was an organized attack by all the landed members against a proposed annual increase of £770 among the more experienced non-graduates. That was why I went, and to my great surprise we defeated them hip and thigh. They consisted of Fletcher of Rosehaugh (a reported millionaire) Sir Ken. Mackenzie (the Prime Minister's recent host) Col. Mackenzie of Orde, Lord Seaforth and a few of their satelites [sic]. Didn't we do well. Mr. Clark and Mr. Burns are now on the grad. Scale.*

Staffing concerns were exacerbated by a lack of appropriate accommodation, as mentioned by Mrs. Gibson in a letter of late 1919:

> *We are finding it most awfully difficult to hear of any lodgings for the teachers. We don't see any way out at all, and it is very hard for Papa being so short of staff and having so many changes now after the war. However he is very patient as you know.*

Both staff and children, and the wider population, were affected by illnesses, some now defeated and forgotten, at least in Scotland. In a letter of January 1920, Gibson wrote of 'poor Lamont,' a contemporary of his daughter's, suffering from tuberculosis, and, later, in June 1922, of spending some time with a former pupil who had contracted TB:

> *Sat. afternoon, walk, & visited Sanatm[64] to see Murdo Kennedy; had tea with Matron. Had Murdo down to tea this afternoon – poor laddie, it is very pitiful.*

---

64 Sanatorium: tuberculosis was endemic in Lewis at the time. Eliminated almost totally by the 1950s via BCG vaccination.

Earlier, in October 1921, typhoid was the prevalent concern as Gibson told his daughter:

> *Dr Porter came in the other night after ten o'clock and stayed talking for an hour. We were hearing from her about the typhoid epidemic. There are now about a dozen notified cases and there seems to be a considerable margin of un-notified as far as one can hear. It is a pity.*

Cases increased quickly to 26.

Measles and influenza both had an effect on the school and community during this period - as letters of April 1921 testify:

> *I got 'Dolly Doctor' to come and give us a hand in school[65]. It was just as well, for Mr. Fleming has been off during the week with influenza. There is a good deal of it about still.*

and:

> *Influenza has now reached the staff. On Friday we had Mr. Fleming, Mr. Kenneth Macdonald and Miss Normanna Macleod all off, & Miss Bellann Morison has been away for a month, but her illness is not influenza.*

In February 1922, measles was prevalent; it continued to spread quickly, and the school was closed.

Worsening Social Conditions

The worsening social conditions and symptoms of poverty of the decade were outlined in the letters of both Gibsons to their daughter, related, where relevant, to school concerns. Ex-Provost Anderson's efforts in ensuring

---

65 'Dolly Doctor' (Donald Macdonald) was to marry Emily Paul, the niece of Lord Leverhulme: Leverhulme gave them a substantial slice of the parish of Uig on the south-west coast of Lewis. They were married in London in April 1923. The marriage lasted until the death of Dr Macdonald in October 1961.

Lewis got a £35,000 share of the unemployment grant were praised in a letter of 1922, whilst the number of applicants for the matron's post in the Louise Carnegie Hostel was seen as an indication of the economic grimness of the times:

> *There are 38 applicants for the Matronship. It is pathetic reading through 38 requests for work at £100 a year.*

Lewis was in deep recession. Mr. Gibson observed that 'the town here is like Sunday all the time; no fishing, no work.'

When the Medical Officer of Health published his report in July 1922, it was to cause a great deal of concern to the various authorities. The incidence of tuberculosis had increased to three times the Scottish level. Malnutrition was rife, a large number had no footwear or adequate clothing and, even of greater concern, some were showing symptoms of disease. When the facts were reported in the national and foreign newspapers because of a grossly exaggerated account in a national magazine, the County Council and other authorities were forced to take vigorous action. A distress fund was launched to raise £5,000.

As a result, mid-day meals were provided where necessary, footwear and clothing on the headmaster's recommendation, and adequate heating of the classrooms provided. Thirty-six pairs of boots and various articles of clothing were issued. Hot meals consisting of soup or cocoa and a roll were also provided for children from outlying areas. However, it was many years before a fully equipped canteen was provided.

Gradually conditions improved but, as many needed operative treatment, a full-time surgeon was appointed, the hospital extended, X-ray equipment installed and further medical service supplied by the appointment of an assistant Medical Officer of Health and district nurses.[66]

The outlook appeared so bleak that over a thousand young people, many of them former pupils of The Nicolson Institute, decided to emigrate in search of the security denied them at home.[xi] The names *Metagama*,[xii] *Canada* and *Marloch* were not easily forgotten by an older generation.

The *Metagama* caused quite a commotion when it arrived in Stornoway. Mr. Gibson was invited aboard for lunch. He and the other guests were shown round the ship and after lunch there were speeches. Mr. Gibson

---

66 Medical conditions included defects in bone structure and indications of former lung disease.

records that there were over 30 'newspaper men' present, at least ten of them from the London Press:

> *Saturday here was a stirring day. I do not think we have ever seen the town, or rather the quays, so crowded. The occasion was the embarkation of about 300 emigrants for Canada. The big ship* Metagama *of the Canadian Pacific Ry. Coy. came in about 10 o'clock & anchored inside the harbour mouth off Stoneyfield.*

Mrs. Gibson also noted an intimation of mass emigration from Lewis, on the famous (some would say infamous) *Metagama*:[xiii]

> *Two girls aged about 16 have just been in asking for Testimonials. They are going to Canada in April. A ship is to come to Sy. for about 400 young men and women. It makes it attractive to them to be picked up here. These lassies struck me as young, young to be starting life on their own. An agent from the Canadian Govt. is here picking them up.*

Emigrants in Stornoway boarding a tender for the Metagama in 1923

In letters of 1922-3, both Gibsons recorded potato and corn failures and lack of work in the fishing industry, all of which undoubtedly exacerbated the emigration exodus. Although both noted that fishing improved in 1924, Mrs. Gibson wrote in that year:

> *Another ship is calling at Sy. tomorrow for Lewis emigrants. Soon the population will be much less if this goes on as it seems it must. Perhaps it is the best way out for these people. Really there isn't anything for them to do here.*

The emigrant ship which sailed from Stornoway on 17th May 1924 was *The Canada*, a White Star Dominion liner of 9,472 gross registered tons. Passengers embarked at Stornoway, bound for Quebec and Montreal.

Lord Leverhulme and Gibson

Lord Leverhulme's ownership of the island was another feature which contributed to mass emigration. During the years 1919-1925, Mr. and Mrs. Gibson recorded many meetings at the Castle with Lord Leverhulme in their correspondence; their commentary on his plans for the island ran through the letters. Mr. Gibson did not always follow Leverhulme's views on local employment. Gibson used the connection in order to provide opportunities for school leavers, contrasting that with Leverhulme's intention in regard to works at Goat Island not to employ men from the districts in which there had been land raids:[xiv]

> *Mr. Fletcher, Lord Leverhulme's Engineering Manager, and I have been making a joint scheme as between the School and the works for taking on Engineering apprentices. I want a preference to be given to our boys who have got their Intermed. Certif., the School to undertake their Continuation educn. during their apprenticeship. I am rather glad that there should be a local opportunity for learning engineering.*

At a visit to the Castle later that year, Gibson reported an 'entertaining debate' between two guests, a Professor Sarolea, who was 'critical of the crofters, especially the raiders' and Dr Robert MacIver, who defended them.

Mr. Gibson's own views are not recorded; instead, he used the occasion to discuss education and 'the school' with another visitor, Dr Macdonald, who was due to visit a number of the rural schools that week.[67] However, in Mrs. Gibson's letter of December 1920, Leverhulme's actions are the subject of regret:[xv]

> *Leverhulme is paying off his remaining workers this week, 400 we hear. Seems a pity.*

As times became hard economically both in Lewis and elsewhere, Mr. Gibson feared that 'the first chapter of the Leverhulme schemes here ends in failure.' Women and children were given permission to gather firewood from the Castle Grounds and several old boats were broken up for fuel. Gibson observed that was a 'good deed in itself.'

The following year, Mrs. Gibson speculated presciently on the effect of the latest raids:

> *The raiders have raided again and Leverhulme has stopped the works again. I wonder if this will be final.*[68]

and Mr. Gibson visited the remnants of the Leverhulme works in May 1921, amidst plunging fish prices:

> *In middle of day on Saturday I went down to the cannery and was shown over by Mr. Fletcher. Saw the refrigerating & canning portions. They cd all start in a few weeks, but the state of the markets*[xvi] *is such that it is unlikely that anything but the laundry will start and the new manure-making process begin.*

---

67 Later to be Secretary (i.e. Head) of the Scottish Education Department. He spoke at Dr Robertson's funeral (see page 108).
68 It was.

In October 1922, Mr. Gibson faced a busy week, including a ball at the Castle:

> *Next week is to be busy – Dr Murray's[69] two addresses; Wed. afternoon, opening by Lord L.[70] of Service Men's Hut; Wed. evening Mr. John Anderson lectures on 'The Nic. Inst. & Beekeeping'[71] (myself in the chair) and on Thur. evening on 'Bees'; Thur. evening, ball at Castle & we are going (not to dance!).*

He reported on the details of the event later in the month:

> *We went to the Castle on Friday evening – about two dozen to dinner. Lord L. was in great fettle again and had several stories – not new perhaps – but new to me… A good dinner it was too; we had soup, salmon, grouse, venison, a swell pudding with fruit salad, a savoury, grapes, and coffee…*
> *'Dolly Doctor' was there looking very well in his kilt…*
> *Mr. Donald & Mrs. Maciver fetched us home in their car.[xvii]*

Despite these social niceties, the dispute over land offered to the community by Leverhulme continued; Gibson commented in October 1923 that the District Committee of Landward Lewis had voted to decline the 500 square miles of land offered to them:

> *I hope we have now heard the last of the land-hunger cry! It will be interesting to see what happens next.*

but reported a few days later that the offer had been accepted in Stornoway, leading to the foundation of the community-owned Stornoway Trust, which exists to this day.

---

69   Local MP.
70   Leverhulme.
71   For which the school had established a considerable reputation.

The following month, and somewhat unusually, Gibson indicated his generally favourable view of Leverhulme:

> *A few days ago we, i.e. Mamma & I wrote a little letter of appreciation to Lord L. about his efforts for the Lewis and his help to the School and the Library. We suggested at the end that we wd. like his photo. He has sent a nice print and a nice letter... He has been very decent with Lewis and the folk. Did we tell you that Katie Murray ('Fishy')'s father gets from him a house at Goathill & a pension of 10/- a week? He has been a good old soul in a number of cases we have heard of.*

As Leverhulme divested himself of Lewis estates, abandoned his projects and moved his focus to Harris,[72] Gibson passed comment:

> *Have you seen in today's paper that Galson Ness, with the Lodge and other houses and indeed the whole northern district of the Island has been sold for £500 which figures out at about 2½d an acre![73] It is pure farce in landlordism.*

Leverhulme was to die in May 1925 and, soon after, work was stopped.

---

72 Leverhulme had abandoned his Lewis projects. But was now trying to re-launch them in Harris, centring on Obbe (now called Leverburgh).
73 Now a community trust.

The Nicolson Institute's 50ᵗʰ Anniversary

In February 1923, Mr. Gibson previewed the Golden Jubilee of The Nicolson due the following week:

> *Do you know, Li'l Sheann, that the Nicolson Institute will be fifty years old next Tuesday? It was first opened on the 27ᵗʰ of February, 1873. Our commemoration will not be elaborate, but I hope to tell the children a little about the Founder, and possibly a half-holiday will be the best way to fix the event in the young folk's memory. On the Wednesday evening I am to redeliver a lecture of 22 years ago on 'The Old Schools of Lewis'. This will give the older pupils and their friends a glimpse of the educational perspective into which the N. I. fits. We are also to have some Gaelic music.*

But, judging by what appears in the Angus Nicolson manuscript and, in an abbreviated form, in the 1973 school magazine,[xviii] this somewhat understated what Gibson had invested in this event:

The Jubilee of The Nicolson Institute was celebrated on 27ᵗʰ February 1923. In addressing parents and former pupils gathered on that occasion, Mr. Gibson gave an account of the history of the school and sketched the past educational conditions in Lewis out of which it had arisen. The material thus dealt with was later put into permanent booklet form[74] by Mr. Gibson and, with the addition of various lists and statistics of interest to the large family of alumni, it became for them a souvenir of the school.

Many of the topics included in the booklet, such as the developments in the curricular field, the aims which inspired them and the need for increased accommodation and educational resources to cater for the steadily rising school population, have been covered above.

Mr. Gibson wished to put on record the support which he had received from the local School Management Committee in the effort to bring secondary education within the reach of pupils of both town and country and from the County administration, first as the Secondary Education Committee (1892-1918) and later as the Education Authority (post-1918). The encouragement given by the Education Department through their officials, and the special aid afforded in the form of additional grants he gratefully acknowledged. He wished to remember with special gratitude the attitude of the two Chief Inspectors, Dr J.L. Robertson and Mr. James

---

[74] Much of it is incorporated in this book.

A. Macdonald, who in succession had charge of the district in the early years and who had done all in their power to advance secondary education in Lewis.

With these he wished to mention the three successive Secretaries to the Scottish Education Department and especially Lord Balfour and Lord Pentland, who had filled the office of Secretary of State for Scotland. They had visited the school, and both had shown, personally and officially, an active interest in its aims and work. His debt to the foundation laid by teachers in other parts of the island was one he wished to acknowledge and especially to past and present teachers in The Nicolson Institute who had devoted many years to its service and of whom many had risen to positions of eminence, either as headmasters, inspectors of schools or lecturers in training centres[75] or universities.

In praising the character of Lewis children, especially in their desire to benefit from education, he stated that financial considerations had not only prevented some from attending university, although eligible to do so, but had also prevented many others from continuing for a fourth year to take an Honours course. During these 25 years, however, nine had gained First Class Honours and six Second Class: two in Classics, two in Mathematics and Natural Philosophy,[76] three in Mental Philosophy, one in Modern Languages, two in History, four in English and English Literature and one in Medicine and Surgery.[77]

In the 1922-3 session, there were 840 pupils on the roll made up almost equally of 'elementary' and secondary pupils. The number of teachers had risen, with 25 in the Secondary Department, nine in the Elementary and four in the Infant Department.

The roll had decreased from 985 in 1911, probably due to the declining population, but it was to pass the thousand mark in the early 1930s. The war years had affected the number of Leaving Certificates gained, but, by 1924, 239 had been passed with a group entry to university. Of individual subjects passed, English easily led, followed by Science which had been compulsory for several years, and was closely followed by Mathematics. Already 43 passes had been obtained in Book-keeping and Commercial Arithmetic at Higher grade level.

---

75 What are now Schools of Education in universities.
76 A term for what would now more typically be called Physics.
77 There is a discrepancy between the Angus Nicolson/Centenary magazine Honours' categories and those of Mr. Gibson's booklet. Mr. Gibson reports two in Mental Philosophy and three in History.

Mr. Gibson summarised the universities attended, and the courses followed: 128 students had attended Aberdeen University; 92 in the Arts, nine in Science and 27 in Medicine; 71 had studied at Glasgow University, with 29 in the Arts, seven in Science and 35 in Medicine; and 38 had obtained degrees at the University of Edinburgh, with 25 in the Arts, three in Science and ten in Medicine.

Additionally, 241 girls qualified at teacher training centres and entered the teaching profession.

Also listed were the names of the various Duxes and their subsequent careers. One is struck by the variety of subjects in which they specialised. Between 1895 and 1925, as recorded by Mr. Gibson, six duxes including Robert Maciver and Donald Maclean, gained First Class Honours.[xix]

Donald Mackenzie (Dux 1900) graduated MA from Aberdeen University with First Class Honours in Mental Philosophy. He also was gold medallist and earned a notable scholarship. He later entered the ministry.

Angus Macleod (Dux 1903) graduated MA with First Class Honours in Mathematics and Natural Philosophy. He also graduated BSc in the same year. In 1924 he was Rector of Oban High School.

Norman Macleod (Dux 1908) graduated with First Class Honours in Classics. In 1924 he was Classics Master at The Nicolson Institute. He was later to become Rector of Madras College, St Andrews.

Jane Gibson (Dux 1916) graduated with First Class Honours in English Language and Literature from Aberdeen University. In 1924, Miss Gibson was Assistant Mistress at Edinburgh Ladies College. When her father W.J. Gibson retired and Mrs. Gibson died, she ceased teaching - to care for him. Comparatively late in life, she married: the Gibson Collection was gifted to Museum nan Eilean in 1992 by the Executors of Lady Urquhart (née Jane Gibson).

Malcolm A. Macdonald (Dux 1922) graduated with 1st Class Honours in Mathematics, and a BA in Mathematics at Cambridge. In 1924 he was still a student at Aberdeen University, but later joined, as we shall see in Chapter 9, the Sun Life Assurance Company of Canada.

Another notable Dux (1911) was Gaelic poet John Munro: Munro (Dux 1911) enlisted while he was still a Divinity student in Aberdeen University. He was commissioned and decorated with the Military Cross. He was killed in action during the heavy fighting in Flanders in 1918.

Mr. Gibson reflected on the Jubilee:

> ...On Tuesday morning I got Mr. Cameron over to the Springfield Building, it being the 27th of Feb., and the 50th birthday of the School. We sang a psalm, he made a prayer, and addressed them in a few words. Then with the aid of the picture from the Sixth Classroom I told the young folk a little about the Founder and about his brothers. Something of the same was then done in the Francis St. building, Mr. White being with me, and again in the Sandwick Rd. building with Mr. Cameron. After this I tackled the Infants, the hardest part of my job. The pupils from 'the tin school'. I had to take them over to the Francis St. building so that they could have sitting room. The whole matter was clinched by a half-holiday, which is now to be taken in perpetuity[78] as marking Founder's Day. After five addresses I felt that I at least had earned my half-holiday.

A plaque erected by the Seaforth Highlanders on the clock tower

---

78   Not now, alas.

Another half-holiday was held that year, as Mrs. Gibson told her daughter:

> *This afternoon the school had a half holiday for the unveiling of the memorial bronze for the fallen Seaforths.*

Mr. Gibson's Retirement Plans Advance

Not much more than two years after the school's Golden Jubilee, Mr. Gibson's own retirement plans were advancing:

> *We are waiting to hear your report on the new bungalows, and how they strike you…Whereas at Corstorphine there wd. be the added advantage that we cd. go in at any time into the Zoo and calm our minds by meditating along with the penguins.*

Mrs. Gibson, however, indicated that the plans were not yet generally known in June:

> *Mr Macdonald the inspector is the only one Papa has said a word to about his retiral and he asked him not to say anything of it till he had his arrangements a bit clearer ahead.*

and advertising for his successor was still not underway in October:

> *Papa's post is not yet advertised as although the comtee. drafted the advert. They are waiting for an Auth. meeting for approval of the terms. It is to be advertised at a salary of £750[79] we hear. Donald Mackenzie, Tain, objected that 'there was no need to pay so large a salary when those holding more important posts got less'. Dr Philip, I presume.*

---

79   £46,000 at current prices.

The occasion of his retirement is recorded in historical archives.[xx] Before Mr. Gibson's retiral on 23rd December 1925, staff and pupils gathered in the Springfield Building at 3pm to honour the occasion and pay tribute with presentations from both as a mark of their esteem. Miss Donaldina Macleod, LLA, French mistress and the first school Dux, spoke of his great service to the school over a period of 31 years, and the greatness it had achieved. A senior pupil, A. Macleod, spoke on behalf of his fellow pupils. After presentations were made, Mr. Gibson spoke of his years in The Nicolson Institute, years that had brought great happiness to him, of which the gifts he had received would be a constant reminder. He was sure his successor would receive the same loyalty.

For Mr. Gibson the years had also brought changes. The mass of dark hair and the large, almost unkempt beard of the early photographs had now turned grey, but the slim figure had hardly changed. The hair, now thinned, was carefully brushed; the beard neatly trimmed; and the grey suits which he almost always wore seemed less sombre. There was now an air of distinction, even of elegance; and the high forehead and steady gaze a sign of the high intelligence and drive which had brought such great achievement.

Later, there was a very large gathering in the Infant Hall when the teachers of the island met to do honour to Mr. and Mrs. Gibson on his retiral and impending departure to take up residence in Edinburgh. Among the guests was Dr J.L. Robertson, who had travelled specially for the occasion; Mr Lang, HMI for the County; the Chairman and Members of the School Management Committee; and the Provost and Senior Bailie of Stornoway representing the community.

Several speakers paid tribute to the debt Lewis owed Mr. Gibson: The Nicolson Institute would be a lasting memorial to his work, having seen it from infancy to high status; others spoke highly of his civility, sympathy, tact and sense of duty.

In his reply, Mr. Gibson said that they would understand that it was very difficult for him to speak to them, but he wished to thank them for the kindness and generosity of their remarks. He then outlined the principles which had guided him in his long career:

> *I hardly know when I began to teach, but I must have started at a very early age. I began regular teaching as far back as 1883, and... I have been at it ever since. I have always believed in the importance and value of democratic education – that every child in our nation has the right to get the best possible*

> *education. More than ever I still have a profound faith in Education and what it can do.... there are born teachers, but I have only come across five or six in my lifetime. The ordinary teacher is not born, the ordinary teacher is made slowly, painfully by conscientiously trying to do the day's work. I was not one of these born teachers. I was one of those who strayed into teaching and being in it did not want to get out.*

Speaking of the island he said he had not only liked being among the Lewis people, but he also liked greatly to be in Lewis. There were two classes of people who came to the island – those who disliked it greatly and were anxious to get out of it, and the other class, those who got caught by its charm.

> *I am not a sentimentalist, but I do love Lewis from the stiff, old, hard gneiss which underlies it up to the things above. I have gone through all the Island. Mrs Gibson and I have camped out in the wilds of the Island... from the Butt of Lewis to the Rodd. I have been in the outlying islands. I spent a while in the Flannans; I have been in Little Bernera, on Pabbay, and three times on the Shiants.*
>
> *I love every bit of it, every rock and stone in it. I will never see anything finer than a Lewis moor with the wind blowing on it and the blue sky over it; nothing is more impressive than to hear the Atlantic surge beating on the rocks at the foot of one of its headlands.*

He concluded by offering advice to young teachers as it was his last opportunity to do so. Thus ended a remarkable career. If, as he said, he was not a born teacher, he was certainly a born administrator and educational policymaker to whom Lewis owes a great debt.

On January 10th 1926, the Gibsons left Stornoway for their Edinburgh retirement home and their 541 letters (1916-1926) to their daughter came to an end.

The Nicolson Institute staff in 1925 (the last staff photo with Mr. W.J. Gibson as Rector)
Back row: Mr. Clement W. Bell (Woodwork), Mr. William Rudland (Janitor), Miss Alina Macleod, Miss Maggie Stewart (Maths), Miss Kathleen R. Harrold, Mr. Norman Macleod (Classics), Miss Helen A. Hart (Housecraft), Mr. Donald M. Macpherson, Miss Annie Morrison, Miss Christina Macleod, Mr. Roderick Macrae (Science Master), Mr. James R. Matheson
Third row: Mr. Donald Mackay, Mr. Kenneth Mackenzie (Maths), Miss C. Macarthur, Miss Margaret Love, Miss Lisa R. Lobban, Mr. William Grant (Commercial Subjects, part-time), Miss Isabella A. Morrison, Miss Mary S. Pope, Miss Marion A. Young (Needlework), Mr. George S. Fraser (Art Master), Mr. John Macrae (Mathematics Master)
Second row: Miss Rose E. Bassin (Music Mistress), Miss Isabella Reid (Infant Mistress), Mr. William A. Macneil (History), Miss Macdonald (Matron of L.C. Girls' Hostel), Miss Donaldina Macleod (French Mistress), Mr. William J. Gibson (Rector), Mr. John M. Pryde (Second Master), Miss Dorothy C. Hutchings, Mr. John Macdonald (Gaelic)
Front row: Miss Angelina MacCallum, Miss Marion Clarke, Miss Alexandrina Macdonald, Miss Louise G. Kent (Gym Teacher), Miss Lillian Macleod, Miss Catherine Macsween (Rector's Clerkess), Miss Margaret Macfarlane

Chapter 9:
Into the 1930s

Mr. John Macrae

John Macrae[i]

Mr. Gibson was succeeded as Rector at Christmas 1925 by Mr. John Macrae, a native of Stornoway. He had been a school student of The Nicolson Institute and had graduated from Aberdeen University in 1905, having entered the Faculty of Arts. He taught for a short time in Thurso, but then returned to The Nicolson Institute as an Assistant Teacher of Mathematics in 1908. Not only did he teach this subject but also English, Latin, History and Geography. Later, he was to devote his whole time to the teaching of Mathematics which his patience and talent made lucid and interesting. He served in World War I. Even before he was demobilised, he was appointed Principal Teacher of Mathematics in 1919.

It was now in 1925 his task as Rector to carry on the tradition of high learning and corporate unity passed on by Mr. Gibson, especially in times of hardship when grants for ·educational purposes were being severely curtailed because of the general economic depression. The employment of teachers was drastically restricted, a reduction in salaries and various bursaries was enforced, and a policy of all-round economy insisted on. The roll was steadily increasing but the demand for further accommodation could not be met. Mr. Macrae's many years of teaching in The Nicolson Institute had given him a deep insight into the principles which had governed Mr. Gibson's educational outlook.

He too was a man of high intellectual stature; an able teacher endowed with an administrative ability of the highest order. His many years of service left him dedicated to the school's welfare and advancement. A strict disciplinarian, and meticulous in all he did, he was intolerant of ill-prepared and slovenly work. One only learned later of his great interest in the general welfare of his pupils: the favours unobtrusively done, and the bursaries found for those who could not otherwise attend university.

Even after becoming Rector, he still taught Mathematics to the sixth-year class. The pocket watch was placed on the table and the length of chalk neatly broken in half, after which the lesson proceeded, tuned almost to perfection. The lessons were often enlivened by his caustic humour, either in praise or condemnation, but never with personal rancour.

It was impressed on the class that, whatever else was neglected, the theorem for the following day was learned and the weekly exercise done before one indulged in sporting activities. There were few outlets for pupils after school. No pupil could become a member of the local YMCA or attend adult dances; and enrolment in the Ross Mountain Battery was apparently frowned on.[80] Pupils made their own amusements and were the better for it. Annual picnics, the younger classes to Arnish and the older classes somewhat further afield, marked the culmination of the school year. School dances took place two or three times a year but were conducted with the utmost decorum, only old-fashioned dances being allowed.

Although Rectoral policy placed great stress on maintaining a high standard in the work of the classroom, the extra-mural life of the school was not neglected. Meetings for musical practice were held on Tuesday evenings and, although most of the members were beginners from the intermediate classes, good progress was made. In 1938, a junior section of the school orchestra was formed with a view to preparing younger school students to enter the senior orchestra as vacancies occurred. Most of the junior members were girls. School concerts were held from time to time.

In December 1937, a staff venture was undertaken when there was a performance of the Gilbert and Sullivan operetta *'Pirates of Penzance.'* The background painted by Mr. Chalmers was a very realistic expanse of sea and rocks, an ideal setting for dashing pirates. Miss Black (piano) and Mr. Chalmers (violin) played the incidental music. Mrs. Pursell designed most of the costumes.

Macrae took a close interest in other school clubs, notably the Literary and Debating Society. With his authority, *The Nicolson Institute Annual* which had lapsed for many years through lack of funds was resurrected. He had

---

80   Perhaps because of the horror of what had followed a different policy in the school pre-1914.

an unusually retentive memory for the names and faces of those he taught and kept in close touch with their movements after leaving school. This was reflected in the wealth of information about the careers of former pupils which appeared each year in the *'Annual'* during his tenure of the Rectorship.[81]

It was only after many years when one met him in the privacy of his own home or elsewhere that his true personality was revealed - the quiet charm and simple dignity. Having viewed him in the past with some degree of awe, one suddenly felt at ease and realised why his staff regarded him with respect and gave him their loyalty because of his dedication to the school and all it stood for.

He retired at the age of 60 in October 1943 on health grounds. His illness, hastened by his devotion to his work and to the youth of the island, and by the death of his wife, left a hint of loneliness because, next to his family, the welfare of the school had absorbed him in unremitting toil. Premature retirement did not come easily, and often the conversation turned to school affairs. However, when he was made an Honorary Sheriff Substitute (October 1945),[ii] he felt he had still a part to play in the life of the community.

He died on 7th May 1954.[iii]

The Nicolson Institute staff, 1930
Back row: *Miss A. Macdonald, Mr. J. Macpherson, Mr. Albert Nicoll, Mr. D.M. Macpherson, Mr. J.C. Rae, Mr. Gordon Urquhart, Mr. Alec Urquhart, Mr. Kenneth Mackenzie, Mr. W. Trail, Mr. G. More, Miss C. Macleod*
Third row: *Miss A.B. Scott, Miss J.A. Mackenzie, Miss A.A. Macleod, Miss M.A. Stobo, Miss Belle Morrison, Miss J.B. Calder, Miss A.M. Cheyne, Miss M. Campbell, Miss Maggie Stewart, Miss A. Macleod, Miss G. Mackenzie*
Second row: *Mr. Norman B. Anderson, Miss Susan M. Craig, Mr. K. Macdonald, Miss D. Macleod, Mr. J. Macrae (Rector), Miss B. Reid, Mr. Rod Macrae, Miss Mary S. Pope, Mr. J.M. Pryde*
Front row: *Miss A. MacCallum, Miss G.M. Black, Miss J. Montgomery, Miss M.A. Feathers, Miss Marion Clarke*

---

81   Some of it used in this book.

The Call of Kinship

As the economic depression of the 1920s deepened, bringing harrowing years of hardship to many, the task which faced Mr Macrae had inevitably become increasingly difficult. However, the gloom was lightened to some extent by the efforts of Thomas Bassett Macaulay, son of Robertson. This second generation Canadian devoted so many years, even at the height of his career, and much of his fortune, to better the conditions in the land of his forebears.[iv] The Macaulay Trust made, and continues to make, a big difference to many things in Lewis, not least to The Nicolson Institute.[82]

There is evidence from T.B. Macaulay's own words that the arrival of Canadian liners bound for Montreal from Stornoway (in the 1920s) with immigrants from Lewis touched him deeply and turned his thoughts to the other side of the Atlantic from which his father had emigrated; Angus Nicolson attributed this to the 'call of kinship,' going on to reference the words of the Canadian Boat-Song:

and we in dreams behold the Hebrides.[v]

The Nicolson Institute football team, 1931
Standing at back: G.M. Pryde
Middle row: Mr. J. Macrae, Mr. W. Trail, D. Morrison, A.D. Mackay, D. Crichton, A.A. Macgregor, H.R. Cullum, Mr. A. Nicoll, Mr. K. Mackenzie
Front row: I.A. Fraser, Mr. W.F. Chalmers, H.S.M. Graham, M. Morrison, M.A. Nicolson

---

82 A school which until the 1950s had no significant in-house library, but relied instead on the town library, destroyed in 1918; and which had few bursaries at its disposal.

In 1928, shortly after John Macrae became Rector, Macaulay began to offer the opportunity of employment in insurance to the older pupils of The Nicolson Institute on passing a special examination designed to test their suitability for this type of work. Many took advantage of this scheme. In 1930, it was reported that nine female ex-pupils and four male ex-pupils had joined the company.[vi] The most distinguished of these Lewis graduates was Malcolm A. Macdonald, the school Dux in 1922, who graduated from the Faculty of Arts in the University of Aberdeen with First Class Honours in Mathematics and a similar BA degree from Cambridge University; qualifications which gained him a high executive position with the Sun Life Assurance Company. But the Canadian Government, alarmed at its own rising rate of unemployment, saw the scheme as a threat to young native-born Canadians and eventually it had to be abandoned.

The rise of the Sun Life Assurance Company of Canada from comparatively modest beginnings to an international commercial enterprise, ranking among the great life insurance companies of the world, was due in no small measure to the vision and drive of the Macaulay family, both father and son.

Robertson Macaulay was born in Fraserburgh, where his father, a native of Valtos in Uig, owned a coastal vessel. He returned to Stornoway at the age of twelve and was first employed in the Estate Office in the building on the site on which the first Town Hall was built. At the age of seventeen, Robertson Macaulay went to work in Aberdeen. Approached by other insurance companies, he elected to accept the first offer and joined the Sun Life Assurance Company of Canada.

Thomas Bassett, Robertson Macaulay's son, joined the company in 1877 at the age of seventeen, the most junior of five clerks. Realising that only limited growth was possible in Canada because of its small population and of the competition from other companies, Robertson Macaulay, with the aid of his son, embarked on a policy of expansion. With a specially drawn up insurance policy, indisputable and unconditional[83] on any grounds, the company established in Britain, and from its London office it soon had agencies in the major cities. Later it opened its first office in Detroit to challenge the huge United States companies. With its reputation for liberal settlement and with most of the American companies still carrying restrictive clauses, it spread from state to state. Shortly after his father was made company President, Thomas B. Macaulay was appointed Secretary. On his father's death in 1915, he became the third President of the Sun Life until his retiral in 1934. This

---

83   i.e. unrestricted in terms of the travel, the occupation, the residence or even the suicide of the policy holder.

was the man who was to play, even from a distance, such a prominent part in Lewis affairs and, not least, in the welfare of The Nicolson Institute.

T. B. Macaulay

The Macaulay Educational Trust for Lewis

As early as June 1925, Mr. Macaulay created by deed of agreement a benevolent trust to be administered by a committee of six. The revenue from this fund, to be called 'The Macaulay Trust', was to provide bursaries for boys to attend a Scottish university, preferably the University of Aberdeen. The bursaries were to be competed for annually and there were to be two or three awarded each year. In granting the awards, Mathematics should have preference over Classics. The express condition laid down, however, was that no bursary could be granted unless, in the opinion of most of the committee, the financial circumstances were such that, without this assistance, the pupil could not take a university course.

In 1929, the scope of the 'Macaulay Trust' was widened to provide bursaries for rural pupils to attend The Nicolson Institute, in addition to those who intended to take a university course, and other educational facilities were provided.

When Mr. Macaulay met the Lewis School Management Committee in October 1929, the 'Macaulay Educational Trust for Lewis' was officially finalised. When the Endowment Commissioners held their enquiry in

Stornoway in 1931, it was obvious that they were aware that it had been framed in such a way that Mr. Macaulay's desire to benefit the island with which he had now such close links could not be altered either by the Court of Session or the Secretary of State for Scotland. At The Nicolson Institute prize-giving held in the newly opened Town Hall where Macaulay and his daughter had presented the prizes, he stated that the welfare of the youth of the island was now one of his main interests; he was to return to the Town Hall in 1929 to unveil a plaque to commemorate the fact that his father had worked on the same site, having himself contributed so much to its redesign following the fire.

The Macaulay Educational Trust for Lewis, Mr. Macaulay informed the School Management Committee, was drawn up to provide better educational facilities for those who for financial reasons could not otherwise benefit. For this purpose, he had invested a sum of £5,000 with a Montreal Trust Company which would be administered by the Provost, the Rector of The Nicolson Institute, the Chairman of the Lewis School Management Committee, the senior Presbyterian minister in Stornoway and the Chairman of the Lewis District Committee. This arrangement was to prevent Trust funds being merged into the general educational funds of the County Council.[84]

Over a period of sixteen years, Macaulay was to donate a sum of more than £100,000[85] to educational and other charitable causes. He had already offered £5,000 to the rebuilding fund for the new Town Hall and to pay half of the debt of £1,400 which remained on the old building. He had donated £12,000 to the public library, £400 for fire-proof doors to it, and £700 to provide books and the means by which each village in Lewis and Harris should have the same facilities, if possible, of a circulating library. To the Lewis Hospital he contributed £17,000 for a new maternity wing, £10,000 towards an experimental farm to convert peatland into arable land, and a similar sum for research to the Agricultural College at Aberdeen. Further donations were to follow, especially a considerable sum to Edinburgh University. For these benefactions, not only to Lewis but also to other Scottish centres, he was the first to receive the Freedom of the Burgh of Stornoway. He also received the honorary degrees of Aberdeen and Edinburgh universities.

It is not surprising, therefore, that in the summer of 1929, even although social conditions were worsening, especially with the now rapid decline in the herring fishing industry, that Stornoway presented an air of expectancy, an almost carnival atmosphere, reminiscent of the early visits to Lewis of Lord Leverhulme. Thomas B. Macaulay, as the principal contributor to

---

84 As we shall see on page 137, a wise precaution.
85 i.e. about £6.5m at current prices.

the rebuilding fund for the new Town Hall, was to perform the ceremonial opening of the new building on 19th June. He had chartered the Canadian Pacific liner, *Minnedosa*, to make the direct Atlantic crossing from Montreal to Stornoway. On board were more than a hundred exiled Lewismen, most of whom had contributed to the rebuilding fund, returning for a brief visit to their native island. South Beach Street, Cromwell Street and the route to the Lews Castle were festooned with flags of all shapes and colours. Ships in the harbour were dressed overall.

Stornoway Town Hall in 1932

Soon after his arrival, Macaulay journeyed to Valtos. There, before a large and appreciative audience, he talked of the past: he had begun, he said, to think of Lewis when so many immigrants were landing in Canada. He felt the call of the blood and decided to do something for Lewis. As to the future, he went on to describe his visit to the experimental farm at the River Creed and had seen bog land being transformed and different crops growing. He finished by saying he would come back as a member of the clan and do what he could to ease their lot. Unfortunately, his plan for land reclamation was to prove a failure. With heavy and prolonged fertilisation to lower the acidity and promote growth, crops were grown, but the experiment proved uneconomic and was finally abandoned. But into the 21st century it is the location of the Macaulay College, founded in 2010, a well-regarded training establishment based on farm management, for young adults with additional social and educational requirements. In that and in other ways, the legacy of T.B. Macaulay lives on.

On Wednesday 19th June 1929, the Town Hall was formally opened by T.B. Macaulay,[86] the son unveiling a plaque to commemorate the fact that his father had worked on the same site, and having himself contributed so much to its redesign following the 1918 fire. On the occasion he was presented with a key, engraved on one side with the Macaulay coat of arms and that of the town on the other side, a representation of the building and the date. This, in his address, he said would be a cherished heirloom in the Macaulay family handed down from generation to generation. When the Provost expressed his regret that they had not the power to confer on him the Freedom of the Burgh, he replied that it was probably as a result of the activities of his ancestors.

On both sides of the new Town Hall stage were hung shields bearing the coats of arms of the Macaulay and Bain clans to add to those of the Stornoway Trade Corporations gifted by Dr J.L. Robertson. John Bain, who had been a school student of The Nicolson Institute, had become President of a chain of banks in Chicago. A brother of the Provost Louis Bain, his donation of £3,500 to the rebuilding of the Town Hall was the second largest contribution.[87] With financial aid from other Chicago passengers, he presented the town with its first motor fire-engine. Both Bain and Macaulay were to receive the Freedom of the Burgh some years later.

T.B. MacAulay's continued interest in The Nicolson Institute was shown on other occasions. When the school was celebrating its Diamond Jubilee in February 1933, he sent a cablegram in which he paid tribute to the tremendous benefit which the Nicolson brothers had conferred on both town and island and wrote that one of the main interests in his life was now the welfare of Lewis. He also sent a cable on the centenary of the founder's birth (1932):

> *By establishing [The Nicolson] Institute the Nicolson brothers [gave] benefit of inestimable value to [the] people of Lewis and through their school they are still working for [the] island and will go on for generations to come...They were not only generous but far-sighted. I am proud to join your splendid school in tribute to the noble founder...*

---

86 An invitation to this event is stored in the archives of Tasglann nan Eilean.
87 The Town Hall, notably its library, had large significance for The Nicolson Institute. It took until the 1950s for The Nicolson to establish a useful academic library of its own.

T.B. Macaulay resigned from the office of President of the Sun Life Assurance Company in 1934 having weathered the chill wind of the stock market panics which was elsewhere to destroy confidence and bring the economies of nations to the verge of collapse. As the cloud of the Depression seemed to be lifting, and now 74 years of age, he gave up his high office, remaining a director until his death in 1942. During these last years, his thoughts must have turned to happier times, and more and more to the island where he had been so warmly welcomed and held in honour and respect.

It is perhaps only fitting that W.C. Mackenzie, former pupil of The Nicolson Institute and a distinguished scholar and historian, and who was also to receive the Freedom of the Burgh, should dedicate his book The Western Isles: Their History, Traditions and Placenames to T.B. Macaulay, Montreal – A true friend and a generous benefactor of the Island that gave birth to his ancestors.[vii]

The Nicolson Endowments

In 1931, The Nicolson Institute adopted a badge of its own. The design was five torches, symbolic of the founder and his brothers; underneath, a motto, 'Sequamur' (let us follow),[88] and at the top a small shield with the initials 'N.I.' inscribed on it. The predominating colours were those of the School navy and gold - while the motto was written artistically in red. Pupils were encouraged to wear the school badge and most of them did so with pride, although many years were to pass before a school uniform was introduced.

The Nicolson Institute badge

---

88 Loosely translated as 'Let us follow the example of the brothers who were our founders.' The number five is somewhat mysterious. There were six adult brothers who had contributed to the school's foundation and growth, albeit some more directly than others. Angus Nicolson wrote in the middle of the 20th century: 'With hindsight one cannot but regret that the six brothers were not represented, as they formed such a close-knit family.'

At this point, many pupils, notably those from rural areas, depended on bursaries to be able to access education from The Nicolson Institute. In 1933, owing to many objections raised against a scheme for new management of The Nicolson endowments (a proposal to make them more available county-wide), a new scheme was submitted to the Ross and Cromarty Education Department by the Educational Endowments (Scotland) Commissioners. Both schemes made provision for special equipment for schools, midday meals for school pupils, the establishment of hostels, etc., but in the first scheme no mention had been made of either school or university bursaries specifically for Lewis pupils. The second scheme, however, was a great improvement on the first, as not only school bursaries but also five university bursaries were granted to Lewis students.

Much credit was due to Mr. Alexander Morison Nicolson of Australia, a nephew of the founder, son of the Rev. Roderick Nicolson and the sole third generation Nicolson member - whose influence was responsible for the adoption of the latter plan. Early in 1932, the Rector, Mr. Macrae wrote to Nicolson explaining the situation and that he and the other Lewis members of both the Town Council and County Council were making every effort to retain the use of the benefit of The Nicolson Bequests for the purpose for which they were intended. As his father had played the most prominent part in fulfilling the wishes of the founder in providing educational facilities in Stornoway and, with his brother Kenneth, had endowed The Nicolson Institute with not only considerable sums of money but also with other amenities, they would be grateful if he could intervene to make representations that the aims of the Nicolson family should be respected.

In his reply to Mr. Macrae, Nicolson enclosed a copy of the cable he had sent to the Commissioners and the letter which followed it to confirm his strong opposition to the proposals of diverting any part of the funds from those laid down in the Deed of Gift.

The letter, addressed to the Secretary of the Educational Endowments Commission, enlarged on the views expressed in his cablegram of the 24th of June 1932:

> *I have carefully studied your Commission's Draft (Section 18) dealing with certain scholastic purposes in the Counties of Ross and Cromarty and which recommendations affected an Institution with which my family has always been closely allied, i.e. The Nicolson INSTITUTE of STORNOWAY (sic). My father and uncles mad e certain definite endowments to The Nicolson Institute and these gifts were made on the distinct understanding that the money was to be used for the education and development of the sons of Crofters and deserving poor people who complied with the terms of the Trust and graduated to be equipped for securing advantages for a special education at The Nicolson Institute.*
>
> *As I am the last living representative of The Nicolson family I felt it was necessary for me... to lodge... my emphatic protest against the misplacement of money that was endowed by my father and uncles for a definite purpose to this fine Institution in Stornoway....*
>
> *These funds in the past have been well spent and have catered for a class of student that has made known throughout the world the name of The Nicolson Institute... I have met men occupying high commercial positions and many of them Master Mariners... others occupying high positions in the commercial sphere – and the opportunities which gave them their early start towards their future success in life having been based on the training received through these bursaries and Educational advantages made possible by the endowment gifts to The Nicolson Institute.*
>
> *Surely... the Commissioners must have found the work that this scholastic Institute has done and the general effect in giving an opportunity to those Crofter lads possessing the natural ability who without this help could have no other future than to remain as Crofters and fishermen. The Knowledge gained in meeting of men who have risen from this Institute... has always filled me with gratitude and admiration for the far-seeing vision of my father and uncles which enabled this money to be provided for utilisation to such effect.*
>
> *I therefore hope that nothing will be done to disturb this Trust from the beneficial work it has so successfully performed in the past and which I am sure will be equally so in the future.*

Shortly afterwards, Mr. Gibson added his plea for their retention to that of Alexander Morison Nicolson. In the discussion over the administration of this fund Mr. Macrae supplied some interesting statistics to justify the retention of the revenue for Lewis: there were 37 schools in the island having a total roll of 4,000 pupils for which the county grants were highly inadequate. Since the introduction of these bursaries, 200 had graduated in arts, of whom over 30 had taken divinity courses, and two of whom had been appointed to Chairs in American universities;[89] 30 had graduated in science; and 80 in medicine; a total of nearly 350, many of whom would not have been able to do so without the aid of the Nicolson Endowments.

The school roll, which had exceeded 950 pupils in 1915, had fallen to 860 by 1919 because of the heavy demand on manpower and the heavy sacrifice in lives. Gibson claimed that nowhere else in the Empire had the toll been so proportionately high.[viii] As the economic depression deepened and emigration continued, by 1928 the roll fell to less than 800. As Sandwick School was now suffering from serious overcrowding, it was decided to readmit the children from the Battery Park and Coulegrein areas, especially as the Town Council intended to extend its boundaries to acquire land for housing schemes.

In 1931, a rather ambitious programme which outlined the progressive provision of new buildings for The Nicolson Institute was proposed. The hope was expressed that a new secondary school building would be erected in Springfield soon. In the light of the economic conditions which prevailed, its fulfilment seemed unlikely, being more of a pious hope rather than a statement of actual policy. A quarter of a century was to elapse before this new secondary building came into existence.

A most interesting staff photograph dates from 1932, pointing up two noteworthy features. It should be noted that women teachers suffered a marriage bar until 1945.[ix] The bar was set by local authorities, not officially from central government. Most authorities in Scotland were heavily influenced by the strong eugenic arguments of the time and brought in a marriage bar in 1923, in an attempt to ensure that educated women stayed at home to produce the next generation. There was also pressure for employment of ex-servicemen in preference to women who would be getting supported by their husbands. Church representatives on education authorities or school boards were very strongly in favour of the marriage bar, so one would imagine that the education authority of Ross and Cromarty was quite rigid in its application of the bar, although

---

89   Possibly Professor Mackenzie, by then in Pittsburgh, and Professor John Macleod, by then in Toronto.

The Nicolson Institute staff, 1932
Back row: *Mr. Bill Trail, Mr. J. Macpherson, Mr. J. Maclennan (Janitor), Mr. W.F. Chalmers, Mr. G. More*
Third row: *Miss J. Montgomery, Mr. Kenneth Mackenzie, Miss I. Mackenzie, Mr. N. Macarthur, Miss Marion Clarke, Mr. Alec Urquhart, Miss C. Macleod, Mr. Albert Nicoll, Miss A. Macleod, Mr. D.M. Macpherson, Miss C. Macsween, Mr. Gordon Urquhart*
Second row: *Miss M.A. Feathers, Miss A.B. Scott, Miss A. Morrison, Miss C. Macarthur, Miss A. Macdonald, Miss M.A. Stobo, Miss J.A. Mackenzie, Miss Belle Morrison, Miss Jessie B. Calder, Miss Gertrude M. Black, Miss K. Grainger, Miss C.A. Smith*
Front row: *Mr. K. Macdonald, Miss Susan M. Craig, Mr. J.M. Pryde, Miss B. Reid, Mr. J. Macrae (Rector), Miss M. Stewart, Mr. Rod Macrae, Miss Mary S. Pope, Mr. Norman B. Anderson*
Sitting: *Miss A.M. Cheyne, Miss M. Campbell, Miss A.A. Macrae*

there is no specific evidence of that. World War II obviously required many women to return to the classroom and the Advisory Council on Education in Scotland Report 1944 recommended *'all obstacles in the way of employment of such (married women) teachers be removed.'* SED Circular 38 made it necessary for education authorities to alter their policies on the employment of married women teachers. The second interesting feature is the remarkable longevity of service of many of these teachers.

Accommodation - the Recurring Problem

By the mid-1930s, with the school roll having grown to more than one thousand, the recurring problem of inadequate accommodation and serious overcrowding of classrooms once again led to urgent demands for further construction. Mr. Macrae made strong representations to the Education Authority that the difficulties in finding accommodation for the increasing number of pupils, especially those in the secondary department, was becoming a problem difficult to solve.

To ease the situation, the Education Authority recommended that the old wood and iron building of the elementary department should be demolished, and a more modern structure erected in its place. It was once again suggested a new secondary building be erected to the east of the existing one in Springfield. A resolution was also passed that the original school which had housed the first pupils should be preserved, when no longer needed for classrooms, as a school museum, a rural library, and the later extension converted to a gymnasium for primary pupils. Mr. Macrae expressed his satisfaction with the proposed building programme, especially the use of the original building as a cultural centre. He, like many others of an older generation, would have deplored its demolition.[x]

By 1934, the decision to build, taken three years earlier, was now long overdue. Cuts in public expenditure, reductions in salaries, and other obstacles during the worst part of the economic depression had militated against a progressive programme to provide further accommodation. In addition to the larger projects already outlined other resolutions were made. This would be followed by the erection of a new secondary block on the Springfield site. As the Burgh boundary had been extended, a further extension to the existing Springfield playground was applied for and granted.

Since taking office, Mr. Macrae's work in the school had been handicapped by the inadequacy of school buildings. In 1936, however, the launching of a five-year plan of reconstruction for the school seemed to be a promise of better days to come. Work on the first instalment had started and, when the whole scheme was completed, a well-appointed modern building would replace all the 'tin' buildings where scholars were wont to *'freeze and fry alternatively.'* In addition, a fine new playing field would extend from Springfield Road up towards Goathill Road. Moreover, it was anticipated that, at a later stage, the plan would involve the construction of new secondary classrooms between the gymnasium and the eastern boundary wall of the school. Ultimately the elementary classes which were then in the *'Tin School'* and in the Sandwick Road School would all be housed in the new building, which would replace the *'Tin School',* and then perhaps the Sandwick Road building would be converted into a gymnasium for elementary classes and, very fittingly, a school museum.

The first section of this new building was opened after the Easter vacation in 1937 and occupied by the pupils of the 'Tin School.' At the time it was described as *'a model of cleanliness and efficiency, a building most favourable to the free development of mind and body,'* and good wishes for equal success were extended to the builder of *'the sister leviathan whose "keel" was being laid alongside.'*[xi]

Almost twenty years were to elapse before the rest of the five-year plan came to fruition - too late for Mr. Macrae to reap any benefit from it.

The new primary building, constructed in two stages to avoid part-time teaching for some classes, was finally opened officially at the beginning of the new session in 1938. It soon became known as the *'Pink Building'* from the colour of cement rendering used. For years it bore the more dignified title of Springfield South. It was in use, latterly for Maths and Geography, until being the first building demolished in the building works of 2011-12.

Increasing School Roll

The Rector, intolerant by nature of the long and frequent changes in decisions regarding building plans for the Secondary Department, repeatedly drew attention to the congestion and inadequate accommodation. The problem was even greater than the renewal of an old building in the elementary department. Since 1929, the school roll had increased by a quarter. The problem of overcrowded classes had become acute and difficult of solution. The Rector had also kept in close touch with Mr. George Thomson, the Director of Education for Ross and Cromarty.[90] In reply to a letter from Mr. Macrae in December 1938, Mr. Thomson stated that provisional arrangements had been made for a detailed discussion between the County architects and those of the Department. The decisions and plans from

---

90 The County responsible for schools in Lewis between 1929 and 1975.

this meeting would then be submitted to the Education Committee in January. As an additional one-storey Art room had been added to provide enough Commercial rooms, this would clearly be open to alteration and lead to further delay. He also agreed with Mr. Macrae that even after the new secondary building had been completed there was use for the original building as a museum, reading room and gymnasium.

This, Mr. Thomson stated, was an excellent idea since, as the original building of The Nicolson Institute, it could well be utilised in fostering school traditions. An interesting footnote was added. If the vacation course in weaving and textiles, which was to be held at The Nicolson Institute during the following summer, proved successful, it might serve as a nucleus for future development as a Technical subject. Although further reconstruction would be necessary, the subject was desirable because of the increasing importance of the Harris Tweed industry. (The subject was introduced many years later in the Lews Castle College.) Regarding the suggestion made by Mr. Macrae that a film room should form part of the new building, Mr. Thomson replied that one of the end classrooms should be fitted for this purpose with a screen table and light excluders. Thus, although Mr. Macrae would not benefit from the additional facilities provided, he played a significant part in its future design.

Further council house building by the Town Council of Stornoway,[91] the centralisation of Technical instruction, and the raising of the school leaving age[92] were certain to increase the numbers of pupils in the post-Primary Department. Mr. Thomson was asked to assess these various factors and determine whether the proposed accommodation submitted by the Ross-shire Education Committee was necessary. To this there could be but the one reply: the population of Stornoway was rapidly increasing because of the continuous drift of people from the more remote rural areas into the burgh and because of high birth rates. The need for these classrooms was even more imperative.

The plans were then returned for further consideration and revision about 1938. At the time the elementary building was being completed, the clouds of war were darkening over Europe, heralding another World War. It is against this background of inevitable war that the negotiations regarding the construction of the new secondary building must be viewed. With priority now given to hasty rearmament, delay in school building was certain. The time of appeasement was past. The guarantee to intervene on

---

91 Mostly not to happen until post 1945.
92 In 1947.

behalf of Poland probably made the abandonment of a school-building programme inevitable. In a few months, air-raid shelters would replace the desired classrooms and the proposed raising of the school leaving age would be abandoned at least for the present.

The time spent would not have been wasted, however, as many of the recommendations made would eventually be put into effect. A Domestic Science room would replace the dining hall and a library be included near the rooms occupied by the English Department. As had happened all too often in the past, by the time this new and large secondary building was completed, there was still a need for further accommodation.

Chapter 10:
The Nicolson, World War II and its Aftermath

On the day Hitler invaded Poland, a large draft of naval reservists was due to sail by mailboat. Many friends and relatives had come from diverse parts of Lewis to see them leave. The following passage from the *Stornoway Gazette*, probably written by James S. Grant, the former Dux of The Nicolson Institute who was now *Stornoway Gazette* editor, described the scene:

> *It was an orderly and strangely silent crowd... From the roof of the Maritime Buildings it was like... a scene from the silent days of the cinema... There was a steady stream of reservists through the crowd and up the gangway, but their leave-taking with their relatives was also silent... the crowd was obedient, almost lifeless.*
>
> *Then, suddenly, the silence was broken. At first a single voice rising tremulously in the air of a Gaelic psalm – a precentor giving out the line. Some of the crowd took up the verse and the solemn words of the 46th Psalm swelled out to the tune Stroudwater...*
>
> *The Loch Ness, listing perceptibly with the mass of men crowded on the shoreward side, slowly began to move from the quay.*
>
> *There was a flutter of hankies from the deck. The crowd ashore poured through the barriers and rushed to the edge of the quay... A full-throated cheer broke out from the crowded deck and waving frantically the crowd ashore responded...*
>
> *A glimmer of moonshine on the broken water in her wake drew attention to the fact that the clouds above had thinned for a moment, but through the haze the moon was a sombre red.*

Many years later, Angus Nicolson speculated that the *'sombre red'* was intentionally used, although the writer could not have foretold the carnage to follow.

For some of the reservists this was to be their last glimpse of home. Many were to crew minesweepers: tackling the new and more deadly undersea weapons – acoustic, magnetic or activated by pressure – took a heavy toll before counter measures were found to lessen their menace. However, few who had passed their schooldays in The Nicolson Institute enlisted in the Naval Reserve unless they had been in the Sea Cadets.

When Chamberlain broadcast to the nation on the morning of 3rd September that the country was now at war with Germany a sense of unreality was felt. The silence of this sunlit Sunday morning seemed to belie the fact that Europe had erupted into violent war. This was followed by a feeling of relief that the long months of anxiety and uncertainty were over. There was no thought of possible defeat, not even later in the nation's darkest hours. A new spirit of defiance had been born which united the nation more firmly than ever before.

At The Nicolson Institute, as elsewhere, windows were made as shatter-proof as possible. After some discussion it was also decided to provide eight large shelters, fully equipped for a prolonged raid, for The Nicolson Institute rather than sandbagged trenches. At the request of the Town Council these were to be open for public use after school hours. Fire drill and dispersal of classes were to be regularly rehearsed. To cater for children who were unable to reach home during the dinner hour it was proposed that the hut at Laxdale Public School should be transferred to The Nicolson Institute where it could be used as a canteen for eighty pupils. A kitchen, made from materials from the Teachers' Hostel, would be sited nearby.

Under the Government sponsored 'Dig for Victory' campaign the Town Council suggested that the area granted as an extension to the existing playing-field should be converted into allotments as no levelling or other improvement had been done. Each secondary class took over an allotment and dug. It was also proposed that the school holiday periods should be arranged to permit school pupils to participate in croft or farm work during spring and autumn. Failing this, school children were to be given leave of absence, especially at harvest time, at the discretion of the head teacher.

Unlike during World War I, there was no mass exodus of older pupils. As conscription had been fixed initially at twenty years of age, there was little disruption in the normal life of the school. Enlistment in the Ross Mountain Battery, which might have brought older pupils into the company of much older men, had been, as we have seen, severely discouraged. The Battery was mainly composed of former pupils, and was actually stationed at its annual training camp when the call came to form part of the Highland Division. A few school pupils, however, joined the Home Guard, and subsequently, in 1942, 1731 Squadron Air Training Corps (ATC) was formed within The Nicolson under the command of Mr. Albert Nicoll, supported by various other members of staff. Recruitment was good and soon the roll reached sixty cadets who met for instruction on Mondays and Thursdays in the Springfield building of the school. The basic training was to prove helpful for those who were later to volunteer for the Royal Air Force.

As in the previous war, the school contributed handsomely to the National Savings Campaign throughout the years of the war. This spirit was also shown in contributions to provide a 'Spitfire' by public subscription in 1940 and in the 'Wings for Victory' Campaign in 1943. Probably, however, their finest contribution was in raising money to purchase a 12-pounder gun for HMS *Stornoway*. Lewis, with its long association with the Royal Navy, had immediately set up a committee to raise money for a vessel to be named HMS *Stornoway*. The raising of the necessary funds proved highly successful. The target of £410 was surpassed even on the first day of collection - when £776 had been raised. By the end of the week £2,718 was raised. The total cost of the vessel was estimated at more than £270,000 (£14m at current prices). Several Lewismen, some in responsible positions, expressed the strong viewpoint that a ship raised by Lewis money should bear a Lewis name and be manned by Lewis sailors, as the greatest expression of patriotic fervour. However, the name *Iolaire* (a disaster not much referred to by W.J. Gibson[93] or his successors) was not easily forgotten, even by the Admiralty. When a naval chaplain from Lewis visited the ship, intrigued on seeing the name, he was shown the plaque on the quarter-deck which informed the ship's company of the details of how the ship had been built '*by the effort of Lewis in 1941*'. He found only one Lewisman on board although three had served on the ship, albeit not at the same time.

A great number of Lewismen, many of them former pupils of The Nicolson Institute, were also serving in the Merchant Navy. Like their fellow Lewismen they too had to suffer the hardships of war with little of the glamour given to those in uniform.

Several months after the outbreak of war, Dr Doig, the Medical Officer of Health, wrote to the School Management Committee asking if it could be arranged that the Boys' Hostel on Church Street:

> *could be made available as an auxiliary hospital in the event of severe bombing or other raid on the island involving casualties outwith the capacity of the Lewis Hospital or the Infectious Diseases hospitals to deal with.*

---

93 Perhaps because his main correspondent Jane was at home on holiday in Stornoway on 1st January 1919 when the *Iolaire* foundered; perhaps because of the few ex-Nicolson school students on board the *Iolaire* - they were mostly rural Lewismen who had left their local school at 14, initially to go fishing, then to join the Royal Naval Reserve and thence to go to naval war in 1914. Somewhat belatedly, in 2019 a Nicolson Institute event focused on the tragic loss of the *Iolaire*. See Chapter 14.

The Naval officer in charge in Stornoway had stated that the Elizabeth Haldane Boys' Hostel would probably be requisitioned to provide suitable accommodation for sick quarters at Stornoway because, although every endeavour had been made to secure a suitable alternative, this had proved unsuccessful. He also informed the Committee that he considered the Education Authority of Ross and Cromarty should without too much difficulty find alternative accommodation for the boys from the hostel as lodgers in various houses in Stornoway. The Scottish Education Department had been informed of the situation.

The Nicolson Institute was to feel, directly or indirectly, the impact of World War II. As in World War I, social activities and other extra-mural activities were almost completely abandoned so that the school could concentrate on the war effort.

In the internal administration of the school, the war created difficulties. As time went on, various members of staff were conscripted to join the armed forces. An effort had to be made to ensure that the standard of work in the school was maintained despite this depletion of staff. Special arrangements had to be made by schools within the County for conducting the Scottish Leaving Certificate[i] examinations. That these problems incidental to wartime were being tackled successfully was made clear by the high level of Scottish Leaving Certificate group certificates which were gained throughout the war years. Mr. Macrae had been quick to realise the potential of film in education, and when funds became available, he had the school equipped with a cinema projector. Another important development in the final period of his Rectorship was the introduction of a full Commercial course.

Retiral of Mr. Macrae

On 27th October 1943, Mr. John Macrae called the school together to take his farewell of the pupils after a life spent in the service of the school. A presentation subscribed to by the pupils was handed over by a representative of Class VI. In replying, Mr. Macrae reminded the pupils that he spoke to them not only as their Rector but as a pupil who had once occupied one of the seats which they shared then. He gave a very interesting account of the history and traditions of the school, telling how when the Secondary Department was opened in 1894, the whole Department had occupied IIC's Room.[94] He said:

---

94 In the Francis Street building where the Secondary Department originated.

The Nicolson Institute staff, 1939
Back row: Mr. S. Smart, Mr. W. Welsh, Mr. W. Macleod, Mr. N. Macarthur, Mr. K. Mackenzie, Mr. J.A. Maciver, Mr. D. Macpherson, Mr. J. Macpherson, Mr. W.F. Chalmers, Mr. D.M. Watt, Mr. H. Macrae (Janitor)
Third row: Mr. G. Urquhart, Miss A. Macdonald, Miss M. Clarke, Miss G.M. Black, Miss J.A.T. Thain, Miss A.M. Cheyne, Miss F. Patrick, Miss C.M. Macdonald, Miss M.P. Maciver, Miss J. Montgomery, Mr. J. Barber
Second row: Miss A. Macleod, Miss C. Macleod, Miss J.B. Calder, Miss C. Mackay, Miss I.A. Morison, Miss J.A. Mackenzie, Miss A. Morrison, Miss S.M. Craig, Miss C. Macarthur
Front row: Mr. A. Urquhart, Miss M.S. Pope, Mr. W. Trail, Miss M. Stewart, Mr. J. Macrae (Rector), Miss B. Reid, Mr. C.G.S. Taylor, Dr G.S. Ferrier, Mr. A. Nicoll

> *I remember very well I received my first lesson in Greek on the blackboard above the fireplace. There were half a dozen of us and the lesson was given by a man who is now a prominent official in the Education Department. There were at that time only three male teachers, including the headmaster, and one lady to do all the Secondary work. But in less than four years the first boys from that class went directly to university.*[95]

---

95 Donald Maclean and Robert Maciver in 1898.

The Nicolson Institute

A class in 1939

Later at a meeting of staff, presided over by Mr. Alex Urquhart, Head of Gaelic, Mr. Macrae was presented with a wallet of notes. Mr. Macrae said that he accepted the presentations with pleasure and the good wishes given with so much sincerity. He had enjoyed his period as Rector. They were strenuous days but that was more than atoned for by the goodwill and fellowship he experienced at the hands of the staff. During his remarks he urged the immediate need for new school buildings *'worthy of our founder, worthy of the town and the Island and worthy of the great work which is carried on here.'* [96] He concluded with the hope that The Nicolson would go from strength to strength.[ii]

Mr. Thomas Henderson

Thomas Henderson

Mr. Macrae's successor in the Rectorship was Mr. Thomas Henderson, MA. For ten years he had been an assistant in the English Department at Camphill Secondary School, Paisley. In 1934 he was appointed Principal Teacher of English in Barrhead High School and in 1937 he returned to Camphill as Principal Teacher of English. It was from there he came to The Nicolson Institute.

---

96 A hope that took another thirteen years to realise.

A scholar and a talented musician, Mr. Henderson was also a dynamic leader. He came to The Nicolson with a fine record of service in youth welfare. He had been especially active in the Boys' Brigade and had a wide experience of the organisation of out-of-door activities such as camping and trekking. His message to the school after taking up his appointment in 1944 was 'Carry on!' - an expression of his own declared aim to continue the honourable record established by his predecessors.[iii]

Soon after, in May 1944, Mr. Alexander Urquhart, MA, who had been Principal Teacher of Gaelic since 1925, was appointed Deputy Rector at the school. Urquhart's appointment, the first of its kind in Ross-shire, was a timely recognition that the administrative burden imposed by a school of the size of The Nicolson Institute was too great for one person to sustain. On his retirement (in 1960) he was succeeded by Mr. Albert Nicoll.

Sometime in the late 1960s, Angus Nicolson wrote an extended tribute to both men, which is worth noting at this point. As Sheriff-Substitute (Mr. Urquhart), Town Councillor (Mr. Nicoll) and members of the County Council Education Committee (both), after retirement they continued to give of their time to public affairs in the community, particularly in relation to the cause of the *'ever-recurring lack of adequate accommodation and other facilities.'* He also commented on the influence both men had on him as a pupil and then as a young teacher, noting that:

> *Although neither is a native of Lewis, there are few more Lewis-minded in outlook... Not only in the narrow confines of the teaching profession but also as both are extremely extrovert, they have made many friends, not only in Lewis, but in many other quarters.*

He felt that either man could have made careers elsewhere but:

> *Their long association with The Nicolson Institute and their regard for both the Island and its people must have aroused a compelling desire to remain.*[97] *Because of their outstanding teaching and administrative abilities, they could have... become rectors of well-known established Scottish schools. That they have not done so has been of inestimable value to Lewis. Both came as Principal Teachers, Mr. Alexander Urquhart as Head of the Gaelic Department and Mr. Nicoll that of History and Geography. One found life congenial in a Gaelic community and the other by marriage into a well-known Stornoway family...*

---

97   Nicoll did leave once for a more senior post elsewhere but returned very quickly.

Lewis could not have found more qualified or forceful advocates to present the cause of The Nicolson Institute; and on a wider scale that of the Western Isles in the educational changes which the new regional zoning scheme will bring.

With the victory in Europe came a renewed interest in school activities which had lapsed during the war years. The Literary and Debating Society resumed its sessions, and a Dramatic Society was formed. With the formation of a Junior Football League in Stornoway, the Nicolson football team came into being again after a lapse of seven years. When the Senior Lewis Football League was reconstituted in 1946, the school decided not to compete. It was generally agreed that the school team lacked the years and the weight which would give it a fighting chance in League contests.[98] In the Junior League, however, the school acquitted itself with credit, not only upholding but also excelling the record of former school teams.

At this time various members of staff who had been on war service began to return. To judge by the lists of former pupils serving in the various branches of the Services which appeared in the 'Annual' from 1940 onwards, the contribution made by Old Nicolsonians to the war effort was impressive. The 'Annual' which was published without intermission during the war years reflected the impact of the war on the internal life of the school. Information about war casualties and honours and promotions in the Forces was regularly recorded in its pages. By 1945, the number of former pupils who had died in the service of their country, although not so staggering as in the World War I conflict, was nevertheless considerable.

The names of former pupils figured from time to time in the lists of honours and awards for gallantry or outstanding war service. Among them were: L/Colonel Malcolm Macewan, DFC, OBE (Military Division) and later the DSO and bar; Colonel John Macsween, OBE (Military Division);[99] Commander D.M. Maclean, DSC;[100] Major Angus Macleod, RAMC, MBE; Captain Donald Macrae, RAMC, MC; Pilot Officer Murdo Macdonald (Dux 1940), DFC; Dr Peter J. Macleod, OBE; Rev Jo Ross, MBE; Major Ivor Macleod, Captain Quentin Mackenzie, Flight Lieutenant Malcolm Macdonald, BSM, H. Maciver[101] and George Henderson, all mentioned in dispatches; Sergeant Marcus Bauer, DCM; Sergeant Malcolm Mackenzie

---

98 A decision later reversed, with decisive results in the 1950s when the school team twice won the (Senior) league (see Chapter 11).
99 Later founding Principal of the Lews Castle College.
100 Later Commodore of the Cunard fleet and Freeman (1961) of Stornoway.
101 Possibly Hector Maciver.

IN EVERLASTING MEMORY OF FORMER PUPILS
OF THIS SCHOOL WHO GAVE THEIR LIVES
IN THE WORLD WAR 1939 – 1945

Rank	Name	Service	Rank	Name	Service
GNR.	JOHN CAMPBELL	ROYAL ARTILLERY	SMN.	DONALD MACLEOD	ROYAL NAVY
C/ENR.	WILLIAM S. CLARKE	MERCHANT NAVY	SMN.	KENNETH D. MACLEOD	ROYAL NAVY
SGMN.	ALEXANDER CRAWFORD	ROYAL NAVY	F/SGT.	HUGH MACLEOD	ROYAL AIR FORCE
F/O.	JAMES P. GRAHAM	ROYAL AIR FORCE VOLUNTEER RESERVE	R.O.	IAN M. MACLEOD	MERCHANT NAVY
GNR.	JOHN HEPBURN	ROYAL ARTILLERY	SMN.	JOHN DANIEL MACLEOD	ROYAL NAVAL RESERVE
CPL.	JOHN R. INNIS	CAMERON HIGHLANDERS	P/O.	MALCOLM MACLEOD	ROYAL NAVAL RESERVE
L.A.C.	RODERICK MACASKILL	ROYAL AIR FORCE	A.B.	MURDO MACLEOD	MERCHANT NAVY
L/BDR.	NEIL D. MACAULAY	ROYAL ARTILLERY	PTE.	MURDO MACLEOD	AUSTRALIAN IMPERIAL FORCE
CAPT.	HUBERT A. MACCALLUM	MERCHANT NAVY	BOSN.	NEIL MACLEOD	MERCHANT NAVY
GNR.	ALLAN MACDONALD	ROYAL NAVY	R.O.	NORMAN A. MACLEOD	POST OFFICE CABLE SHIPS
CARP.	ANGUS MACDONALD	MERCHANT NAVY	SMN.	ALEXANDER MACMILLAN	ROYAL NAVY
WTR.	DONALD ANGUS MACDONALD	ROYAL NAVY	A.B.	JOHN M. MACRAE	MERCHANT NAVY
SMN.	IAN O. MACDONALD	ROYAL NAVY	SGT.	HECTOR MACRAE	PIONEER CORPS
SGT.	MURDO MACDONALD	ROYAL TANK REGIMENT	CPL.	DONALD MACRITCHIE	SEAFORTH HIGHLANDERS
P/O.	MURDO MACDONALD, D.F.C.	ROYAL AIR FORCE	P.O.	WALTER MATHESON	ROYAL AIR FORCE
A.B.	MURDO M. MACDONALD	ROYAL NAVY	F/O.	ALASDAIR D. MORRISON	ROYAL AUSTRALIAN AIR FORCE
CADET	JOHN MACGUCKIN	MERCHANT NAVY	SGT/NAV.	DONALD MORRISON	ROYAL AIR FORCE
F/SGT.	ANGUS MACIVER	ROYAL AIR FORCE	L/SMN	JOHN MORRISON	ROYAL NAVAL RESERVE
A.B.	DONALD MACIVER	ROYAL NAVAL RESERVE	CPL.	DONALD MURRAY	ARGYLL AND SUTHERLAND HIGHLANDERS
F/SGT.	ALISTAIR R. MACKAY	ROYAL AIR FORCE	A.B.	JOHN ANGUS MURRAY	MERCHANT NAVY
SGT/P.	DONALD MACKENZIE	ROYAL AIR FORCE	SMN.	NORMAN MURRAY	ROYAL NAVAL RESERVE
SGT.	KENNETH MACKENZIE	ROYAL AIR FORCE	A.B.	ANGUS NICOLSON	MERCHANT NAVY
PTE.	JOHN N. MACLEAN	GORDON HIGHLANDERS	SMN.	DANIEL NICOLSON	ROYAL NAVAL RESERVE
SMN.	NORMAN MACLEAN	ROYAL NAVAL RESERVE	L/SMN.	MURDO NICOLSON	ROYAL NAVAL RESERVE
SPR.	WILLIAM T. MACLEAN	ROYAL ENGINEERS	A.B.	MURDO D. NICOLSON	MERCHANT NAVY
SGMN.	ALASDAIR MACLEOD	ROYAL NAVY	A.B.	DONALD C. SMITH	MERCHANT NAVY
C/ENGR.	ALEXANDER MACLEOD	MERCHANT NAVY	F/SGT.	HUGH J. SMITH	ROYAL AIR FORCE
E.O.	ALEX M. MACLEOD	MERCHANT NAVY	SMN.	JOHN MACDONALD SMITH	UNITED STATES MERCHANT MARINE
CPL.	ANNA M. MACLEOD	AUXILIARY TERRITORIAL SERVICE	CAPT.	MALCOLM SMITH	ROYAL NAVAL VOLUNTEER RESERVE
A.B.	DONALD MACLEOD	MERCHANT NAVY	SPR.	NEIL M. STEWART	ROYAL ENGINEERS
SMN.	DONALD MACLEOD	ROYAL NAVAL RESERVE	ENGR.		MERCHANT NAVY

A memorial plaque, now situated in the school foyer

and Flight Sergeant John Maciver, Croix de Guerre; Sergeant Hector Macleod and L/Corporal Callum J. Macdonald, MM; William Mackenzie, BEM; Leading Seaman Kenneth Macphail, DSM.

Mr. Henderson's Rectorship was of short duration. He bade farewell to The Nicolson Institute in January 1947 to become Rector of Musselburgh Grammar School. He had come to the school at a time when war-time restrictions of materials, combined with a drastic lack of accommodation, made for difficulties of administration, but despite these problems the school's record of achievement was well maintained under his direction. The very successful school concerts run during his time as Rector reflected the personal interest taken by him in the musical life of the school. By his patronage he also did much to stimulate interest in another area of special appeal to him - the youth movement, both in The Nicolson and in Lewis generally.

'Donny B' MacLeod's War-time Recollections

The broadcaster, 'Donny B' MacLeod, wrote in the 1973 *Centenary Magazine* of his war time years in the school. 'Donny B' MacLeod (1932-1984) was a Grampian TV presenter, subsequently best known for presenting the afternoon show, Pebble Mill at One. His description provides an evocative pupil's eye view of the school at this particular time:

'Donny B' MacLeod

From what seemed the high wall of the pink school all the way to Mossend stretched a sheep-haunted bulrush wilderness and where the new school (i.e. 1956 building) now stands we dug for Victory in the school allotments. The Francis Street building smelled of chalk and cold stone, of wet raincoats and coal fire. I was a town sophisticate who sold 'Gazettes' on a Friday and strings of skeds[102] to cailleachs[103] on Saturday mornings…We saluted teachers on the street and Pavlovian reflex still causes an involuntary twitch of the right arm when I meet them today. The upper lab was full of strange devices . . . moth-eaten stuffed birds in glass cases and an unfortunate flayed frog mutely protesting his crucifixion in formaldehyde. The lower lab, like the music room, was a corrugated iron shed where the aroma of Miss Craig's baking from next door battled with the miasma of leaking Bunsen burners. The 'library' was three cupboards outside Class VI in Springfield where Albert Nicoll dispensed Scott, Dumas and Henty, and the yellowing photographs of the school football teams of yore stared out in Corinthian poses. The teachers all seemed ancients of days and when later I returned as a member of staff I discovered that they had aged not a whit and then a pupil asked me where I had served in the war! And of course the great pitfall is for me to say that despite it all I preferred the cosy gas light, the draughty old rooms, the tin sheds and the outside privies to the modern sophistication of the new Nicolson. And I'm going to plunge straight into it and say, hand on heart, that I did.

---

102 Herring in Stornoway slang.
103 Elderly ladies in Gaelic.

Chapter 11:
Post-War Nicolson, 1945-1968

Mr. C.J.S. Addison

Mr. C.J.S. Addison

Mr. Henderson was succeeded as Rector by Mr. C.J.S. Addison, a Dux of Grove Academy, Broughty Ferry, who had graduated with First Class Honours in Classics from Edinburgh University and took a First in Classical Tripos from Cambridge. He held lectureships at Aberdeen and Liverpool Universities until 1941 when he joined the Intelligence Corps. After the War, he lectured at University College, Dundee, until his appointment as Rector of The Nicolson Institute in 1947. He wrote in the school annual:

> *18 years ago, when I first became acquainted with Lewis, I little dreamed that one day I should be called to be Rector of The Nicolson Institute. We in the South knew of its existence, of course, thinking of it chiefly as a fertile source of ministers, doctors and schoolteachers.*[i]

Demographics and Accommodation

The formidable problem of shortage of accommodation which had dogged his predecessors became even more intractable when Mr. Addison took office. It was exacerbated by societal and educational changes, and both local and national policy changes. High post-war birth rates, and the building of housing in Manor Park, Kennedy Terrace, Plasterfield and Parkend, fed more pupils into Sandwick and Stornoway Primaries and The Nicolson. The raising of the school leaving age to fifteen in 1947; the right of everyone to secondary education which had been confirmed under the Education (Scotland) Act 1945; the development of 'pre-nursing' and commercial courses which attracted good numbers; and the introduction of O Grades in 1962, all led to increased numbers during Addison's Rectorship.

The dispersal of this volume of pupils through many buildings, not all within the school area, imposed a severe strain on pupils and teachers. The prospect, however, that work might soon begin on the long awaited new secondary school building was becoming brighter. Meanwhile various expedients had to be resorted to. Under a government scheme to contain the sudden bulge in the school population by the provision of temporary accommodation (HORSA i.e., Hutting Operation for the Raising of the School-Leaving Age), six classrooms were constructed in 1949. These were designed to house classes in Domestic Science and Technical subjects. (Some were still in use into the 1980s.) Around 1953 this 'temporary' accommodation was supplemented by the construction of wooden huts to provide ten classrooms. These measures were palliatives which eased the problem: they did not solve it, leading to:

1949-50 football team

...these uniquely nomadic school pupils who had to migrate regularly through the town between lessons to attend classes in church halls, drill halls, hostels, canteens etc.[ii]

With the opening in 1950 of new canteen premises to replace the corrugated iron hut in which the school meals service had been inaugurated in 1944 to serve 120 pupils,[104] the number of pupils that could be catered for now increased considerably. At an early stage in the history of the school the need for such a service was fully recognised, especially for pupils from outlying areas, but for financial reasons only very tentative efforts could be made to meet it.

At the close of session 1949-50, the Rector announced the introduction of a standard school dress to help promote a spirit of unity and loyalty. The school badge introduced in 1931 could now be worn to better advantage. The uniform took the form of blazers (for boys) and navy-blue skirts worn by the girls.[105]

That spirit of unity was already seen wherever former pupils of The Nicolson met, especially furth of their native island; with the mention of their old school a certain rapport was established. The reality of this bond was well illustrated in August 1950 when members of the Class VI of 1925 held a re-union dinner in the Masonic Hall. The occasion received generous coverage in the *Stornoway Gazette*. Its editorial comment testified to the success of the 'Nicolson Experiment' in terms of unity, loyalty and ties that bound from Lewis to Hong Kong. The speeches at the reunion were:

an admirable blend of personal reminiscence, class gossip and concern for the continued well-being of the school.

---

104   A wartime measure, as we have seen, to improve the safety of school students at lunchtime.
105   Photographic evidence, courtesy of Sandy Matheson, suggests that uptake was uneven.

The Nicolson Institute staff, 1947
Back row: Mr. Angus Macleod (Janitor), Mr. Ian Paterson (English), Mr. Kenneth Mackenzie (Maths),
Mr. W.F. (Bill) Chalmers (Art), Mr. Gordon Urquhart (Maths), Mr. William Macleod (Classics), Mr. John Reay (Handwork),
Mr. John Macarthur, Mr. Alasdair Macleod (Primary), Dr George S. Ferrier (Science), Mr. Charles G.S. Taylor (Languages),
Mr. James Thomson
Third row: Miss Ena Smith (Maths), Miss Gertrude M. Black (Science), Mrs. M. Hunter (Boys' Hostel),
Miss Mamie Macdonald, Miss Marion Clarke, Miss Anne Cochayne (Gym), Miss Jessie B. Calder (Needlework),
Miss Janet Macleod, Mrs. Jessie Mackay, Miss Isabella Morrison, Miss Maclean (Commercial Subjects),
Miss Annie Mackenzie (Singing), Miss Joan Montgomery
Second row: Miss Kate Macsween (Secretary), Miss Maudie Maclean, Miss Peggy Macdonald, Miss Chrissie
Macarthur, Miss Cheyne, Miss Anchris Ross, Miss Isabella Morrison, Miss Jean Mackenzie, Mrs. Fletcher (Boys' Hostel),
Miss Christina Macleod, Miss Annie Morrison, Miss M.M. Macleod, Miss Helen Ann Maciver
Front row: Mr. Albert Nicoll, Miss I. Craig (Domestic), Mr. John Angus Maciver (First Master, Primary),
Miss Belle Morison, Miss Maggie Stewart, Mr. Cecil J.S. Addison (Rector), Miss Annie Campbell (Infant Mistress),
Mr. Alex Urquhart, Miss M.S. Pope, Miss Ina Macdonald, Miss Isabella Macrae

Class VI of 1925 reunion dinner, outside the 'Technical' in Springfield (with four teachers and some spouses), August 1950
Back row: *Mrs. R. Smith, Donald Montgomery, Roderick Smith, W.J. Cameron,[106] John Morrison, Mrs. Macleod (Christina Mackay), Madge Gunn, Christina Maciver, Mrs. Maclean (Miss Hart), Donnie Matheson*
Middle row: *Ancrise Ross,[107] Mary Smith,[108] Di Mackenzie,[109] Mrs. D. Macdonald, Miss Maggie Stewart,[110] John Macdonald, Miss Bassin,[111] Mrs. Murdo Macleod, Mrs. A.J. Maclean, Mrs. Norman Macleod, Mrs. D. Matheson*
Front row: *Alex John Maclean, Donald Macdonald, Murdo Macleod, Norman Macleod*

---

106 Dux in 1925. Son of Stornoway Free Church Minister. His mother was a friend of Mrs. Gibson decades earlier.
107 N.I. teacher
108 N.I. teacher
109 N.I. teacher
110 Dux in 1910. Joined school staff in 1919.
111 She had joined school staff in 1920.

In 1953, the Secondary Department was divided into four 'Houses' named after the first four Headmasters or Rectors - Sutherland, Forbes, Gibson and Macrae.[112] The four clan crests on the cover of the school magazine of that year symbolised the houses. The Hebridean Spinners' Association presented the school with a handsome shield for inter-house competition. It was hoped that the house system would generate within the school community a spirit of healthy competition in all areas of endeavour.

For three reasons, 1954 was a notable year in the history of the school. One was the winning of the BBC radio contest, 'Top of the Form', by a team from The Nicolson under the direction of Mr. A. Nicoll. The victory of the four boys brought pleasure not only to The Nicolson but also to Old Nicolsonians throughout the world. To mark the success of the boys, Stornoway Town Council presented to the school a handsome lectern, which is still in regular use.

The winning Top of the Form team in 1954

---

112   Now five: the fifth is called Addison House. Ironically it is a House for Gaelic-medium school students. Addison, fluent in French and German, did not ever master Gaelic.

A school student of that era recalled:

> *In 1954 - the school winning the final of the Top of the Form Nationwide inter schools quiz show v Methodist College Belfast (Boys). The scores were very close right up until the end before the NI prevailed. I still remember the sense of pride we all felt (pupils and staff) following this achievement which certainly put the school even more on the map. The successful team was Ronnie Urquhart (son of Alex Urquhart),[113] Alasdair MacLean, Ian MacKay and William McTaggart.*

The second event was the commencement of work on the long-awaited new secondary building in Springfield and, associated with it, the progress made with part of the school's new playing fields. All looked forward eagerly to the time when the days of constant migration of classes would come to an end and when every boy in the school who wished to play football would have the opportunity to do so.[114]

The third feature of this session which made it a memorable one was the initiation by the Rector of a series of continental tours, mostly to France, which proved highly successful.

---

113 The late Ronnie Urqhart pursued a successful career as a teacher and headteacher. Photograph courtesy of Stornoway Historical Society.
114 At the time of writing (about 1972), the concept of girls playing football was yet to surface. The film *Gregory's Girl* lay somewhere in the future (1981).

The Nicolson Institute staff, 1954-55
Back row: *Mr. A. Macleod (Janitor), Miss Vida Macleod, Ms Campbell, Mr. Bill Young, Mr. William Macleod, Mr. Duncan Maclean, Mr. John Macarthur, Mr. Bill Cameron, Mr. J. Mackenzie, Mr. J. Macleod, Mr. A. Macleod, Mr. N. Macleod, Miss Annie Morrison, Miss Christine Macleod*
Fourth row: *Miss Bella Macleod, Miss Maggie Mary Macleod, Miss Maudie Maclean, Mr. Bill Chalmers, Mr. Wallace Short, Mr. Fraser Edwards, Mr. Angus Nicolson, Mr. Bert Evans, Mr. Calum Macinnes, Mr. Murdo Smith, Miss Joanna Montgomery, Miss C. Macarthur, Mr. Neil Morrison (Janitor)*
Third row: *Miss Gertrude Black, Miss Annie Mackenzie, Miss Macsween, Mrs. Nan Cunningham, Miss Jessie Mackenzie, Miss Cathie Macleod, Miss Dolina Morrison, Mrs Mollie Morrison, Miss Marion Clarke, Mrs Jean Maclean, Miss Cathie Stewart, Miss C. Macleod, Miss M.A. Maciver, Miss Freda Patrick, Mrs. F. Mackenzie, Miss Ena Smith*
Second row: *Dr G.S. Ferrier, Miss J. Cowie (Matron EH), Mrs. Fletcher (Matron LC), Miss Di Mackenzie, Miss Ancris Ross, Miss Annie Mackay, Ms Bella Finlayson, Miss Murdina Macleod, Miss Greta Henderson, Miss Mary Ann Maciver, Mrs. J. Mackay, Miss Jessie B. Calder, Miss Bella Morrison*
Front row: *Mr. Charles G.S. Taylor, Miss Chrissie Macarthur, Mr. Kenneth Mackenzie, Miss M. Macdonald, Mr. Alex Urquhart, Mr. Cecil J.S. Addison, Miss Maggie Stewart, Mr. John Angus Maciver, Miss A. Macdonald, Mr. Albert Nicoll, Mr. Gordon Urquhart*

Football Glory

As we have seen in Chapter 10, when the Senior Lewis Football League had been reconstituted in 1946, the school had decided not to compete, as the school team would not have had a fighting chance in League contests. This decision was later reversed, with decisive results in the 1950s[115] when an outstanding Nicolson Institute football team won the Senior League title twice, in 1955 and 1957. Alasdair Morrison from Lochs, the goalkeeper, wrote of their successes and the impact on the wider school:

> *The 'fifties' was certainly looked upon as an exciting and enjoyable time at the school. This was in no small measure due to the great success of the football teams at that time... The staff also showed much interest and support, some of whom are featured in the team photographs. Bill Young, our P.E. teacher, was the chief source of encouragement...*
>
> *The significant high points, of course, are the 1955 and 1957 league winning teams - quite an achievement considering that we played against grown men. Our final game in 1957, against a very strong Stornoway Athletic team, will long live in my memory. It was a very close exciting game which we won. Fortunately for us, D. M. 'Safety' Smith missed a penalty - a draw would have prevented us from winning the league. Three days later at Goathill, we defeated the North of Scotland Senior Schools cup holders, Inverness Royal Academy, 3-1. For our entire team (bar one player) this would be our final game for the N. I. - a great way to finish!*

---

115   The NI school team, except when playing against other schools, typically included some staff. In school photographs of the time, they were dignified by the title of Mr.

1955 League Winners
Back row: Mr. A. Nicoll, Mr. K. MacKenzie, G. Matheson (Tong), Mr. C. MacKay, J. M. Graham (Back), A. Morrison (Lochs) J.D. Mackenzie (Callanish), Mr. W. Young, C. MacKenzie (Stornoway), Mr. D. MacDonald, Mr. A. Nicolson
Front row: Mr. W. Chalmers, I.M. Matheson (Back), M. A. Macleod (Back) M. MacAulay (Carloway), D. M. Campbell (Ness), N. MacArthur (Carloway), D. M. MacLean (Back), N. Murray (Back)

1957 League Winners
Back row: Mr. W.F. Chalmers, Mr. D. Mackay, Mr. Macdonald, Mr. K. Mackenzie, Mr. W. Young
Middle row: M. Morrison, C.A. Maciver, R.J. Macleod, A. Morrison, N. Macarthur, P.N. Macdonald
Front row: A.J. Macarthur (Team Secretary), N. Smith, A. Macdonald, D.M. Campbell, N. Gillies, B. Urquhart, J. Macarthur

The New Building[116]

Thursday 10th January 1957 was an historic occasion in the life of The Nicolson Institute. On that day the new secondary department, at the time the largest in the Highlands, was formally opened by Sir John Stirling, KT, County Convener of Ross and Cromarty. It had taken three years to build, at a cost (including the adjoining playing fields) of £300,000 (£7m at current prices). It was designed to accommodate 750 school students. This building had existed as a dream for many years, but in his speech Sir John Stirling informed his audience that if it had been built when it was first planned the accommodation would have become quite inadequate by that time.

The Opening Ceremony of the Nicolson Institute Springfield Road extension, 10th January 1957
On the platform were members of the Education Committee of Ross and Cromarty County Council.
Left to right: Ex Provost Smith, unknown, Rev R. Macdonald, Sir John Stirling, C.J.S. Addison (Rector), Rev Jenkins, unknown, Mr. Maclintock, Mrs. Addison, Provost Mackenzie, Rev Angus MacCuish, unknown, unknown

---

116   Quickly dubbed by Jacques Mesleard, French teacher, as 'Versailles'. The Francis St. building he knew as the 'Bastille'.

One sixth year school student of that era recalled:

Moving into the new school - being able to spend the last two terms of our school life in brand-new surroundings was very uplifting. That same school year several young teachers, mostly mainlanders, were appointed to the school. This gave the staff a noticeable freshness with the older experienced teachers creating a good balance.... My main memory... of... the school during the fifties (is) the camaraderie, esprit and sense of belonging to something special. The N. I. was certainly a school of which the staff and pupils could be proud. There were certainly some very high academic achievers in its history... Many progressed to higher education, later excelling in various careers and professions...[iii][iv]

Another student wrote of producing an essay on the topic of moving into the new building for which he was praised by his English teacher, Fred Webster, whom he described as 'such a good teacher, ahead of his time in his methods.' The other memories were of the huge Assembly Hall and the modern gym facilities.

However, another student of the late 1950s and early 1960s recalled rather less approvingly that there was no provision of Gaelic learners' classes and had the impression that the middle-class town children were privileged over those from the rural areas.[v]

Another account gave a different perspective on the language issue:

We had to go to the Nicolson that afternoon and meet the Rector, Mr. Addison in the Assembly Hall. He asked me my name and I quietly said, "Annie Macdonald."

He looked at the records and said, "Annie Macdonald 1A – French and Latin."

"No!" said the bold Niseach, "French and Gaelic!"

"No!" he repeated. "French and Latin!" I still insisted that I was going to study Gaelic and I was allowed to do that. I have never really found out if others had the same experience.[vi][117]

---

117   The issue of course was not peculiar to Stornoway. See pp 83-139 of the wonderfully erudite, if educationally depressing, book: Rebanks, J. (2015) *The Shepherd's Life: A Tale of the Lake District*. London.

The ominous note in Sir John Stirling's remarks soon proved to be only too true: the accommodation problem had not yet been solved. A development soon to take place, however, gave promise of relief. This was the divorce of the Primary Department from the Secondary in 1961 and its being constituted a separate school - The Nicolson Primary School. The first headmaster of the new school was Mr. John A. Maciver, who since 1946 had held the appointment of First Assistant in the Primary Department of The Nicolson Institute. It was hoped that, with the migration of the primary school to a new home which was being planned for it elsewhere, The Nicolson Institute (now a purely secondary school) would be able to take possession of the vacated premises. This, however, did not happen until 1969 when The Nicolson Primary moved to its new home in Jamieson Drive and was renamed the Stornoway Primary School. However, this was certainly not the end of the 'accommodation' saga.[118]

The Library and Curricular Developments

As the 1950s and 60s progressed, a number of developments were worthy of note.

When Mr. Addison took up his appointment as Rector in 1947, he stressed the importance in a school as large as The Nicolson Institute of a well-stocked library. He appealed for books to be sent in.[vii] By 1962, much had been done to meet his wishes in this respect: the accession register showed a total of 6,049 volumes on the shelves and the level of borrowing was satisfactory. By 1967, the number had risen to 9,000. The routine work of the library was carried on by library prefects and by a professional librarian whose services were shared with the Stornoway Public Library.

Several changes occurred in the curriculum of the school, as noted earlier. In 1954, a one-year intensive course in Commercial Subjects was introduced in Class IV. Applicants for this course from the third year in The Nicolson and from rural junior secondary schools had to pass an examination in English and in Arithmetic. The course was designed to equip pupils for secretarial posts in local offices. Later, a two-year pre-nursing course was introduced to which entry could be gained by passing the same entrance examination as for the commercial course. This course, organised by the school in liaison with the Lewis Hospital, prepared girls for admission to training as student nurses working towards the State Registered Nurse qualification. With the introduction of the Scottish Certificate of Education Ordinary Grade examination in 1962, the practice

---

118   An issue that remains to this day despite the 2010s rebuilding of the entire school.

The Nicolson Institute Primary staff, 1962
Back row: *Miss A.M. Maclean, Miss K.A. Macarthur, Miss M.P. Henderson (Needlework), Miss Murdina Macleod, Mrs. M. Smith, Miss Jessie Mackenzie, Miss Mary Smith, Miss Alma Kerr, Miss I.M. Morrison*
Middle row: *Mrs. A. Kennedy, Mrs. K.A. Macgregor, Miss W.M. Macleod, Miss Bella Macleod, Miss M. Campbell, Miss C. Mackay, Mrs. C Macarthur, Miss M.M. Morrison, Mrs Janet Hunter, Miss C. Nicolson (Occupational Centre)*
Front row: *Mr. Alex Macleod, Mrs. J. Mackay, Miss J. Montgomery, Miss C.M. Macdonald (Infant Mistress), Mr. John Angus Maciver (Head Teacher), Miss K.B. Crichton*

The Nicolson Institute Primary staff, session 1965-66, on the occasion of presentation of prizes by Provost Ann Urquhart
Back row: Mr. John A. Maciver, Mrs. Mary Smith, Mrs. Jean Kennedy, Mrs. Mollie Morrison, Mrs. Morag Maciver, Mrs. C. Macarthur, Mrs. Anna Macarthur, Mrs. Mary Mackenzie, Miss W. Macleod, Miss Bella MacLeod, Mr. John Macarthur
Middle row: Miss Catriona Mackay, Miss A. Maclean, Miss Mary Smith, Miss Mary Ann Maciver, Mrs. Mary Ann Macinnes, Miss Greta Henderson, Miss Murdina Macleod, Miss Katie Crichton, Mrs. Anna Mackinnon, Miss Jessie Ann Mackenzie, Miss K.M. Murray
Front row: Mr. Duncan Morison, Mrs. Jessie Mackay, Mrs. Zena Macgregor, Mr. Gordon Urquhart, Mrs. Ann Urquhart, Mrs. Alma Jamieson, Mrs. Alice Mackay, Mrs. Anna Kennedy, Miss Catherine Nicolson, Miss Mamie Macdonald

The Nicolson Institute

The Nicolson Institute staff, 1958-59

began of presenting pupils from both these courses for a limited number of subjects at that level.

In Science, radical developments took place in the early 1960s. Up to that time all branches of the subject had come within one department under one Principal Teacher, the legendary 'Doc Ferrier.' In 1963, however, a separate department in Biology was inaugurated under its own Principal, the first incumbent being Dr A. Fraser in 1964. After the retiral of Dr Ferrier, who had been Principal Teacher of Science for 25 years at The Nicolson Institute, Chemistry and Physics branched off as separate and autonomous departments. With typical wit, 'Doc' noted that it had taken three people to replace him.

The whole national examination procedure was reviewed during this period. With the introduction in 1962 of the 'O' Grade examination (to be taken in Fourth Year) came a dramatic rise in the number of post-Third Year classes in The Nicolson Institute.[119] As a result, subject sections began to proliferate in some departments - in English, for example, where in 1961 there were two sections presenting candidates for Higher English in the SCE examination; by 1972 there were eight such sections.

Not all school students of the time were complimentary about the teaching they received, some comparing it unfavourably with their Junior Secondary experience, describing some teachers as *'terrifying'* and *'disinterested'*.[viii]

Other memories of The Nicolson of the 1960s included a teacher smoking in the side room beside his laboratory during lessons and a French teacher being buried under an avalanche of books as a prank was played on him.[ix]

Less happily, there were recollections of excessive belting[x] and, specifically, the 'sting of collective punishment' when individual miscreants could not be identified.[120] The source of the latter reminiscence observed that pupil indiscipline could also be a problem:

> *I remember two lovely but inexperienced art teachers who struggled with my class. One day I saw the first of these teachers buying* The New Statesman *in town and I was tempted, but much too timid, to tell her that I too was an NS reader. Probably a wise decision: it's not likely that she'd have been impressed by being chatted up by a spotty 11-year-old from her troublesome class.*

---

119 As happened right across Scotland. Possibly on a nationwide basis one of the most successful innovations in Scottish secondary schools.
120 In defiance of a code of practice of the time - which however had no statutory power.

He spoke too of:

> *some great teachers... challenging and inspiring... (and) of friendships which have lasted a lifetime.*[xi]

Another school student of roughly the same era described the school as being like many other Scottish secondary schools of its time, with teacher attention focused on potential academic achievers and others treated with indifference. He felt there was a lack of support for those experiencing difficulties, and:

> *...extensive, and often arbitrary, use of corporal punishment in years one to three.*

He did, however, feel that things improved from Fourth Year onwards, with a focus on pupils who would be measured in Highers, 'O' Grades and the newly introduced Sixth-Year Studies, with opinions being sought on occasion, rather than facts being recalled.[xii]

A later change in the examination structure was indeed the introduction in session 1967-68 of Certificate of Sixth Year Studies examinations[121] to be taken by post-Higher pupils in certain subjects. Several departments in the school participated in the new scheme from its inception, and in general the examination seemed to be welcomed for the sense of purpose and direction which it gave to post-Higher work in the Sixth Year. The post-Higher Sixth Year curriculum however remained problematic in many Scottish schools, including The Nicolson Institute.[122]

In addition to these changes, a process of critical reappraisal was going on in all subjects during these years. It concerned both subject content and techniques of presentation. The most significant development work was concerned with the introduction of a new syllabus in several subjects - for example, in Mathematics, all the Science subjects and Modern Languages; but no subject in the school was immune from the prevailing climate of change and rethinking of old approaches and attitudes. One manifestation of the trend was the increasing use, within the limits imposed by finance, of various technological aids such as films, tape-recorders and record players. Language laboratories, television sets and video-tape recorders were however still for the future. Laptops, electronic whiteboards and other wizardry lay even further ahead.

---

121 Roughly equivalent to the modern 'Advanced Higher'.
122 For smaller secondary schools, it was hard to provide a range of post-Higher studies. The problem persists to this day.

Retiral of Mr. Addison

Mr. Addison retired in April 1968. During his tenure of office many changes had taken place in the character of Scottish education, some of them of quite a revolutionary nature, and they were reflected in the general organisation of the school. The school roll had continued to rise and, although there was a corresponding increase in the staff, in some departments a serious staffing shortage created administrative problems from time to time.

During the final year of his Rectorship, Addison's health began to give way and he had to depart on sick leave for an extended period. Hopes that he would be able to return to duty were not realised and, finally, during a brief visit to Stornoway, he bade farewell to his colleagues on the staff at an informal gathering where they extended to him and Mrs. Addison their best wishes for many happy years of retirement. He lived in retirement in North Berwick to a great age.

There are varied views of Addison's tenure of Rector, ranging from the critical[xiii] to giving credit for guiding the school through:

> *... some of the most difficult years of its development with... skill and patience (often sorely tried under pressure).*[xiv]

Class photo, 1967

The Nicolson Institute Choir, 1968, with Head of Music Bill Short and Music teacher Betty Mackenzie

Nicolson Institute football team in 1968. Note the Sequamur school badge.

Chapter 12:
Into the 1970s and the School's Centenary

Mr. Edward Young

Addison's successor was Mr. Edward Young, MA, Principal Teacher of English at the Bell-Baxter High School, Cupar, Fife. A former pupil of Dalziel High School, Motherwell, and an Honours graduate in English of the University of Glasgow, Mr. Young assumed the Rectorship at a time when the winds of change continued to blow across the educational scene and important developments were in the offing, not least among them being the raising of the school leaving age to 16 with all its implications for the sole senior secondary school in Lewis.

Edward Young

On arriving at The Nicolson Institute, his first main task was to introduce the principles of comprehensive education. In 1969, the distinction between 'academic' and 'non-academic' pupils was removed with the introduction of the 'common course' in First and Second Year. Pupils had two years to find their feet and to develop their potential before being differentiated in Third Year into Scottish Certificate of Education work or into a Leavers' Course which prepared them for employment at fifteen or sixteen.

Senior Register class, 1969-70

S6, 1969-70

The fact that the common course allowed young people to study both French and Gaelic ('Native' Speakers or Learners) meant that The Nicolson Institute became the only school in Scotland at that time in which all pupils could study Gaelic as well as another Modern Language. A pupil of the time, a school leaver in 1968, called this a 'visionary change' at a time:

> when Gaelic, to paraphrase the Irish author Myles na Copaleen, 'was neither popular nor profitable.'

On 1st September 1969, as the renamed Stornoway Primary School moved to new premises in Jamieson Drive, the vacated buildings were occupied by The Nicolson Institute. One youngster of that era recollected:

> ... the move in September 1969 to Jamieson Drive from the Clock School. Did we really, as Primary 2 pupils, carry our own trays up Goathill Road as my memory tells me we did? It seems a world away from our own era of risk assessments and rules and regulations![i]

The departure (circa 1971) of the late Terence Twatt (by then Depute Rector) to become Rector of Oban High School and his replacement by Alan Whiteford as Depute saw corporal punishment become significantly less a tool of senior management. A probationer teacher of the early 1970s recalls:

> The Nicolson Institute struck me as a generally relaxed institution compared with some of the schools I had experienced as a student teacher in Glasgow. School students were noted, for the most part, for their reticence. Nevertheless, some teachers made extensive use of corporal punishment and regarded the prospect of its abolition - then a matter of some active national debate - with horror.[ii]

By 1983, the use of corporal punishment was beginning to be phased out in state schools after two Scottish mothers won an action in the European Court of Human Rights. Use of the Lochgelly Tawse and any other form of corporal punishment was finally banned in state schools in 1987, with Scottish private schools following suit some 10 years later in 1998.[iii]

The Swimming Pool Saga

Today, there is no trace of the original building of The Nicolson Institute. The clock tower, which can be seen today, was an addition in 1902, with a clock and chimes installed in 1905. The Clock School, as it became known, was demolished in 1972 to make way for The Nicolson-Lewis Sports Centre and swimming pool, which incorporated the Clock Tower.

From the mid-1940s, there had been numerous unsuccessful attempts to persuade successive local authorities to build a swimming pool in Stornoway. In 1957, the sad drowning of a teenager at the Braighe further fuelled these demands. George Macaulay, YMCA President, was instrumental in the YM's decision to offer £1,000 towards any fund concerned with the establishment of a swimming pool in Stornoway. Neither the County Council nor the Town Council was prepared to take the lead, and stalemate ruled until 1962, when a meeting of the YMCA led to the formation of the Lewis Swimming Pool Committee.

Several years of fund-raising followed, including a succession of annual carnivals, and in the autumn of 1970 the Honorary Burgh Treasurer announced to the Town Council that the County Council had accepted the project. Then the Scottish Education Department mysteriously *(but temporarily)* mislaid the documents!

Heated debate at a meeting of the Lewis Amenity Trust concerned possible sites for the pool, ranging from the Porter's Lodge, Cuddy Point, the Gas Works, the grounds of the new Stornoway Primary School on Jamieson Drive, to the site of the Clock School building.[iv]

The focus of attention settled ultimately on the Clock School building with the alternatives of total demolition or of retaining the Clock Tower within the new construction. The final decision was to retain the Clock Tower, and the school was demolished in 1972. The new Nicolson-Lewis Sports Centre and swimming pool was formally opened on 26 October 1974 by Mr. Donald Stewart, MP.

Demolition of the Clock School in 1972

As we have already seen, Angus Nicolson wrote critically at the time of the decision to demolish the Clock School:

> *Even at that time, probably more than the utilitarian present, the Sandwick Road School had come to be regarded as of considerable historic value, especially by those who had received their early years of schooling there. In its walls were incorporated the two commemorative plaques, one in honour of its founding and the other of its founder. On the wall facing Sandwick Road there had been fixed a large bronze memorial tablet presented to the Town Council of Stornoway by the Seaforth Highlanders in honour of the many Lewismen who had served in this famous Highland regiment and especially those who had given their lives in the many campaigns in which it had fought. It had been loaned temporarily to The Nicolson Institute because of the many former pupils who had served in its ranks. Over the years it had become a permanent fixture.*

One cannot but wonder if the original school could not have been retained with only the headmaster's house and the later extension demolished. The clock tower, a later addition, stands seemingly forlorn and incongruous without the building it was intended to adorn... The first school had considerably more historic and architectural value than other buildings for whose preservation demands have been made.

By the time the decision was made to retain the original school as a museum and rural library centre there had been acquired a collection of various items, some of rather a motley nature, but others of intrinsic value. At the further end of the upper corridor of the Springfield building one recalls a large glass-fronted case containing geological specimens, prehistoric stone implements, arrow tips, hammer heads, stone axes and scrapers. In another were cups and shields either won outright or presented such as the plaque made of oak from the 'Victory' to commemorate the Battle of Trafalgar. Lining the walls were photographs of successive school football teams, of various individuals who had rendered notable service to the school such as Dr. J.L. Robertson, and of those who by acts of bravery for which they had been decorated had brought a certain degree of honour to the school. Perhaps, as tradition dies, so does pride in achievement. Once removed they are no longer replaced.

Here also are relics when life in Lewis had a harsher reality than the present: a pot chain which once hung from a thatched roof over the central peat fire, a cruisgean whose dim light from seal oil provided the only illumination, a length of siomain fhraoich (heather rope) to hold down the thatch with the aid of stones, and a wooden boat bailer. Probably the article of greatest intrinsic value is a craggan of Lewis pottery. There are also 'adder' stones...

There is also a table which once graced The Nicolson home which was presented to the school by Miss Donaldina Macleod, a former teacher, who lived in 77 Kenneth Street. Thus, if over the intervening years the original plan had been put into practice, a valuable collection might have been assembled in the original school to which many former pupils would have contributed.

The School Centenary

In 1973 the school leaving age was raised again, this time to sixteen, and new provision was deemed necessary for the '*less academic*' pupils. Young's solution was to introduce a highly flexible set of options in Third and Fourth Year, allowing pupils previously dubbed 'non-certificate' to take up to five Ordinary Grade subjects. This led in many cases to these pupils staying on to take Higher Grades successfully in Fifth Year.[123]

The year 1973 also saw a historic landmark in the history of The Nicolson Institute as various events were held to celebrate the one hundredth anniversary of the founding of the school, culminating in a Centenary Dinner in the newly completed Cabarfeidh Hotel. The main toast 'To The Nicolson Institute' was proposed by Sir Norman Graham, Secretary of the Scottish Education Department, and other speakers included BBC presenter 'Donny B' Macleod, a former pupil and Art teacher in the school, and Western Isles M.P., Donald Stewart. A special film of all the events of the centenary year was made by staff, and a centenary magazine was produced.

The Nicolson Institute Staff Centenary Dinner was held at the Cabarfeidh Hotel in February 1973, attended by 200 guests.
Back row: *Mr. E. Young, Rector; Mr. D.B. Macleod; Mr. D. Stewart M.P.; Sir N.W. Graham, Secretary of the Scottish Education Department; Mr. A. Matheson, Provost*
Front row: *Mrs. Stewart, Mrs. Macleod, Mrs. Young, Mrs. Matheson*

---

123   This was a common trend in Scottish secondary schools of the time.

In 1973, the centenary of the Nicolson Institute, the Freedom of the Burgh of Stornoway was conferred on the school. The photo shows Murdoch MacLeod, Town Clerk, reading the citation; Edward Young, Rector, who received the honour on behalf of the school; Sandy Matheson, Provost of Stornoway, who presented the Freedom scroll; and Rev Angus MacCuish, minister of Stornoway High Church and chaplain of the school, who delivered the prayer at the event. The item held by Mr. Matheson and Mr. Young is the Freedom casket, a hand-crafted wooden model of the Clock School. The model is hollow and the cavity containing the scroll was accessed via a small door at one end of it.

Malcolm Macdonald, coxswain of the Stornoway Lifeboat; Ann Urquhart, Provost from 1965 to 1968; and Edward Young, Rector, pictured at the ceremony to confer the Freedom of the Burgh of Stornoway

In the centenary school magazine in an item entitled *'The Present and the Future,'* Young wrote about changes in the school since his arrival and what might happen in coming years. The common course for First Year, including both French and Gaelic, was a change in 1968, followed by the fuller development in Session 1969-70 by which time all of First Year were grouped in a common course without streaming (except for a small group of *'tutorial'*[124] pupils) for two years, before the choice of subjects offered on entrance to Third Year and embarking on S.C.E.[125] work, or following a leavers' course to prepare them for employment on leaving school at fifteen or sixteen.

Mr. Young looked forward to 1973-74, where he hoped that more choice would be available for all, following the Raising of the School Leaving Age (RoSLA). This tied in with 'a more intimate tie-up' with Lews Castle College, where new facilities would be:

> ... available to our Leavers'[126] group for two half-days a week in Class III and four half days a week in Class IV. At the College, pupils can have 'taster' courses in Class III in subjects such as Seamanship and Navigation, Building Construction, Textiles, Business Studies, Catering and in Class IV move on to select and concentrate on their main vocational interests.

General education would continue to be provided in school to this group of pupils, giving a balance of experience, Mr. Young felt.

He also wrote at some length of the expected impact of local reorganization, with 'the Long Island'[127] coming under one education authority. He predicted a fully comprehensive school for Uist,[128] and the continuing function of The Nicolson in the further secondary education of Lewis pupils, with the rural schools continuing to provide for the first two years of secondary education.

As in earlier decades, there would be a further demand on the school's resources as a result of changes, and a new building programme was beginning to get under way. Still further would be needed, as the school's population continued to grow from the 1,200 at the time of the centenary.

---

124 What might today be called 'learning support'
125 Scottish Certificate of Education
126 i.e., those intending to leave age 16.
127 Lewis and Harris: geographically one island. But historically Lewis had been in the County of Ross and Cromarty and Harris in Inverness-shire.
128 Eventually realised as Sgoil Lionacleit in 1988, a move we are told fuelled by the school inspectorate. And what is now Castlebay Community School in Barra also came to cater for 3-18-year olds, as did the Sir E. Scott School in Tarbert, Harris.

Mr. Young spoke of the 'three natural units' into which the school was divided, to allow an Assistant Headmaster to take charge of each, an organisational structure which he felt countered:

> *the tendency towards impersonality, the individual becoming lost in the mass... We cherish personality and the individual in Lewis: we must ensure that this remains a fundamental concern of the school in the future...*

On the other hand, he saw positives in a large school population: flexibility; more educational opportunities; a *'multiplicity of drive, energy and expertise'* amongst these.

The Senior Management and Guidance Staff, 1972-73
Back row: Mr. J. Macleod, Assistant Principal (Guidance); Mr. R.J. Macleod, Principal Teacher (Guidance); Mr. A. McCormack, Assistant Principal (Guidance); Mr. M. Macleod, Principal Teacher (Guidance); Mr. N. Galbraith, Assistant Headmaster; Mr. J.M. Graham, Assistant Headmaster.
Front row: Miss M. Mackay, Assistant Principal (Guidance); Miss A. Maclean, Principal Teacher (Guidance); Mr. E. Young, Rector; Mr. A.D. Whiteford, Deputy Rector; Mrs. C. MacLeay, Assistant Principal (Guidance); Mr. G. Moody, Assistant Headmaster

Also in the 1973 school magazine was an item still of historical interest, a message of greetings from the oldest surviving member of staff, Mr. Murdo Morrison, MA, FEIS, of Troon, Ayrshire, who celebrated his 100th birthday on 19th November 1972. Mr. Morrison began his professional career in The Nicolson Institute in 1900 as Principal Teacher of Classics; he ended it as Director of Education of Inverness-shire in 1937 when he retired at the age of 65, having held that post since it was instituted in 1919.

Mr. Morrison wrote in glowing terms of the *'considerate and inspiring'* Rector under whom he had served, Mr. Gibson, particularly his *'wide and clear outlook'* and *'his organizing foresight,'* including the introduction of Technical Education to the school curriculum. His praise of the pupils and his fellow staff was also fulsome in his *'heartfelt tribute'.*

As indicated in his piece for the Centenary magazine, during Young's Rectorship, several serious attempts were made to address the continuing accommodation problems which seem to have been an almost permanent feature of Nicolson life. In 1969, with the opening of the new Stornoway Primary School, the old primary building, known affectionately as *'Pinkville'* after an interesting experiment in external decoration, became the new home of the Mathematics and Geography departments. Next, a new Science block was constructed mainly accommodating the burgeoning Biology department; and a new Home Economics suite, with up-to-date facilities, was built around an open-plan area. These buildings were much needed.

The School Roll Peaks

The 1970s saw the school at its most populous, with the roll peaking at over 1400 following the raising of the school leaving age to 16 in 1973 and the addition of senior pupils from Barra, Uist and Harris, as a result of local government reorganisation.

Another new purpose-built block for Art and Music arrived in 1976. At the very end of Mr. Young's tenure of office, the construction of a new wing for English and History, incorporating a Drama studio, meant that at last the old Francis Street building, the original Secondary Department, was taken out of school service to become the Stornoway Museum.[129] Mr. Young had chaired a national Working Group on the importance of Drama in Scottish education.

During this period Comhairle nan Eilean also spent considerable sums refurbishing the older parts of the school, a process which neared completion as the new millennium approached. However, none of the new buildings described in this section survived the new build of 2012.

---

129 And now (in the 2020s) a centre for developing e-learning materials, known as e-Sgoil.

The Nicolson Institute staff, 1973
Back row: Mr. G.A. Cuthill, Mr. D. Macdonald, Mr. I. Macsween, Mr. D. McLauchlan, Mr. D.J. Maclennan, Mr. C. Torrance, Mr. J. McDougall, Mr. N. Lyon, Mr. J. Maciver, Mr. A. McCormack, Mr. M.J. Macleod
Fifth row: Mr A. Hillocks (Jan.), Mr. I.R. Smith, Herr K. Schmutzler, Mr. J. Crombie, Mr. J. Garvie, Mr. A. Crichton, Dr P. Hopkins, Mr. M. Macleod, Mr. R. Maciver, Mr. R.J. Macleod (b), Mr. A. Nicolson, Mr. K. Mackay, Mr. R.J. Smith, Mr. N. Mackay
Fourth row: Miss D. Macdonald, Miss C. Mackenzie, Mrs. B.E. Macleod, Mrs. C. Murray, Miss C. Macdonald, Miss A. Macdonald, Miss J. Macdonald, Miss R. Tulloch, Miss J. Sutherland, Mr. N. Campbell, Mr. A.N. Macleod, Mr. J. Macleod, Mr. C. Macleay, Mr. J. Macaskill, Mr. M. Macleod, Mr. A. Leonard, Mr. J. Cunningham
Third row: M. J. Mesleard, Miss M. Aitken, Miss M. Munro, Mrs. J. Macdonald, Mrs. F. Macleod, Mrs D. Finlayson, Miss C.M. MacCuish, Miss J. Mackenzie, Miss M. Macleod, Miss J. Gray, Mrs. C. Macleod, Mrs. C. Macleay, Miss M. Macleod, Miss E. Macleod (sec.), Mrs. W. Prince (lib.), Miss C. O'Connor (sec.)
Second row: Mrs. M. Maclennan (Admin. Asst.), Mrs. D. Morrison, Mr. D.J. Maciver, Mr. R.J. Macleod (a), Mr. M. Macleod, Mr. W.W.C. Scott, Mr. N. Macleod, Mrs. Z. Nicoll, Mr. R. Mackenzie, Miss M. Mackay, Miss M. Gilbert, Mrs. N. Whiteford, Miss A. Macaskill, Mrs. Kirkness
Front row: Mr. T.R. Clark, Mr. D. Mackay, Mr. R.L. Dawson, Mr. R.W.A. Scott, Mr. J. Robbie, Mr. N.R. Galbraith, Mr. A.D. Whiteford, Mr. E. Young, Mr. J.M. Graham, Mr. G. Moody, Mr. H.W. Evans, Dr A. Fraser, Mr. T. McCallum, Miss I. Mackenzie, Mr. I.A. Mackinnon

Fashions also changed during Mr. Young's tenure. A school student, spoke of living in an age when the boys' hair grew longer and the girls' skirts became shorter, quoted from the school logbook of January 1968:

> *Blitz on hair – 8 boys in VI ordered to remove their side whiskers and have their hair cut.*

She pointed out that the logbooks did not record the blitz on skirts:

> *We well remember an afternoon when all girls from Class 4 upwards were ordered to appear in the Assembly Hall after lunch. There, skirt length was closely examined by Miss Gertie Black, a Science teacher who also had the title of 'Woman Adviser'. If a skirt was deemed to be too short, the offending garment would be pulled down to lengthen it. This was possible because school skirts were not designed as mini-skirts, but most girls had the habit of giving the waistband a few turns to shorten the skirt once they left home (where mini-skirts did not generally meet with approval). They could be lengthened again on the way home.*

Miss Black was one of six retirals in 1968. She had waged a losing battle against the mini-skirt. The campaign against long hair proved to be equally futile.

A young probationer teacher of the early 1970s has, 50 years on, good memories of both Edward Young and The Nicolson. Not only did he provide advice and encouragement, but he introduced him to fishing:

> *… I think I may be one of a very few probationer teachers rowed up and down the loch at Keose by the Rector... I spent many happy years fishing all over Scotland thanks to E.Y.'s enthusiasm and generosity.*

Mr. Young had a clear vision and strove for high standards, expecting a lot from his staff and from himself. He guided the school with a quiet, but firm and effective, style. The same member of staff gave the following example of that approach:

> *I visited the Acres one Sunday evening (just after the hotel had been opened)[130] and the next day EY mysteriously appeared*

---

[130] The only hotel in Stornoway at the time to open its public bar overtly on a Sunday.

> beside me in the Crush Hall and mentioned that he had heard reports and advised against a repeat as he feared it might damage my standing in the eyes of the town. There was no hint of disapproval just a real concern about the effect it might have on me, a friendly piece of advice quietly offered by a decent man; he was a thoroughly decent man trying to do a very difficult and politically demanding job.

Another teacher of the time spoke of his attraction to the idea of teaching in the Western Isles, inspired by:

> Frederick Rea's 'A School in South Uist': his account of moving from Birmingham to become headmaster of Garrynamonie School in the early 20th Century.

In the summer of 1970, he and a colleague, required to spend two weeks in a school before embarking on their year's teacher training at Moray House, decided to combine visiting Lewis and Harris with their teaching practice, aware of the school's 'great academic tradition.' He was impressed with Mr. Young's willingness to meet them, and agreed with his view that they would learn a lot from the Principal Teacher of English, Alan Whiteford. Both he and his colleague returned to permanent posts in the school following teacher training.[131] He felt:

> ...very privileged to join the staff of The Nicolson in the early 1970s. Edward Young had been appointed a few years previously as Rector, full of enthusiasm and determined to create a team spirit in which every member felt valued, and shared a determination to strive for the highest standards in every aspect of school life. He once shared his strategy with me: 'Notice everything, criticise rarely, encourage and praise at every opportunity.' Any achievement, whether in an academic or extra-curricular context, resulted in a visit to your door the following day.

He also described Mr. Young as being a stern disciplinarian when required, as befitted a man with a military background. He was to be seen, clad in his gown, patrolling corridors during every break, checking on latecomers, both pupils and staff. However, positive staff-pupil relationships

---

[131] Tom Clark, the author of this piece; stayed in The Nicolson Institute for his entire career.

were developed at this time through a wide range of extra-curricular activities, encouraged by Mr. Young, and leading to what he felt was a very happy school.

A colleague had slightly different memories:

> *I returned to the Nicolson in 1973 as a teacher – It was the year the school leaving age was raised to 16,[132] with the result that we had quite a few reluctant conscripts in classes, none more so than in my R.E. class. In those days the Ross and Cromarty application form asked all applicants, 'Are you willing to teach RE?' Most applicants said they would, with the result that you ended up teaching at least one RE class. My class consisted of fourth year girls, desperate to be anywhere other than school.*

Her first classroom was in the 'North Huts,' one of the HORSA huts built as a temporary solution to the previous RoSLA in 1947, but she was then allocated one of the 'South Huts' beside the 'Pink School', sharing the staffroom there with Maths, Geography, English and Learning Support staff. Many anecdotes were told in that staffroom of Mr. Angus Nicolson who had recently retired and was prone to the odd Spoonerism:

> *In his retirement speech, he claimed to be 'strumduck' by the generosity of his colleagues. He had also been known to ask a pupil to 'Go to Asia and get a map of Room 4.'*

Another memorable presence in Springfield South was Roddy MacIver, latterly Principal Teacher of Maths, and a stickler for correct usage of English:

> *... if a pupil came to his room on a message from another teacher, asking to speak to a particular pupil, he had to choose his words carefully. If he asked, "Can I see Donald Morrison?" Roddy would say, "Donald Morrison, stand up." He would then turn to the messenger and say, "Can you see him now?" He would get apoplectic if anyone referred to 'O Levels', reminding them in no uncertain terms that 'O Levels' were the examinations in England, but that in Scotland you took 'O Grades.'* [v]

---

132 Something that probably will never happen again.

A Richness of Experience

During 1973, the school organised the first massive fundraising event to finance extra-curricular activities, a sponsored walk by all pupils and staff across the less accessible hinterland of the island originally called the 'Moor Toor,' in subsequent years becoming the institution affectionately named 'The Bog Slog,' still an occasional source of income for the School Fund. The next decade saw an unprecedented flourishing of school sporting, musical and other clubs, many originating in the Friday afternoon 'Activities' sessions introduced by Mr. Young, when all staff abandoned their normal subjects and offered pupils a wide variety of indoor and outdoor activities in which they had an interest. As a school student of the time recalled:

> *Folk Singing with Dr Whiteford to Golf with Mr. Whiteford; Canoeing with Mr. Moody to Mural Painting (halfway up the main stairs) with Mr. M. A. MacLeod and Wild Flower Collecting in the Willowglen with Mrs. Frances MacLeod.*

As a direct result, pupils during this period enjoyed a richness of experience within both the curricular and extra-curricular life of the school, involving regular expeditions to St. Kilda, Mingulay, the Shiant Islands, Loch Langavat and Rhenigidale; clubs, societies, musical and dramatic productions; and a whole range of sports, many involving fixtures against mainland schools, that can seldom have been emulated.

The 'Blog Slog', an annual fund-raising walk across the moor from Barvas to Stornoway, c. 1972 (courtesy Tasglann nan Eilean)

The Senior Debating Society, Burns' Supper

The Archery activity

This richness also stemmed in no small measure from the large intake for the first time, with the inception of Comhairle nan Eilean in 1975, of senior pupils from Harris, Uist and Barra who - as hostel residents - were enthusiastic supporters of many of these after-school and weekend activities. During this period the school roll peaked, making The Nicolson one of the largest secondary schools in the north of Scotland. Whilst the later opening of Sgoil Lionacleit in 1988 and the upgrading of Sir E. Scott and Castlebay Schools in 1992 were much to be welcomed in these communities, there is no doubt that pupils from the other islands enhanced the school community and that their presence was a memorable feature of the 1970s and 80s.

Senior Badminton Champions

The Canoeing activity

The Golf activity with Mr. Young

Sports Day, Springfield Road

Sports Day, Senior Girls' Long Jump

Table Tennis champions

Hector Morrison debating

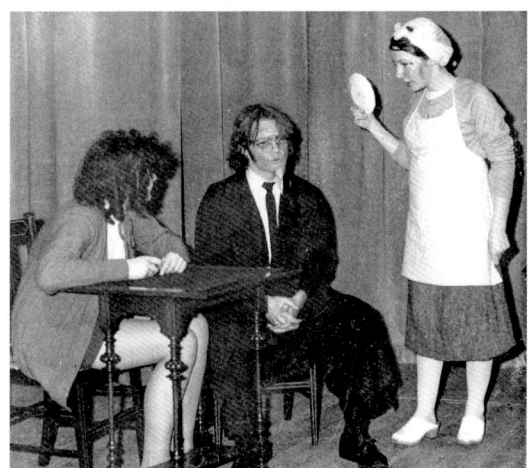

Dramatic production

Dramatic production of Before You Roast Your Beef, June 1967

Backstage, dramatic production

Photos of activities circa 1972, courtesy Tasglann nan Eilean

Unfortunately, because of the massive campaign by Scottish teachers during the mid-eighties to improve pay and conditions, many of these voluntary activities were boycotted by staff. At the end of this period of industrial action, the government adopted a much more legalistic stance towards the teaching and non-teaching duties of staff, and much of the goodwill that had previously existed in schools towards voluntary non-contractual activities disappeared.

Sadly, this aspect of school life has never fully recovered, although a few committed staff have continued to give huge amounts of their free time to organise sports teams, choirs and cultural visits.[133]

A letter published in the *Stornoway Gazette*, on 6th November 2003, under the heading, 'Whiteford: Thanks to a great teacher' paid a posthumous tribute to Alan Whiteford's teaching and gave a sense of the school in the Young/Whiteford era. Alastair McIntosh wrote:

---

133 As of 2022, the school estimates that the recovery is now substantial.

I was saddened to read in the Gazette *of the passing of Alan Whiteford, teacher of English at The Nicolson Institute.*

Having been what in those days was called a 'slow developer' at school, I vividly recall struggling with a number of subjects when I first went to the Nicolson in 1967. Strange though it may seem as one who now makes his living as a writer and public speaker, English was one of these bewildering realms.

By sheer good fortune Alan Whiteford then arrived on the scene. Our class - 1F - had him for several months. I still remember sitting electrified through the first lesson he gave us. Alan... deepened our capacity to use language to communicate feeling. He taught poetry as a tool of the heart's empathy. My own output in this regard was a few lines called 'The Elephant Hunt'. ... I couldn't believe it when the grade came back as 'Excellent'. It was the first time I'd ever got 'Excellent' for anything in school. So it was that Alan's teaching stimulated not only creativity, but also a confidence that could have consequences far beyond the English class.

Another thing that Alan did was that he encouraged as many of us as he could so persuade to study for Spoken English examinations... Alan had evidently recognised that kids raised in Lewis could benefit from being cultivated in their public speaking ability. He therefore took the trouble of arranging for an examiner from a rather Victorian-sounding institution called the English Speaking Union to come to the school once a year and listen to our presentations. These Spoken English examinations were taken out of pleasure, not fear... one last word of thanks to a great teacher who, along with several others at the Nicolson during Eddie Young's era, gave me the tools of my trade and maintained the esteem of the school.

Let it just be added that physical parting does not diminish the presence of figures like Alan Whiteford. The Spirit lives on. Through so many of us, it will continue to serve the whole community.

S1 Boys' register class, 1971

S1 Boys' register class, 1971

A windy day for a photo of the Gaelic choir, 1975

A horse feeding on Springfield Road

Feeding the hungry pupils

In the canteen

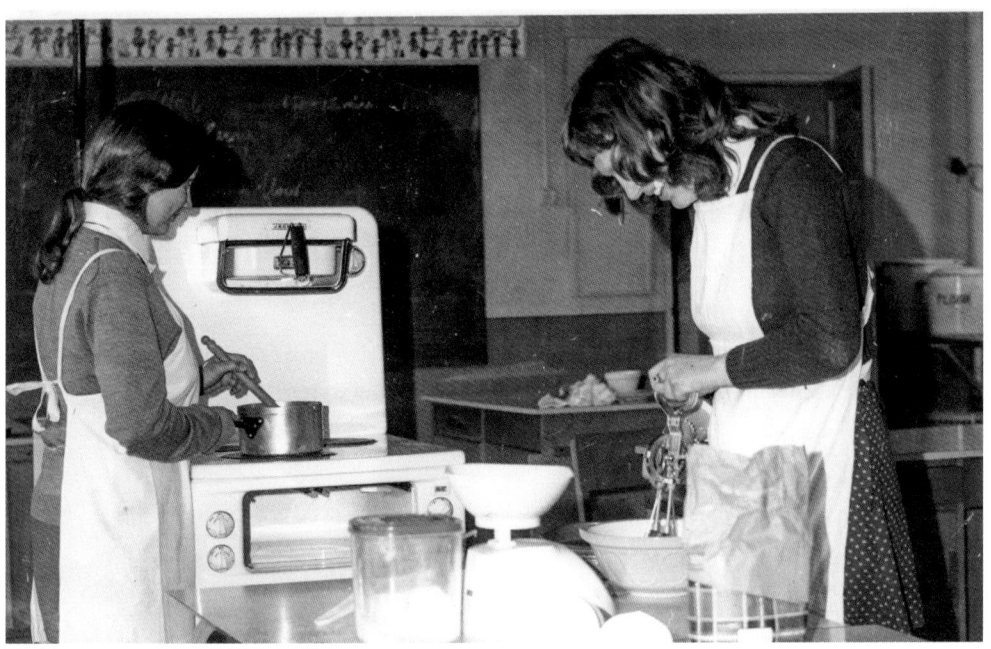
Preparing food in a Domestic Science class

Typical classroom arrangement of the era

The Nicolson Institute

S1 pupils in 1972

Mass gathering of pupils and staff between main building and Science block in 1980 to mark national achievements with an aerial photo
Photo by the Scottish Daily Express

Chapter 12: Into the 1970s and the School's Centenary

The business of learning, 1970s

French class in the Language Lab with Mr. Dawson, 1970s

Under 16 football team, mid 1970s

Senior hockey team, mid 1970s

Utilising new technology in a Business Studies class

Working on Airfix models at Activities, 1973

The Nicolson Institute Top of the Form team, 1974
Standing: *John A. Morrison, Philip Campbell, Martin Flett, Peter Farquhar*
Seated: *Kirsty Macdonald, Joan Ross, Jane Cardwell*

Junior hockey team, early 1970s

Junior football team, 1974

Senior netball team, 1976

Junior netball team

Rugby team, 1973

Senior football team featuring staff as well as pupils, 1974

Staff football game, 1970s

The Nicolson Institute senior rugby team won the North of Scotland Schools League and the North of Scotland Sevens Championship in 1978-79. Several of the team went on to play for the North Select v Glasgow. On the left is Mr. T.R. Clark and on the right the referee is Mr. E. Young, Rector.

Netball team, 1972-73
Back row: *Isobel Macintosh, Kathleen Macleod, Donna Maciver, Iona McCallum*
Front row: *Catriona Mackenzie, Jane Aird, Murdina Macleod*

The choir under the direction of Mr. R. Scott, Principal of Music, Photo by Scottish Field, 1972

Senior boys' cookery class, photo by Scottish Field, 1972

Art class with Mr. Robertson, pre-dating new Art block, photo by Scottish Field, 1972

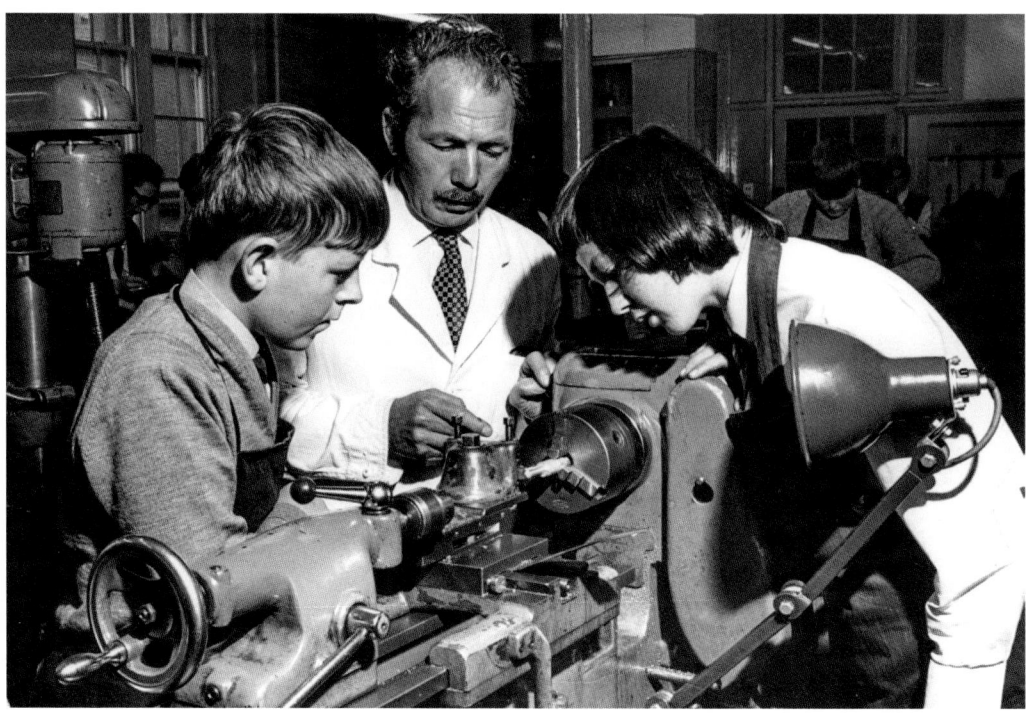

Mr. W. H. Evans, principal technical teacher, instructing pupils in the use of a metal lathe in the metal shop
Photo by Scottish Field, 1972

Murder in the Red Barn, Drama production, 1976

A musical performance

Androcles and the Lion, Junior Drama production, 1974

Junior Drama Club, 1976

Staff musical performance, early 1970s

The Nicolson Institute won the TV quiz 'First Class' in December 1984, defeating Elgin Academy in the final.

A Finance Committee meeting, mid 1970s

Dissecting in biology in the 1970s with Dr Alasdair Fraser, Head of Biology

A lively debate, circa late 1960s. The challenging debater is Malcolm Nicolson.

Colourful boys' register classes of the 1980s

Prefects, 1986-1987 with Mr. Whiteford, Mr. Young and Mr. R.J. Macleod

Prefects, 1989-1990 with Mr. R.J. Macleod and Mr. Macdonald

The Nicolson Institute staff, 1987

The Nicolson Institute staff, 1981

The Nicolson Institute staff, 1983
Back row: Mr. M. Dunn, Mr. I. Macarthur, Mr. N. Macarthur, Mr. R.M. Scott, Mr. K. Mackay, Mr. A.G. Morrison, Mr. D.J. Maclennan, Mr. M.A. Macleod, Mr. R.J. Macleod (b), Mr. N. Mackay, Mr. R.J. McAlpin, Mr. T.R. Clark, Mr. G. Paterson, Mr. I. Campbell, Mr. K. McBride
Sixth row: Mr. N. Eadie, Mr. D. McLauchlan, Mr. D. Leadbitter, Mr. N. Lyon, Mr. I.A. Macsween, Mr. J. Macleod, Mr. A. McCormack, Mr. D. Macdonald, Mr. D. Murray, Mr. K. Inglis, Mr. J. Macrae, Mr. R.J. Smith
Fifth row: Mr D.J. Maciver, Mr. S. Mackenzie, Mr. J. Cameron, Mr. D. Conners, Mr. M.J. Macleod, Mr. K. Maciver, Mr. D. Macleod, Dr R.A. Whiteford, Mr. D. Stevenson, Mr. M. Macphail, Mr. W. Stewart, Mr. A. Mackinnon, Mr. S. Oakley, Dr A. Fraser
Fourth row: Mrs. R. Murray, Miss C. Mackay, Miss C. Macleod, Miss C. Aitken, Miss S. Picken, Miss A. Graham, Miss J. Sutherland, Miss J. Wallace, Miss C.A. Stewart, Miss C. O'Connor, Mrs. C. Morrison, Miss C. Cunningham, Mrs. C. Macleay, Mrs. C. Macleod, Mr. G. Ponting, Mr. K. Maclennan
Third row: Mrs. D. Gunn, Mrs. A.Y. Stewart, Miss K. Murray, Miss E. Macleod, Mrs. J. Scott, Miss K. Macdonald, Mrs. J. Imrie, Miss M. Nicholson, Miss K. Mackay, Mrs. H. Simmons, Mrs. C. Kennedy, Mrs. B.E. Macleod, Mrs. N. Whiteford, Mrs. J. Macdonald, Mrs. M. Macleod
Second row: Miss J. Macleod, Miss C. Mackenzie, Mrs. D. Finlayson, Mrs. D. Morrison, Miss B. Macleod, Mrs. I. Dawson, Miss M. Campbell, Mrs. M. McCormack, Mrs. A. Graham, Miss M. Mackay, Miss C. MacCuish, Mrs. A. Nicol, Miss M. Macleod, Mrs. P. Shaw, Mrs. M. Maciver, Mrs. A. Maclean
Front row: Mr. N. Macleod, Mr. R.L. Dawson, Mr. R. Scott, Mr M. Macleod, Mr. G. Moody, Mr. A.D. Whiteford, Mr. E. Young (Rector), Mr. J.M. Graham, Mr. R.J. Macleod (a), Mr. R. Mackenzie, Mr. R. Maciver, Mr. C. Macleod

The Nicolson Institute staff, 1989
Back row: Mr. D.J. Maclennan, Mr. I. Macarthur, Mr. M. Macphail, Mr. I. Brady, Mr. D. Maclean, Mr. D.S. Murray, Mr. A. Crichton, Mr. A. Dunlop, Mr. A. Macphee, Mr. P. Dickie, Mr. D. Macdonald, Mr. R. Johnstone
Fifth row: Mr. I. Macsween, Mr. N. Macarthur, Mr. R.M. Scott, Mr. A. Maclennan, Mr. N. Mackay, Mr. R.J. Smith, Mr. D. Motion, Mr. D. Dunne, Mr. J. Macleod, Mr. W. Stewart, Mr. D.D. Maciver
Fourth row: Mr. A.G. Morrison, Mr. P. Havilland, Mr. D. Macleod, Mr. M. Macdonald, Mr. D. Leadbitter, Mr. J. Thomson, Mr. R.J.G. McAlpin, Dr R.A. Whiteford, Mr. N. Eadie, Mr. A. McCormack
Third row: Miss M. Finlayson, Mrs. A. Graham, Mrs. A.J. Murray, Mrs. R. Murray, Miss M. Martin, Mrs. P.M. Nicholson, Miss K. Macdonald, Mrs. L. Maclennan, Mrs. A.Y. Stewart, Mrs. C. Kennedy, Miss C.M. MacCuish, Miss C. Aitken, Mrs. M. Mackinnon, Mrs. B. Smith
Second row: Mrs. C. Morrison, Mrs. D. Finlayson, Mrs. B.E. Macleod, Mrs. I. Dawson, Mrs. D. Gunn, Mrs. J. Smith, Mrs. P. Shaw, Mrs. H. Maciver, Mrs. M. McCormack, Mrs. N. Whiteford, Mrs. S. Morrison, Mrs. C. Murray, Miss M.J. Macleod, Mrs. M. Maclennan, Mrs. J. Mackay
Front row: Mr. W.G. Paterson, Mr. N. Macleod, Mr. R.L. Dawson, Mr. R.W.A. Scott, Mrs. M. Macphail, Mr. G. Moody, Mr. A.D. Whiteford, Hu Ming (Chinese visitor), Mr. E. Young, Mr. R.J. Macleod, Mr. M. Macleod, Mr. R. Mackenzie, Mr. T.R. Clark, Mrs. M. Maciver

Chapter 13:
The Last Decade of the 20th Century

Mr. Donald J. Macdonald

Mr. Donald J. Macdonald

Following the retirement of Mr. Young and of his Depute Alan Whiteford in 1989, there was a double change in the school's top management with the appointment, first, of Dr Alan Fraser, formerly Principal of the Free Church College in Lima, Peru, as Depute and then of Mr. Donald J. Macdonald as Rector. Mr. Macdonald, a Glasgow Highlander with Ness connections, had experience of local government administration before becoming Rector of Thurso High School and then of The Nicolson Institute. A reputation for amiability followed him from Thurso to Stornoway.

Mr. Macdonald's first innovation was to reorganise the timetable into eleven half-hour periods per day, operating mainly as doubles or triples, which allowed longer blocks of time for practical classes; and the continuation of the same class over the lunch hour solved the problem of security for pupils' bags. He also allocated additional time for Guidance, incorporating a weekly assembly for each year group, and removed the afternoon interval to allow an earlier closure for pupils at 3.40pm.

He set up a Gaelic-medium stream in the school, and added a new house, Addison House, for Gaelic-medium pupils.[134]

A school student of the time recollected:

> *I started in 1990 in first year of The Nicolson. Prior to starting, I and my school mates had one visit to the secondary to walk round the various buildings. There were approximately 12 registration classes in S1, with about 20 in each. This resulted in only about two from my P7 class being allocated to each S1 registration class.*
>
> *The outstanding memory for me was the sheer size of the school's estate. There were 10 buildings and a great deal of the school day time was wasted walking from building to building as we changed subjects. Some students could take quite a while! There was a sense that the more 'important' subjects, such as English, Maths and Sciences were allocated better buildings. In my view, the worst building was reserved for Art (a subject I enjoyed enormously).*
>
> *The Rector was not really involved very much in the day to day running of the school. There were three Depute Heads,[135] each allocated to two years of the school (S1 & S2; S3 & S4; S5 & S6).*
>
> *I enjoyed my 5th and 6th year most (my 6th year as a prefect) as there was much more freedom for students in their final two years. Science and reading did not interest me much, but I loved Art and technical drawing subjects.*
>
> *At that time, some people would leave at the end of their 4th year, often to join Lews Castle College and learn a trade. Virtually no-one would leave at the end of 5th year but continued to their 6th year.*

---

134 Gaelic as a subject had been available in the school for many decades. But the study of other subjects through the medium of the Gaelic language was an innovation.
135 Actually, Assistant Rectors at that time.

Another school student of that era reminisced:

> I spent the first two years of secondary education at Lionel school. I started at The Nicolson in 3rd year in 1991. The Rector was Mr. MacDonald.
>
> In the June before I started at The Nicolson, the students had to shadow an older student for a day to experience life at the school. There was no organised system. Each had to find someone themselves. Fortunately, I was able to follow my friend's sister.

These recollections probably mirror many of those of those who came into S3 in The Nicolson having come from their local rural secondaries at the end of S2:

> My memory of the transition between early secondary education at Lionel School and moving into 3rd year at The Nicolson was initially one of horror because of the sheer volume of numbers in the 3rd year. I went from being one of 32 in S2 in Lionel to one of over 300 in my S3 N.I. year (with school students coming not just from S2 in The Nicolson but from S2 classes in Lionel, Shawbost, Leurbost, Back and Bayble schools). It was a massive change and being away from home for the first time compounded this.
>
> I found it difficult to know where to go for the various classes and the 'Crush Hall' with first to fifth year all together was terrifying. As a new 3rd student, I found it confusing and had to use a map for a while to negotiate the school.

Despite these initial concerns, this particular student thrived in the new setting:

> *But I grew to enjoy school and acquired new friends at the N.I. I got used to the size and used to being away from home.*
>
> *I did not feel disadvantaged at all regarding capabilities with the curriculum and moving from S1/S2 at Lionel to S3 at The Nicolson. Most of my Lionel colleagues went into the Credit classes with me (as opposed to Foundation classes). Prior to the transition, there had been presentations from The Nicolson staff and Lews Castle School staff followed by individual meetings with teachers. Students were free to choose (with guidance from parents) whether they wished to move to The Nicolson or the Castle School. Some of the quieter students chose The Castle School as it was smaller and similar in size to Lionel School.*
>
> *I loved Maths and that was mainly to do with the superb teaching and attitude of Mr. Macsween. He gave me my love of Maths and my love of school.*

The delights of the S5 Degree Trip, where up to 40 pupils visited higher education institutions in Aberdeen, Edinburgh and Glasgow to gain an insight into the courses on offer, were also highlighted as welcome innovations at that time.

During the 1990s strengthening of the school's international links came with the formation of active partnerships with two schools in widely separated parts of the world. Significantly, and quite by chance, the partner schools were located in places that had historic links with the Nicolson family: Suzhou No. 10 Middle School in Jiangsu Province, China, is close to Shanghai where the company of Jardine Matheson has its headquarters and where Alexander Morison Nicolson was tragically killed; and Pendleton High School, South Carolina, is not far from the site of the cotton plantation in Mississippi owned by his brother Kenneth Nicolson.

There were subsequent reciprocal visits by staff of The Nicolson and of No. 10 Middle School; and one later school trip to China. Since 1994, there have been annual exchange visits, involving over the first five years some 22 staff and 110 students from each school, between The Nicolson and Pendleton High School. These experiences enriched all those involved in three very different areas of the world.[136]

---

136 The Pendleton Partnership continues to flourish, although now a community-led one, rather than school-led. It marked its 25th anniversary with a group from South Carolina visiting in the autumn of 2019.

The Nicolson Institute staff, 1989-1990

Chapter 13: The Last Decade of the 20th Century

Long-serving staff members Mr. Murdo Macleod and Mr. R.J. Macleod pictured at their retiral in October 1997

Further innovations in the last decade of the 20th century included the introduction of an informal school uniform: royal blue sweatshirts for S1 and S2 pupils, and a navy blue version for the older year groups, both featuring the letters 'ni' in cursive lower case letters. A black v-neck pullover emblazoned with the school badge was also introduced for senior pupils.

S6 pupils also began to hold a Christmas Dinner Dance during these years, and a Leavers' Ceremony to mark the end of their school careers became part of the calendar.

125th Anniversary

In February 1999, with the school heading to the end of its 125th year of existence, a special anniversary dinner was held. All the guest speakers were school alumni: Matthew Maciver, ex-Rector of the Edinburgh Royal High School and Chief Executive of the General Teaching Council for Scotland; Maggie Cunningham, BBC broadcaster and producer; Sandy Matheson, former Convener of Comhairle nan Eilean Siar; and Margaret Dobson, Medical Ward Manager at the Western Isles Hospital. It was an opportunity for looking back and looking forward.

A Curious Interlude

The last years of the 20th century saw increasing pressure to bring together The Nicolson Institute and the Lews Castle School[137] (the latter providing

---
[137] Not to be confused with Lews Castle College. Although it often was.

vocational courses for about 150 Third and Fourth Year pupils). In 1998, in the context of significantly reducing school rolls, a proposal from the then Director of Education to rationalise education provision in Stornoway was accepted by Comhairle nan Eilean Siar. The proposal involved the closure of The Nicolson Institute and the more vocationally orientated Lews Castle School. A new school with two distinct streams, academic and vocational, would be established. Of course, this would mean the requirement for a new name, marking the end of the highly regarded and respected title 'The Nicolson Institute'. The proposal to identify a new name, however, provoked a furious reaction. A campaign to save The Nicolson Institute name was mounted, achieving thousands of signatures in a very short time.

Advertisements for the recruitment of a new management team were published early in 1999 and a new Headteacher, Mr. Kevin Trewartha, was appointed, as well as a Depute Head Teacher for each of the two streams, and several Assistant Head Teacher posts. Many people throughout the Scottish Educational fraternity were intrigued to see such adverts when they knew The Nicolson already had an existing Management Team. This, however, was an appointments process for a different school. It just happened to be called 'The Nicolson Institute!'

In the event, the project foundered in the Court of Session in July 1999 on a technicality, namely that the School Board of the existing school had not been fully consulted on the proposal. There had actually been an assumption that, as the parent members of the Board had resigned in June 1998, it no longer existed. However, it did in fact still exist, as one co-opted member had not resigned, and the Board was capable of being constituted and, therefore, should have been consulted. Consequently, the judge, Lord Maclean, ruled that all the associated decisions taken after October 1998 to create a new school with new management appointments were null and void and must be set aside.

Local Council elections were held in May 1999 and the new Council decided that a fresh examination of secondary education provision in Stornoway be undertaken. After much deliberation and careful planning, with legal advice taken at every point, it was decided that Lews Castle School be closed. The Nicolson Institute was tasked to develop vocational courses in collaboration with Lews Castle College. Application for capital funding for new building provision was made and eventually this was achieved. Lews Castle School was kept open until 2002 to allow the last Third and Fourth Year pupils to complete their courses.

The Nicolson Institute staff, 1992
Back row: Mr. D.J. Maclennan, Mr. L. Mitchell, Mr. R. McAlpin, Mr. R.J. Smith, Mr. N. Mackay, Mr. C. Rigg, Mr. A. Dunlop, Mr. D. Leadbitter, Mr. A. McPhee
Fourth row: Mr. A.G. Morrison, Mr. I. Nicolson, Mr. N. Mackinnon, Mr. N. Eadie, Dr R.A. Whiteford, Mr. J.A. Morrison, Mr. R.M. Scott, Mr. A. Graham, Mr. W. Stewart, Mr. M. Macphail, Mr. J. Gatensby
Third row: Mr. N. Macarthur, Mr. J. Bain, Miss L. Macaulay, Mrs J. Smith, Mrs. B.E. Macleod, Mrs. G. Corden, Mrs. H. Bayly, Miss J. Brand, Mrs. M. Mackinnon, Miss Ireland, Mrs. L. Maclennan, Mrs. I. Dawson, Mr. R. Davidson, Mr. K. Smith
Second row: Miss C. MacCuish, Miss K. Macdonald, Mrs J. Imrie, Mrs. D. Gunn, Mrs. M. Macphail, Mrs. J. Mackay, Mrs. C. Murray, Mrs. H. Maciver, Mrs. P. Shaw, Miss C. Stewart, Mrs. C. Morrison, Mrs. A.J. Macleod, Mrs. J. Mackenzie, Miss M. Nicholson, Mrs. C. Macleay

The Nicolson Institute staff, 1996

6th year, 1999-2000

Prefects with Dr. Fraser, Mr. Macdonald and Mr. R.J. Macleod, 1993-94

Chapter 13: The Last Decade of the 20th Century

Prefects with Dr Fraser, Mr. Macdonald and Mr. R.J. Macleod, 1994-1995

Prefects with the Rector, Depute Rector and Assistant Rector, 1996-1997

Chapter 14:
Into the 21st Century

As we have seen, the new millennium began with The Nicolson Institute having expanded to include the pupils of the Lews Castle School, following a sometimes controversial process to amalgamate the two as a new school. At the same time, further changes were brought to the whole of the Scottish teaching profession by the McCrone agreement of 2001.

In April 2004, Mr. Iain A. MacKinnon (one-time Principal Teacher of Geography) was appointed Acting Rector in advance of Mr. MacDonald's retirement. During his months in the Acting Rector post, Mr. MacKinnon focused on introducing more consistent methods of quality assurance across departments, following the HMIE inspection earlier that session.

A colleague commented:

> *In the short time between Donald Macdonald's retiral and the appointment of Derek Curran, Iain did a good job of getting the staff focused on some of the issues highlighted for improvement by the Inspectorate. He set up a number of short life working groups on areas such as Improving Attainment, Assessment, Pastoral Care etc.; and members of the Senior Management Team were each assigned to coordinate and monitor the work of a group of departments. He also had the personality to empathise with staff and pupils and was grateful for all assistance and cooperation. I enjoyed working with him.*

Derek Curran

Prefects with Dr Fraser, Mr. Macdonald and Mr. Clark, 2001-2002

The Nicolson Institute staff, 2001-02

Prefects with senior staff, 2003-2004

S5 Register class, 2003-4

The Senior Management Team in 2004
Left to right are Mr. A.G. Morrison, Head of Junior School; Dr A. Fraser, Depute Rector; Mr. D.J. Macdonald, Rector; Mr. T.R. Clark, Head of Senior School; Mrs. A.Y. Stewart, Head of Middle School; Mr. J. Bain, Head of Guidance

The Nicolson Institute

The Nicolson Institute staff, 2003-04

The Nicolson Institute staff, 2004-05

Back row: R. Fraser, A. Threshie, W. Boyd, S. Oakley, I. Morrison (technician), R.J. Smith, A. Campbell, W. Stewart, C. MacLean
Fourth row: S. Macritchie, C. Maciver, K. Macdonald, N. Eadie, A. Mackay, R.G. McAlpin, A. Macphee, I. Morrison, J. Hallahan, J. Goldman
Third row: M. MacArthur, S. Campbell, M. Macdonald, E. Smith, K. Macdonald, M. Smith, C. Kennedy, M.M. Kennedy, J. Macphail,
Second row: M. MacKinnon, G. Cunningham, M. Sheppard, D. Macdonald, C. Rigg, J. Thomson, M. Macleod, R. Craigie, B. Smith, J. Brand
Front row: W.G. Paterson, Z. Stewart, A.G. Morrison, A. Fraser, I. MacKinnon, T.R. Clark, I. Sinclair, M. Macphail, R.M. Scott, F. Murray

Mr. T. Clark (Depute Rector) and Mr. I. Mackinnon (Acting Rector) with S6 pupils, 2004-05

Late in 2004, Mr. Derek Curran was appointed as the school's seventh Rector.[138] Mr. Curran, a native of Edinburgh, took up post in April 2005; he was the last Rector to occupy the Rectory on Goathill Crescent, the house being sold by Comhairle nan Eilean Siar after his two-year tenure of the post. A moderniser, Mr. Curran focused his efforts on strengthening the school's middle leadership, with Principal Teachers encouraged to serve short periods on the Senior Management Team (formerly the Board of Studies) and to pursue short improvement projects, with all promoted staff attending a residential leadership course in North Uist.

These years were also notable for the number of probationer teachers who took up one-year appointments in the school. The revised probationary system had come in as part of the 2001 McCrone Agreement and saw probationer teachers (in exchange for a generous one-off payment) being deployed in any education authority in the country as demand dictated. Session 2005-6 saw thirteen probationers in the school, the vast majority of whom had no previous connection with the island, but who added much to the life of the school.

Another innovation of the McCrone Agreement was the introduction of the new post of Business Manager to schools of 500 or more pupils. The Nicolson Institute, being the only qualifying school in the Western Isles, saw Mrs. Anne Morrison appointed as its first holder of this post. Mrs. Morrison, a native of New Zealand but married to a local businessman, was appointed in 2004. The idea behind this position was the removal of much non-educational administration from School Management Teams, with, for example, the management of non-teaching staff falling into the remit of the Business Manager. Mrs. Morrison served in the post until her death in February 2016, setting a high standard for this new role.

The McCrone Agreement had also been responsible for bringing a new, much flatter, management structure to Scottish schools. The posts of Assistant Principal Teacher, Senior Teacher and Assistant Head Teacher (or Assistant Rector) all disappeared, with schools having multiple Deputes from August 2003. Dr Alan Fraser was the school's final 'Senior Depute,' being joined on the Management Team by three further Deputes (formerly Assistant Rectors) with the change in nomenclature.

The Scottish Schools (Parental Involvement) Act 2006 saw the replacement of the previous School Boards by Parent Councils across the country. The support provided by The Nicolson Institute Parent Council to successive Rectors and Senior Management Teams was a welcome aspect of school life since its inception.

---

138 Only from W.J. Gibson onwards was the head of The Nicolson Institute designated 'Rector'.

The Nicolson Institute

Prefects with Dr MacLean and Mr. Curran, 2005-06

Prefects with Dr MacLean, 2006-07

The Nicolson Institute

The Nicolson Institute staff, 2006-07

Sporting Successes

Sport flourished in the school in the first two decades of the 21st century. Both boys' and girls' football teams, at Junior and Senior levels, reached Scottish Cup Finals between 2000-1 and 2006-7, with the under-15 boys bringing home the Cup that year. The Junior Girls appeared in the final in successive years, winning the Cup in 2011-12. The Senior Girls triumphed in 2014.

The Senior Nicolson Girls' football team won the Scottish Cup in 2014

The girls made the North of Scotland Cup practically their own during these years, going on six- and seven- year winning streaks.

Other notable sporting stars during this time were Kara Hanlon (swimming) and Eilidh MacKenzie (cross country), both of whom represented Scotland with distinction. Numerous staff and pupils represented the Western Isles at Island Games throughout Europe during this period.

In March 2007, Mr. Curran returned to Edinburgh as Head Teacher of Forrester High School, leaving behind a successful application for The Nicolson Institute to become part of the so-called 'Schools of Ambition' programme, a Scottish Government initiative. The Nicolson Institute bid was represented by the acronym GIVE (Gaelic; ICT; Vocational Education; and Enterprising Learning), summarising the key areas which would be the focus of developments over the years of the initiative.

Mr. Kevin Trewartha, CfE and the New Building

In the meantime, Mr. Kevin Trewartha was appointed to succeed Derek Curran, firstly on an interim basis and subsequently to the substantive post. Mr. Trewartha had previously been appointed as Rector of the joint schools in 1999, as we have seen but, as we have also seen following a Court of Session intervention, had served as Head Teacher of the Lews Castle School until its closure in 2002.[139]

Kevin Trewartha

During Mr. Trewartha's four-year tenure, the decision was made to go ahead with a new school building, and he was heavily involved in the consultation and planning stages of the development. Capital funding negotiations for new school building provision is always a slow and tedious process and this took several years to achieve. A stand-alone organisation, Sgoiltean Ùra,[140] oversaw the process; The Nicolson Institute build was one of six new schools planned and built at that time in the islands. One of the most important decisions at this point was the positioning of the new building on the existing site rather than on a green field site in or near to the town. Whilst there would be obvious constraining factors associated with this choice of site, many contributors to the debates, both official and unofficial, felt that the decision was the correct one, keeping, as it did, the school in the same geographical area as the previous buildings,

---

139 Two senior members of Comhairle nan Eilean Siar's Education Department (both now retired) have provided this clarification of an interesting if obscure episode in The Nicolson Institute history.
140 'New Schools': A Public-Private partnership. Nationally still an area of controversy.

and incorporating Springfield North (the Technical or Pentland Building), Matheson Hall (the Infant School) and the Clock School Tower variously in the design. In addition to the fundamental question of site, Mr. Trewartha and his management team were involved in design discussions, in team visits to new-build schools in other authorities, and, increasingly as the project progressed, in more detailed specifications of departments and classrooms.

One particularly challenging element of the process was the need for temporary accommodation for the Maths, Geography, RME,[141] and Technical departments as, first, Springfield South (The 'Pink School') was demolished to create the main site of the new building itself, and then Matheson Hall and Springfield North were decanted to prepare these buildings for their new incarnations.

Session 2010-11 began with the afore-mentioned departments based in 'portacabins' in the Springfield North playgrounds and with a building site in the area between Springfield and Sandwick roads. These arrangements were not without challenges.

At the same time, a national change was being implemented in the education system as a whole: Curriculum for Excellence (CfE). First mooted in 2004 under a Labour-Liberal Scottish Executive, the development had been taken up by the incoming minority SNP Government in 2007. There appeared to be cross-party support for the basic premise of a streamlined system from 3-18, with greater challenge and individualisation for learners as they progressed. However, the reality was much less straightforward, with weighty ring-binders landing on teachers' desks, laying out in minute details the 'Experiences and Outcomes' for pupils in nine curricular areas from Early Years to the end of S3 (the Broad General Education or BGE).[i] Secondary teachers nationally raised concerns about the possible dilution of individual subject areas, and staff in The Nicolson Institute were not immune from these worries. On one occasion, reassurances were sought from the then Chief Executive of the General Teaching Council (GTC), a distinguished former pupil Matthew MacIver, at a staff meeting in the Assembly Hall, as reports and rumours of Interdisciplinary Learning (IDL) replacing discrete subject teaching caused alarm. Mr. MacIver attempted to allay such fears.

Despite the inevitable instability and disruption both locally and nationally of these years, activities such as debating, school trips, sports competitions and musicals continued to be enthusiastically embraced. Mr. Lu, an exchange teacher from China, spent the best part of session 2008-9 in the school, with a group of staff and pupils making a reciprocal

---

141 Religious and Moral Education.

A group in Pendleton in 2016

A concert in Pendleton in 2018

Pendleton trip

visit in August 2010. The exchange visits to Pendleton High School, now on a community rather than a purely school basis, continued and further partnerships were established with schools in Prince Edward Island and Germany. Unfortunately, the inadmissibility of 'home stay'[142] arrangements on school trips meant that these partnerships were short lived.

One downside of the imminent new building was that the existing school was becoming shabbier, providing a marked contrast between the state-of-the-art technology in many classrooms and the rather less than 'fit for purpose' accommodation. The School of Ambition focus on ICT coincided with the authority-wide roll out of equipment, which saw electronic whiteboards being introduced into many classrooms during this period. Another focus of the School of Ambition programme was Vocational Education; one element of this was the provision of Media Studies courses, tapping into the expansion of both local and national Gaelic media, and bringing former pupils in the profession (journalists Michael Buchanan, Torcuil Crichton and Derek MacKay) to address school prize giving ceremonies.

---

142 A 'home stay' is defined as individual pupils being assigned to host families for their accommodation during a trip, as opposed to the group being accommodated together in a hotel or hostel. This practice was not viewed as safe by the local authority (as screening of host family members could not be carried out) and any school trip planning to use such accommodation would not be given the required permission to go ahead.

The First Female Rector

Frances Murray

Mr. Trewartha had once commented at a Principal Teachers' Meeting where the new building was the focus of discussion that he might, Moses-like, not be there to see the 'Promised Land', and that proved to be the case. Late in 2010, he announced his intention to retire, leaving the school in January 2011, just as construction of the new school was ready to begin. The earlier retirements of Dr Alan Fraser and Mrs. Zena Stewart had heralded several new faces on the Senior Management Team. They were joined in March 2011 by Mrs. Frances Murray, the first female Rector of the school. Mrs. (later Dr) Murray was a native of Stornoway and a former Dux and had served as Principal Teacher of English from 2003-7 before becoming Depute Rector from 2007-10. She had then spent a year in the Education Department as Learning Community Principal for the Broad Bay area before being appointed as Rector in January 2011. The Education Department caused some disquiet by announcing that the title of Rector would no longer be used, and that the new incumbent would be the 'Head Teacher'. Pupils immediately launched a petition calling for the title to remain, and a compromise position was suggested, whereby 'Rector' would continue to be used within the school, with the less traditional

Prefects with Mrs. Macdonald and Dr Murray, 2012-13

form of address used by the Comhairle. The reasoning offered at the time appeared to suggest that the Education Department believed that the use of 'Rector' in one school was incompatible with equity across the islands. A further comment about the title being 'outdated' did not take account of the large number of schools across Scotland where 'Rector' continued to be used. It was an unfortunate aspect of the process with some media coverage focusing on the controversy over the change in title rather than the appointment.

Like her predecessor, the new Rector found the early months in post dominated by the on-going implementation of CfE, with the 'Senior Phase' developments, including new qualifications, now added, and the local management of a school in transition between two eras.

The Move to Sandwick Road

Following an HMIE inspection in June 2011, the 2011-12 session was the last in the *'old building'* (or, more properly, 'buildings') with planning for the move to the new premises gathering pace. The summer holiday period was designated for the physical movement of the vast amount of equipment, materials and associated paraphernalia, with the demolition of the 1956 Springfield Road building, still known to many as the *'new building',* along with the 1970s Science, Art and Music blocks, and the 1990s English and History wing. In its place, the new car parks, bus park, rugby pitch and garden were constructed.

The school opened to staff on 13th August 2012, with pupils arriving in stages later that week. A suspected chemical leak on the first Friday of term saw the building evacuated and pupils dismissed early, with social media reports and national media interest heightening concerns. Despite this early set-back, the school community settled into the new building comparatively quickly. Public interest was also keen, and staff became very accustomed to conducting guided tours around the new premises. Inevitable comparisons to the previous set-up suggested more crowded social areas, but this was balanced by the benefits of having the whole school in the one building (with the link to the refurbished Technical Department considered) and consistently good accommodation across all departments. The school building was now managed by a private company, FES,[143] and both staff and pupils, used to a system where the janitor or 'janny' was part of the school staff, had to adjust to a new way of working.

---

143 The property management system for the school. For private companies to manage school property was a Scotland-wide phenomenon which remains problematic to this day (2022). At the very least it adds a level of external bureaucracy to school management.

Canteen staff in the new building

The front of the school

Pupils in the courtyard on the opening day

Pupils with the Technical block in the background

Photos of new school by Leila Angus

Prefects on the opening day

The courtyard looking down from the Technical building

Professor Donald Macleod unveiling the commemorative plaque at the official opening in 2012

The platform party at the official opening in 2012

Many visitors to the school, particularly those who themselves had frequented a previous version as pupils, commented on the pleasing blend of the modern and the traditional in the new building. The refurbished Matheson Hall, no longer part of the school as such, now housed the MSM[144] system for the Comhairle as a whole, whilst the Clock Tower, now situated in the front courtyard of the new building, was brought back into proper prominence after years of appearing to be overlooked.

---

144 An information management system.

Musical performance at the official opening of the school

Within the new Assembly Hall, the Dux, Rector and School Captain boards and lecterns had been relocated, and the World War II Memorial was situated in the front foyer, under the motto of the old burgh of Stornoway: *'God's Providence is our Inheritance.'* A series of murals painted by former Principal Teacher of Art, Mr. Gordon Paterson, and telling the history of the island, had been relocated from the old Assembly Hall to the corridors of the first and second floors. In contrast, a new art installation, commissioned for the building, by the Edinburgh-based artist, Donald Urquhart, and depicting the colours of the Lewis landscape through a series of long three-sided tubular hangings, was placed in the main atrium.

The official opening of the new building took place on 2nd October 2012 with the formalities being carried out by the late Professor Donald MacLeod of the Free Church College. Earlier in the day, the school held its own informal ceremony in the courtyard.

Expansion of Gaelic Medium Education (GME)

And what of the education being offered in the new building? The HMIE inspection of 2011 had demanded a faster pace of provision of Gaelic Medium Education (GME). These pupils who were experiencing their Primary Education through the medium of Gaelic were entitled to receive a *'substantial proportion'* of their Secondary Education through Gaelic, where staffing allowed. In the years between the inspection and the 150th Anniversary, that provision had grown to include up to ten subjects being delivered through Gaelic to pupils in S1 and S2. In addition, pupils were able to continue with History and Modern Studies to Scottish Qualifications Authority (SQA) National 5 level, with the first cohort gaining certification in August 2015. Such provision was, and continued to be, dependent on the availability of Gaelic-speaking staff in these subjects who were willing to teach through the medium of Gaelic. The experience of pupils who followed this route was an overwhelmingly positive one. However, as the percentage of pupils coming into Secondary Education through GME continued to grow, it was clear that political commitment, both locally and nationally, would need to be made if the number of subjects available through GME could be sustained, never mind increased.

By 2023, a fifth of the school's pupil population were Gaelic Medium pupils, with the proportion nearer a quarter in S5 and S6. Exam results of GM pupils were above the school average, and, since 2004, when the first GM pupils reached S6, a high proportion of School Duxes had been from Addison House. This represented a considerable advance on attitudes to Gaelic education in Stornoway in the early 1970s, a time when GM in The Nicolson or even in Stornoway Primary School would have been largely unthinkable.

Senior pupils, writing in 2022, gave very positive feedback on their school days and their Gaelic Medium educational experience in particular:

> *Leis gun robh mi fhìn ann am Foghlam tro Mheadhan na Gàidhlig, bha mi ann an taigh "Addison" san sgoil. Cha bhithinn a-riamh air na caraidean as fheàrr a th' agam fhaighinn an-diugh mura bithinn ann an Addison oir 's e sin far an do choinnich sinn uile. 'S e na daoine a choinnicheas tu an rud as fheàrr mun sgoil (a bharrachd air Macaroni Mondays!), oir tha e a' toirt dhut caraidean agus ceanglaichean làidir a bhios agad gu bràth tuilleadh.*
>
> Because I was in Gaelic Medium Education, I was in "Addison House" in school. I wouldn't have the best friends that I have today if I hadn't been in Addison because that's where we all met. The best thing about school is the people that you meet (other than Macaroni Mondays!), because it gives you friends and strong relationships that you will have forever.
>
> Alice MacMillan

In a creative piece, another pupil wrote of the benefits of being bi-lingual:

> *Tha sia bliadhna air a dhol seachad. Chaidh e seachad cho luath. Tha Catrìona a-nis gu bhith deiseil a' bhliadhna mu dheireadh aice san sgoil. Tha i air tòrr ionnsachadh, caraidean ùra fhaighinn, foghlam buannachdach fhaighinn, tòrr chothroman diofraichte san sgoil agus taghadh mòr airson a dhol dhan oilthigh. Tha Catrìona air a bhith ann am Foghlam tro Mheadhan na Gàidhlig agus tha Gàidhlig mar phàirt mhòr den sgoil. Bha tòrr chothroman agus taghadh de chuspairean ann dhi anns a' chlas Ghàidhlig. Leis gun robh i dà-chànanach, b' urrainn dhi leudachadh air a' Ghàidhlig agus a' Bheurla aice.*
>
> Six years have passed. It went by so quickly. Catrìona is almost finished of her last year in school. She has learnt a lot, made new friends, received beneficial education, had many different opportunities in the school and big choices to make for going to university. Catrìona has been in Gaelic Medium Education and Gaelic is a big part of the school. There were lots of opportunities and choices of subject for her in Gaelic class. Because she was bilingual, she could expand her Gaelic and her English.
>
> Iona MacInnes

The many opportunities afforded pupils in GME were the topic of one contribution:

> *Tha an sgoil seo air mòran chothroman a thoirt dhomh, bho turas-sgoile gu Lunnainn anns an dàrna bliadhna. 'S e turas inntinneach a bh'ann agus thug e dhomh mòran sgeulachdan a dh'fhaodas mi innse! A bharrachd air a sin, chaidh mi air turas a Ghlaschu airson duaisean FilmG (farpais airson filmichean Gàidhlig). Tha siubhal a' còrdadh rium gu mòr agus tha mi taingeil gu bheil an sgoil seo air cothroman a thoirt dhomh sin a dhèanamh oir tha fios agam nach bi mòran sgoiltean eile a' dèanamh sin.*
>
> *The school has given me many opportunities, such as a school trip to London in second year. It was an interesting trip, and it gave me lots of stories I can tell! As well as that, I went on a trip to Glasgow for the FilmG Awards (a competition for Gaelic films). I enjoy travelling and I am grateful that this school gave me these opportunities because I know that there are many other schools where this doesn't happen.*
>
> Rebekah MacKenzie

As appropriate for senior pupils, there was an element of reflection as their school days neared the end:

> *Tro na bliadhnaichean, ged a tha an obair air fàs nas dorra, tha an dùbhlan a thaobh a bhith ga h-ionnsachadh gu mionaideach an còmhnaidh air a bhith inntinneach dhomh. Chanainn gu bheil taing agam ri thoirt dha na tidsearan agam air sgàth 's mar a chum iad an obair gu tur tarraingeach. 'S ged a tha deuchainnean air m' fhàgail le criomagan de fhalt liath agus oidhcheannan gun chadal, b'fhiach e oir chan atharraichinn càil mu mo làithean-sgoile oir 's iad na làithean a bhios còmhla rium gu bràth tuilleadh.*
>
> *Through the years, although the work grew harder, the challenge of more detailed learning has always been interesting to me. I would say that I am grateful to my teachers for always keeping the work interesting. Even though the exams left me with strands of grey hair and sleepless nights, it was worth it because I wouldn't change anything about my school days because they will be the days that stay with me forever.*
>
> Kitty MacIver

A philosophical note completed the reflections of a Sixth Year boy:

> 'S ann tric a chluinnear na faclan "Cha dèanar buannachd gun chall" ach thathar a' tuigsinn, às dèidh gach buannachd a gheibhear a-mach às an sgoil, 's e an rud as dorra dhuinn uile, an call a th' againn an sgoil fhàgail. Leis an doras a' dùnadh air foghlam àrd-sgoile, tha ar làithean mar sgoilearan air a thighinn gu ceann. Ach, le sin air a ràdh, cha do dhùin doras nach do dh'fhosgail doras agus leanaidh na làithean buidhe sgoile sinn fad ar beatha. 'S ged a tha an t-àm ann a-nis an sgoil fhàgail, às bith dè tha air cùl an ath dhoras, thèid sinn uile air adhart le cuimhneachain shona agus gàire oirnn oir is e a h-uile latha latha sgoile!
>
> *You often hear the words "There's no win without loss" but it's understood, after every success you get from school, the hardest thing for us all, the loss we feel in leaving school. With the door closing on secondary education, our days as pupils are coming to an end. But, having said that, one door closes and another opens and the halcyon days of school will stay with us all our lives. Even though it's now the time to leave school, no matter what is behind the next door, we will all go forward with happy memories and a smile because every day is a school day!*
>
> Luke MacLeod

The school's Music and Gaelic Departments continued, as in previous decades, to prepare pupils for local and national Mods, with considerable success. A senior pupil reflected on the importance of Gaelic song, both in terms of words and music, in sustaining the language:

> *'S e an dòigh anns a bheil ceòl Gàidhlig an-còmhnaidh ag innse sgeulachd cumhachdach dhan neach-èisteachd an rud a tha ga dhèanamh cho sònraichte. Tha cuspairean leithid dòigh-beatha, tìr dachaigh nam bàrd agus faireachdainnean domhainn, làidir tric a' nochdadh ann an ceòl Gàidhlig. Feumar aontachadh gur e dòigh glè inntinneach sgeulachdan is cunntasan pearsanta a chur an cèill a tha seo gus dealbh fìor, nàdarrach a thoirt seachad dha dòigh-beatha nan eilean tro na linntean. Chan e a-mhàin na facail a tha prìseil, ach cuideachd na fuinn thraidiseanta; tha iad gu tur eadar-dhealaichte ri ceòl a chluinneadh tu an àite sam bith eile agus 's iad a tha a' cruthachadh bun-stèidh airson nan seinneadairean fhèin a' lìonadh leis an stoidhle agus dealas aca fhèin.*
>
> *What makes Gaelic music so special is that it always tells a powerful story to the listener. Subjects like the way of life, the poet's homeland, and strong, deep feelings, often appear in Gaelic music. It has to be agreed that this is a very interesting way to relate stories and personal accounts, giving a truly natural picture of the island's way of life through the centuries. It's not only the words that are so precious, but also the traditional tunes; they are completely different from music that you hear in other places, and it creates a foundation for the singers themselves to fill with their own style and enthusiasm.*
>
> Iona Davidson

A New School Day and the National Qualifications Debate

A new configuration of the school day was introduced by the authority in session 2014-15. This so-called 'asymmetric week' saw seven 50-minute periods per day on Monday to Thursday, with a shorter Friday of five periods. The school day thus finished at 1.15 p.m. on a Friday. This new 33 period week was not universally popular with staff or parents, but pupils quickly adapted to the concept, enjoying their Friday afternoons of freedom from classes. Teaching staff, nominally contracted to a 35-hour week (but most working far in excess of this), were also entitled to leave the school at 1.15 p.m., but many chose to use all or some of the time to prepare for the following week.

A further development during these years was a Scottish Government one: Developing Scotland's Young Workforce sought to ensure that school prepared all young people for life and work beyond, focusing on enhanced provision of vocational education. By 2020, young people in S5 and S6 were able to choose to undertake Foundation Apprenticeships in place of traditional qualifications in areas such as Care and Engineering. The school's long-standing partnership with the Lews Castle College continued to provide vocational alternatives for pupils from S3 upwards. A new attainment measure of 'Positive Destination' (pupils leaving school to enter Higher or Further Education, employment or training) was introduced by Education Scotland, and The Nicolson Institute scored consistently highly (97%+) throughout this period, thanks in no small part to excellent partnership with the Careers Service, Skills Development Scotland.

Meanwhile the new SQA qualifications aligning with Curriculum for Excellence were introduced, again not without controversy. Many teachers felt that the time period for the introduction of the 'National Qualifications' was rushed. The first cohort of S4 Nicolson pupils who sat National 5 exams (replacing Intermediate and Standard Grades) did so in 2015, many having selected eight subjects at this level; subsequent cohorts were restricted to a maximum of seven.

At the Heart of the Community

Charitable involvement was another notable feature of life in the school during these years, as had been the case throughout the school's history. Annual events included the Children in Need extravaganza held every November and organised by the S6 pupils, becoming a 'YouTube' hit in later years. Another event run annually by the S6 was the Coffee Morning in aid of the local Bethesda Hospice, a regular beneficiary of school giving. From 2015 onwards, the school's RME Department enthusiastically embraced a national competition, The Youth Philanthropic Initiative (YPI), sponsored by the Wood Group. The YPI challenge involved competing groups of S5 pupils championing a local charity, with the winning group being awarded £3,000 to donate to that organisation. Strong connections were made between pupils and local charities, anchoring these young people in the heart of their community.

With many other charitable activities taking place, the school was consistently raising well in excess of £10,000 on an annual basis, a testament to the generosity of the local community as much as to the hard work of staff and pupils. Given the debt which the school's own origins owed to charity, it was heartening to note the continuation of this tradition with young people benefiting from the Macaulay Educational Trust for Lewis, set up in the 1920s (see Chapter 9). From 2015 onwards, the fund was accessed to help run the annual Ceangal event, which allowed the incoming S6 pupils to spend two days exploring the ties ('ceangal' meaning a tie or a link) between their school subjects, the local community and economy, and their heritage. As with many of the extra-curricular activities in which the school was involved in this period, the help and cooperation of the community was vital and much valued.

A visitor from previous decades, or indeed centuries, whilst being quite possibly discombobulated by some of the new technologies (for example, pupils and staff paying for school lunches by fingerprint recognition) would still have seen much which was recognisable: the school crest and motto commemorating the founding Nicolson brothers continued to appear on school documents, uniforms and memorabilia; school sports teams continued to flourish, including a particularly successful era for girls' football from the turn of the century onwards, as we have seen; pupils experienced foreign cultures through school trips, just as had been the case in previous years, with continental skiing trips and regular excursions to Rome and Pompeii amongst these.

The school had become involved in social media, with a Facebook page and Twitter accounts for sport and Gaelic: the pluses and minuses of the new wave of communication were demonstrated at this time.

During difficult and, indeed, tragic times in 2017-18, the important role played by the school's pastoral staff was emphasised; Guidance teachers and the wider school support staff were increasingly called upon to support young people and their families as concerns, both national and international, over mental health, bullying, anxiety and self-harm, were echoed locally. A number of further measures, such as school-based counsellors and Community Learning workers, were employed, in recognition of the challenging and difficult circumstances which many young people faced.

Commemorating the *Iolaire*

Two large scale collaborations marked the school's commemoration of the *Iolaire* centenary. In March 2018, following months of work with the Stornoway Amenity Trust, a cairn and plaque were unveiled in the town's Carn Gardens beside the recently refurbished Town Hall. The cairn featured 201 stones which had been collected from the villages and towns of those lost, locally and beyond. Pupils were integral to the design and development phases of the project: 201 S3 pupils walked in procession from

The Nicolson Institute staff, 2018-19

Chapter 14: Into the 21st Century

273

the school to the Town Hall to represent those lost, and School Captains and pipers participated in the ceremony. Dr Murray, Rector, observed that several of the lost and of the survivors had been former pupils of the school, and many were no older than the senior pupils now present.

At the end of the year, months of work culminated in a spectacular memorial event; one of a series of four concerts held in the islands' secondary schools in the autumn and winter of 2018. Under the banner of *Dìleab*, each commemorated aspects of the effect of the Great War on the Western Isles. Under the musical direction of Principal Teacher of Music, Mrs. Avril Allen, in collaboration with the Islands Council's Multimedia Unit, the concert was a fitting and highly moving memorial. Held in the adjoining Sports Centre to maximise audience numbers, the concert saw pupils of the school, joined by local adult choirs and performers, and pupils of Stornoway and Laxdale Primaries and Sir E. Scott School, perform to a uniformly high standard. A senior pupil wrote of her participation and the impact the event had on her:

> *Nuair a bha mi sa cheathramh bliadhna, fhuair mi an cothrom pàirt a ghabhail ann an Dìleab. Bha an cuirm Dìleab a' comharrachadh ceud bliadhna bho chaidh an* Iolaire *fodha. Bha seo na phàirt chudromach dhòmhsa oir thug an cuirm seo buaidh mhòr orm. Dh'ionnsaich mi mu cho tiamhaidh 's a bha call an* Iolaire *agus a' bhuaidh a dh'fhàg e air ar n-eilean. Aig a' chuirm, fhuair mi an cothrom òran a ghabhail leam fhìn agus sheinn mi "Mar a Chaillear an* Iolaire*" le Murchadh MacPhàrlain. Ged a bha mi gu math nearbhach oir bha an t-uabhas dhaoine ann, 's e faireachdainn air leth shònraichte a bh' ann.*
>
> *When I was in fourth year, I got the opportunity to take part in Dìleab. The Dìleab concert marked one hundred years from when the Iolaire was sunk. This was important to me because the event impacted me greatly. I learned about how sad the loss of the Iolaire was and the impact it left on our island. At the concert, I got the chance to sing solo and I sang "How the Iolaire was lost" by Murdo MacFarlane. Even though I was very nervous because there were many people present, it was an incredibly special feeling.*
>
> *Alice MacMillan*

Two weeks later, many were also involved in the community event held one hundred years to the day of the loss of the *Iolaire*. School prefects served as 'door openers' for the then First Minister and Prince of Wales as they arrived at the ceremony on 1st January 2019, and pupils dropped flowers at the site of the tragedy from aboard the *M.V. Loch Seaforth*. The *'torch of remembrance,'* as described by Dr Murray, at the Dìleab event, had been passed to the current generation. Many commentators spoke of the quiet dignity and respect of the pupils, as the silence which had surrounded the Iolaire in previous generations and classrooms was lifted.

The Covid Pandemic

In common with that in all other schools, and in society as a whole, life in The Nicolson Institute changed irrevocably in March 2020, with the advent of the Covid 19 pandemic. The school was completely shut to pupils from Friday 20th March, with all learning switching to online platforms. The implications for staff, pupils and families were immense; national examinations which had survived two World Wars were cancelled, and alternative methods of certification had to be put in place. Pupils and staff had to become familiar with teaching and learning at home, and support had to continue to be provided to those who required it. Not all families had access to the necessary technology; local and national government focused on providing it. From June, staff began to return to school to plan the reintroduction of pupils after the summer, in an almost surreal atmosphere. Activities which would normally have taken place in the summer term were cancelled, truncated or moved online. A commemoration of the 70th Anniversary of St. Valery took place in the school courtyard with a small audience and socially distanced school musicians.

Session 2020-21 was dominated by the continued restrictions necessitated by the pandemic. Pupils returned in August to social distancing, staggered lunchtimes, and hand sanitising stations at doors. In the course of the autumn term, mask-wearing and testing were added before another lockdown in January 2021. A return to online teaching and learning followed, with an eventual partial return for senior pupils in March. A second year of disruption to exams was inevitable, and schools were again obliged to make alternative arrangements. Prize Giving and Leavers' Ceremonies were conducted online in June 2021, with parents still unable to enter the school building.

Willie Campbell, Jane Hepburn and Neil Johnstone with the choir behind them at the Dìleab performance

Senior boys singing at the Dìleab production

Pipers at the Dìleab performance

The massed bands closed the event

Whilst restrictions were somewhat lifted by August 2021 as a result of widespread vaccinations, there were actually far more cases locally as the autumn and winter progressed, with staff and pupil absences alike disrupting education. By March 2022, two years on from the first lockdown, most aspects of school life were returning to normal, but the effects of these two years on the education of the young people involved were still to be fully understood:

> *Ged a tha an Corona-bhìoras air buaidh mhòr a thoirt air ar sgoil gu h-iomlan tro 2020 agus 2021, bha cùisean fhathast fìor mhath dhuinn agus bha àm sgoinneil againn fhathast san sgoil….*
>
> *'S e an dleastanas a tha oirnn a bhith a' coimhead às dèidh ar n-àite fhèin anns an sgoil air a' chòigeamh bliadhna an rud a tha air còrdadh rium as motha. Tha e math àite a bhith againn dhuinn fhèin air falbh bho na sgoilearan eile, gu h-araid aig àm a' Chorona-bhìoras.*
>
> *Although the Coronavirus had a big impact on our whole school throughout 2020 and 2021, things were still excellent for us and we still had a brilliant time in school…*
>
> *On Fifth Year it's our duty to look after our own place in school and that was something that I enjoyed most. It's a good to have a place for ourselves away from the other pupils, especially during the pandemic.*
>
> Alison Graham

In February 2022, Dr Frances Murray announced her intention to retire at the Easter holidays, after eleven years in post. Her years as Rector were marked by change at local and national level, culminating in the effects of the pandemic. A month after retiring, she was elected as one of only two female Councillors on Comhairle nan Eilean Siar. Depute Rectors, Mrs. Fiona Cunningham and Mr. Angus MacKay, both had spells as Acting Rector at the end of session 2021-22 and at the start of session 2022-23, respectively.

Ms. Jennifer Cairns and the 150ᵗʰ Anniversary

Jennifer Cairns

Ms. Jennifer Cairns, formerly a Depute Head in Bellahouston Academy, Glasgow, was appointed as Rector in July and took up post in October 2022, the second female to do so.

On Monday 27ᵗʰ February 2023, pupils, staff and former staff of the school gathered in the front courtyard, in the shadow of the Clock Tower endowed by Roderick and Kenneth Nicolson, to mark the school's sesquicentenary. A cold but beautifully sunny morning saw the school flag raised, whilst the audience listened to the school's pipe, brass and ceilidh bands play. Both the Rector, Ms. Cairns, and Mr. Richard Fraser, Principal Teacher of RME and Music, spoke of the school's heritage. Neither shied away from the more controversial aspects of the founding family's history, echoing Mr. Angus Nicolson's view that the brothers' contribution be seen as a joint legacy.

However, both celebrated the huge part the school went on to play in the landscape of island life and Scottish education: what began in 1873 as an elementary (or primary) school with 105 students under Mr. Sutherland, grew under Mr. Forbes's first steps to establish secondary education, and flourished under Mr. Gibson supported by Dr Robertson, with the first school students, Donald MacLean and Robert MacIver, going directly to the Universities of Aberdeen and Edinburgh in 1898.

It would be impossible to enumerate those who have followed in their footsteps, benefiting from the legacy of Alexander Nicolson and his brothers, or to list the achievements of alumni of the school in academia, education, music, art, broadcasting, literature, or politics.

As well as looking back, the anniversary celebrations also provided an opportunity to look forward. With a review of aspects of Scottish education on-going, the SQA exams could look very different in coming years, and a continued emphasis on vocational options in the senior school seems very likely in the current climate. A 'harmonised timetable,' shared with the other secondary schools in the authority, has been mooted for a number of years, but practicalities have meant that this remains unresolved; the expansion of electronic learning, following its widespread use during the pandemic, has been similarly controversial. The hoped-for further growth of Gaelic Medium Education is very much constrained by staffing issues, despite local and national political support. All this is for the future and a matter for conjecture.

However, what is incontestable is that Alexander Morison Nicolson, through his donation to his native town, was more than successful in his stated aim of being the *'indirect means of rendering some assistance'* to generations of young people.

Current and former Nicolson Institute staff, 27th February 2023 (photo by Malcolm Macleod)

The Nicolson Institute

6th Year with Mr. Mackay, 2022-23 (photo by Malcolm Macleod)

Appendix 1:

Rectors and Head Teachers of The Nicolson Institute

John Sutherland	1873-1882
John Forbes	1882-1894
William J. Gibson	1894-1925
John Macrae	1925-1943
Thomas Henderson	1944-1947
Cecil J.S. Addison	1947-1968
Edward Young	1968-1989
Donald J. Macdonald	1989-2004
Derek Curran	2004-2007
Kevin Trewartha	2007-2011
Frances M. Murray	2011- 2022
Jennifer Cairns	2022-

Appendix 2:

Duxes of The Nicolson Institute (awarded at end of S5 until 1982)

1895	DONALDINA MACLEOD
1896	DONALD J. MACLEOD
1897	DONALD MACLEAN
1898	ROBERT M. MACIVER
1899	MARGARET MACLEOD
1900	DONALD MACKENZIE
1901	MARY CRICHTON
1902	MARGARET MACLEOD
1903	ANGUS MACLEOD
1904	JOHN MACLEOD
1905	CATHERINE J. MACLEOD
1906	ISABEL MACKENZIE
1907	JOHN N. ANDERSON
1908	NORMAN MACLEOD
1909	MURDO MURRAY
1910	MAGGIE STEWART
1911	JOHN MUNRO
1912	WILLIAM MACLEOD
1913	JOHN MACLEOD
1914	MURDO MACLEOD
1915	JEAN M. MACKENZIE
1916	JANE GIBSON
1917	ALEXANDER M. MURRAY
1918	HENRIETTA MACKENZIE
1919	JOHN SMITH
1920	ALEXANDER MILNE
1921	ANGUS M. MACKENZIE
1922	MALCOLM MACDONALD
1923	ALEXANDER SIMPSON

1924	MURDO MACDONALD
1925	WILLIAM J. CAMERON
1926	MALCOLM M. MURRAY
1927	NEIL R. MACKAY
1928	JAMES S. GRANT
1929	STEPHEN M. MACLEAN
1930	JOHN MACDONALD
1931	DONALD R. MACKENZIE
1932	RODERICK M. ROSS
1933	MARGARET MACGREGOR
1934	JOHN K. MACIVER
1935	JAMES THOMSON
1936	JOHN SMITH
1937	RODERICK MORRISON
1938	ISHBEL M. MACRAE
1939	DERICK S. THOMSON
1940	MURDO MACDONALD
1941	NORMAN GRASSIE
1942	WILLIAM MORRISON
1943	HENRIETTA MACDONALD
1944	MAIRI B. MACLEOD
1945	JOHN W. MACLEOD
1946	MURDO MACLEOD
1947	DONALD MACKAY
1948	IAN G. S. FERRIER
1949	DONALD MACKAY
1950	JOHN R. MACAULAY
1951	IAN B. PATERSON
1952	JOHN P. MACGREGOR
1953	ANN URQUHART
1954	RONALD J. URQUHART
1955	ALASDAIR MACLEAN
1956	CATHERINE MACIVER
1957	MALCOLM W. MACARTHUR
1958	JEAN A. HARTHILL
1959	CATHERINE MACDONALD
1960	RODERICK MACIVER
1961	RHODA MACDONALD
1962	MAIRI D. MACKINNON
1963	CATHERINE A. SMITH
1964	IAIN SMITH
1965	ALASDAIR SMITH
1966	FINELLA MACKENZIE/MIMA H.S. MORRISON
1967	KENNETH MACKINNON
1968	RODERICK D. MACKENZIE
1969	SUSAN MACIVER/THOMAS STRACHAN
1970	CHRISTINE M. MACASKILL
1971	CATHERINE S. MACCUISH
1972	HECTOR MORRISON/ERICA MACDONALD
1973	JOAN ROSS
1974	ALASDAIR I. MACLEOD
1975	LEWIS M. MACKENZIE

1976	DONALD J. MURRAY
1977	RICHARD A. SPEIRS
1978	W. DAVID GALLOWAY
1979	MANDY MACKENZIE
1980	IAIN D. CAMPBELL/FRANCES M. MACFARLANE
1981	RODERICK M. MACRAE
1982	RODERICK M. MACRAE
1983	WILLIAM MACLEOD
1984	DEREK MACLEAN
1985	D. WILLIAM M. STEWART
1986	CAROLYN M. BURNS
1987	HEDDA M. MACLEOD
1988	ROBIN J. WATSON
1989	FRANCIS J. MACNEIL/DAVID MACKENZIE
1990	HELEN A. MACCUISH
1992	DONALD A. MACLEOD
1993	PEIGI S. MACKAY
1994	LEWIS CAMPBELL
1995	ELEANOR J. HOTHERSALL
1996	PETER MACKAY
1997	IAIN MACDONALD/JOHN MACLEOD
1998	CAITRIANA M.M. NICOLSON
1999	CATHERINE E. DICKIE/MARGARET A. MACKAY
2000	ALISON MACRITCHIE/ANDREW JOYCE
2001	CEIT ANNA MACLEOD/ALASDAIR GRAHAM
2002	EILIDH NICHOLSON
2003	HANNAH MACKENZIE
2004	GINA MACLEOD
2005	CHARLES MACLEOD
2006	FLORA E. IMRIE
2007	RORY S. KNOTT
2008	AMANDA M. MACASKILL
2009	KAYE MACLEOD/RACHEL THOMSON
2010	ALLAN MACMILLAN
2011	CIORSTAIDH MACIVER
2012	ALEXANDER WADE
2013	ANNABEL MACLENNAN
2014	ANDREW HAY
2015	RUARI MACPHERSON
2016	GWION AP RHEINALLT
2017	HANNAH SKINNER
2018	KATHLEEN SMITH
2019	JAMIE TYLER
2020	LEWIS CUNNINGHAM
2021	EILIDH WILSON
2022	CAMERON MACKENZIE/ABHISHEK SHADAKSHARI
2023	IONA DAVIDSON

Appendix 3:

School Captains of The Nicolson Institute

(A male and female captain in every year with the exception of 2008 and 2009)

1968 MURDO MACPHAIL; ANNA I. MACLEOD
1969 MALCOLM NICOLSON; CHRISTINE MACKINNON
1970 ALASDAIR FRASER; NETTA MACIVER
1971 DONALD J. MACLEOD; SHEENA P. MACIVER
1972 HECTOR MORRISON; ERICA MACDONALD
1973 MARTIN FLETT; PEIGI M. MACARTHUR
1974 ALASDAIR MACDONALD; RUTH CARRINGTON
1975 ANGUS MACLEAN; ISABEL MACLEOD
1976 DONALD J. MURRAY; CATHERINE MACDONALD
1977 ROBERT D. MACLEOD; AGNES MACLEOD
1978 JAMES THOMSON; MARGARET LOVE
1979 MALCOLM F. MORRISON; MARY C. MACLEAN
1980 DUNCAN J.A. MACLEOD; JANET MARTIN
1981 ALASDAIR I. THOMSON; EILIDH MACLEOD
1982 ANGUS MACPHERSON; ANNE M. MACLEAN
1983 EDWARD G. SMITH; SHEILA A. MACKENZIE
1984 OMER N. AHMED; EILIDH M. MACKENZIE
1985 HARRIS CAMPBELL; MAIREAD DAWSON
1986 IAIN M. MACLAY; SAMANTHA BOLTON
1987 GEORGE M. MACLEOD; SALLY MACAULAY
1988 GORDON MURRAY; CATRIONA E. MORRISON
1989 RODNEY K. JAMIESON; MURIEL A. MACKINNON
1990 W. IAIN POPE; ANNE THOMSON
1991 D. ROSS MURRAY; FIONA A. MACKENZIE
1992 RICHARD A. EMERSON; PEIGI S. MACKAY
1993 DEREK MACKAY; JOANNA FINLAYSON
1994 MURDO A. MACLEAY; ANGELA MACLEAN
1995 WILLIAM MACAULAY; EILIDH WHITEFORD
1996 JONATHAN A.G. DAVIES; HANNAH GOLD
1997 GRAHAM MARTIN; JOANNA M. FERGUSON
1998 ALASDAIR MACDONALD; LESLEY A. ROSS
1999 THOMAS C.G. DAVIES; JOHAN W. DUNLOP
2000 ALASDAIR W.E. WHITE; ALISON H. NICHOLS
2001 NICOLAS DAVIES; ANNA REEVES
2002 SEAN STEPHEN; ALISON SMITH
2003 ANDREW MACIVER; IYEGBE IREDIA
2004 CHARLES MACLEOD; JUDITH MORRISON
2005 RICHARD MIDDLEMISS; HANNAH SMITH
2006 WILLIAM J. MACLEOD; CATRIONA J.M. REEVES
2007 ALASDAIR R. MACLEAN; ANNE R. DICKIE
2008 ESTHER SMITH; RACHEL A.M. THOMSON
2009 ALASDAIR GILLIES; CHARLES MORRISON
2010 JAMES THOMSON; CHRISTINA L. MACLEOD
2011 DOMHNALL BARDEN; RHODA MACLENNAN

2012 ALASDAIR C. MACLEOD; ANNABEL MACLENNAN
2013 PETER McNEILL; GEMMA MACDONALD
2014 TEARLACH BARDEN; ELEANOR SMITH
2015 LEWIS MACMILLAN; MEGAN DAVIES
2016 HARAN RABE; HANNAH SKINNER
2017 ANIL THAPA; CAITLIN MACKENZIE
2018 JOHN ALASDAIR BAIN; ANNIE BARBER
2019 DANIEL MACDONALD; JOHANNA McCARTHY
2020 CAILEAN MACLEOD; JULIET McKENZIE
2021 TAM DUDLEY; KATE MACMILLAN
2022 GREGOR MOFFAT; MOLLY MACDONALD
2023 THOMAS DAVIS; DULCIE FRASER-MACDONALD

Appendix 4:

A History of the Hostels

In 1917, the Carnegie UK Trust proposed to build two school hostels, one for boys, one for girls.[i] The former Imperial Hotel on South Beach Street opened as a hostel *'for 50 female scholars'* in 1922.

The Stornoway Historical Society carried out extensive research on this subject a number of years ago. The findings were drawn together by Anna Tucker and published in 2016. Anna was a major contributor to the research. A summary follows:

In October 1922, the Carnegie Trust handed over to the education authority a former hotel in Stornoway which they had purchased, adapted, and equipped as a school hostel for 50 girls and resident staff - the Louise Carnegie Hostel.[ii] A point of interest in the founding of this hostel is that it was intended to assist in ensuring continuance of the supply of teachers to the schools of Lewis. This is shown by the following excerpt from the Deed of Disposition in 1922, which states that the Trust:

> *resolved to establish a hostel in Stornoway for the accommodation of 50 female scholars and students and especially of such of said scholars and students as proposed to become teachers in the public schools in the county.*[iii]

The Louise Carnegie Hostel (1922 to 1972) was bought initially to provide 50 beds for girl pupils of The Nicolson Institute. The Imperial Hotel on the corner of South Beach and Kenneth Street had closed for business in 1921. The building was considered very suitable for use as a hostel and was bought by the UK Carnegie Trust on behalf of the Education Authority. After closure as a hostel in 1972, the building served as the HQ of the Education Department until the new Council HQ on Sandwick Road was established in 1979.

The Elizabeth Haldane Hostel[iv] (1928 to 1988) was built initially to accommodate boy pupils of The Nicolson Institute. It opened on Church St in 1928.[v] The new structure embraced the original building on the site, known as 'The Cottage'. Earlier residents at The Cottage included Dr Amy Weir Macdonald, Stornoway's first woman doctor and daughter of James Galloway Weir who was MP for Ross & Cromarty from 1892 to 1910. Sir James and Lady Matheson stayed at The Cottage for a short time during the construction period of Lews Castle. In 1967 the original Elizabeth Haldane/Cottage building was demolished and a new 3-storey hostel bearing the same name was built on the same site.

The Gibson Hostel (1954 to 1985) housed boy pupils who were moved from the Elizabeth Haldane. The E.H. then became the home of first and second year girls who would move to the Louise Carnegie on third year. When the Gibson Hostel closed in 1985, the building became the TVEI Centre, with a training restaurant, a hairdressing training studio, and a film editing studio. Facilities were shared between The Nicolson Institute and Lews Castle School (which had come into existence in 1976 when the new Lews Castle College buildings were commissioned). Due to dangerous structural defects in the Castle building, the Lews Castle School was totally relocated to the Gibson building from August 1988, where it remained until the school closed as an educational entity in 2002.

The Macrae Hostel (1969 to 1995) opened in 1969 on Torquil Terrace; this was to be the last of the four hostels serving The Nicolson Institute. By the mid-1990s, only a small number of pupils from Ness, South Lochs and Uig were resident in hostel accommodation. Even with just one hostel remaining in Stornoway in the 1990s, there was substantial surplus capacity and the Macrae became financially non-viable, closing its doors in 1995. The building lay vacant for a couple of years before being completely destroyed by fire on a Saturday night, a very ignominious end to the history of school hostels in Stornoway.

It should not be forgotten that Lews Castle College had a functioning hostel within its precincts, operational from 1953 to about 1983. Miss Margaret Hood Macleod ('Big Maggie'), a Glasgow lady of Lewis parentage, was Matron of that hostel for many years.

Hostel: Dolina Maclennan *(circa 1951)*
Going to Planasker School (which closed in 1973) she had tuition in both English and Gaelic. Passing the 'qualifying exam', she progressed to The Nicolson Institute in Stornoway. That was a two and a half hour bus journey from her home so she lived away from home, in lodgings in 1950 for her first year (listening to the *Tennessee Waltz and Your Cheatin'Heart* at a travelling fair). She stayed at the Louise Carnegie Hostel for girls after First Year. Girls from the districts of Uig and Lochs got home once a term, the rest residing in the hostel only Monday to Friday.

"The regime was tremendously strict," she said.

Each weekday evening, they had to be indoors from 7.30 pm with a study period until 9 pm. Lights went out at 10.30 pm.

The weekend regime for the minority who did not go home was, by contrast, lighter. She records midnight feasts, although Sunday saw two church attendances, albeit with woodland walks in the afternoon.

Hostel: Anon. *(circa 1959)*
I learned three lessons in the Gibson Hostel:
How to smoke;
How to gamble; and
How to drink alcohol.
It took me some time to unlearn these lessons.
(Note: this story is hotly contested by a near contemporary resident of the same hostel.)

Elizabeth Haldane Hostel and the Louise Carnegie Hostel: Annie MacSween *(1960s)*
I passed the qualifying exam in the spring of 1962 while suffering from mumps! I was the older of two sisters and throughout my early years I thought my parents loved my younger sister more than me because they did not banish her to Stornoway to be educated. She was allowed to go to Lionel Junior Secondary School!

At that time the first and second year girls from Ness, Barvas, Shawbost, Carloway, Uig, Bernera and South Lochs were boarders in the Elizabeth Haldane Hostel on Church Street. I was in Dorm. 1 on the ground floor and next to me was the late Normanna Gunn who had been on my class in Cross Primary. There were 6 of us in that dorm. At the beginning of the term the first years had to undergo a kind of baptismal ceremony when nicknames were given to the first years by the second years. A horrible experience!

At that time the resident teacher in the hostel was Miss Gertrude Black 'Gerty' who was an Aberdonian and a science teacher in the school. The Matron was Janet Cowie from Stornoway. They both ruled with a rod of iron and saw themselves very much as being 'in loco parentis'.[145] Every evening the girls had to be back in the hostel for studies and a teacher was present overseeing matters. I am not sure if the hour and a half of studies were used for the studying of school subjects by all those who were there!

By the early 60s, bus services had improved and the hostel girls were allowed home most weekends. This had not been the case for girls who had been in the hostel before then. On Monday mornings I had to walk to the main road in North Dell at 6 a.m. to catch the school bus. This was because some teachers who were living in Stornoway at weekends had to take the return bus to be in their classrooms for 9 a.m. I suffered from travel sickness many a time and Mondays were not pleasant. On a few occasions – usually when there was snow on the ground the Ness girls stayed in the hostel over the weekend. We had to attend church on the

---

145 Slightly begging the question of what 'in loco parentis' means.

Sunday and most of us chose to attend St Columba's Church which was next door – and the services were shorter.

During my second year in the hostel, I was upstairs in a dorm with girls from Gravir. On Wednesdays we had a dorm inspection after school, and I had to ensure that the dorm was clean and tidy. To this day some of them remind me that I used to say to them, "Poilisigibh sin gus am bàsaich sibh!" - Polish that till you die!

After a few months I was transferred to the Louise Carnegie Hostel on South Beach – where An Lanntair is today.

Hostel: D.S. Murray *(circa 1970)*
They wouldn't get off with it nowadays.

Our arrival at the Gibson Hostel at the age of eleven or twelve occurred the afternoon before term began. Only a few words were exchanged between the matron and our parents before the latter left us on our own – often for the first time – and journeyed home again. We then made our way to the dining room to be greeted by the senior pupils.

"They're tiny," they guffawed when they saw us. "We were never as small as that."

Remarkable conversations occurred, too, in the rooms where we were meant to sleep. Among the eight boys congregating in our dorm that year, seven were from Ness. One can only wonder what the poor soul from Bernera thought as he lay there, listening to all that strange talk of Skigersta and Eoropie circling his ears.

The strangeness continued over the next few years. The long hours 'studying'. The wielding of the belt. (Between school and hostel, one of my classmates received thirty-six strikes one day.) The bullying of some senior boys who acquainted us each night with the soles of their slippers. The days when we were "grounded" inside the building's doors. There was even the moment we were "baptised" once again, our bodies raised and lowered into baths brimming with water.

"Your name is now Rufus … Bisto … Dokus…" the older boys would declare. "What is it?"

"Rufus … Bisto … Dokus…" their victim would answer the moment water drained from his ears.

"Good! Remember you now answer to that name!"

Yet, somehow, we survived. Indeed, we thrived upon our friendship. The hour even came when the Bernera boy in our midst understood what the Niseachs around him were talking about when they mentioned Fivepenny or Adabrock.

The most astonishing miracle of all had clearly occurred.

Hostel: Anon. *(circa 2000)*
I stayed at the Macrae Hostel in Stornoway (Monday to Friday) for my 3rd and 4th years only. It was not compulsory for students to stay at a hostel. When I moved into 5th year, a friend and I decided to travel from home each day rather than stay in the hostel in Stornoway. This involved travelling by bus, leaving home at 7.30 and returning around 5pm. A long day.

The fact that I had experience of hostel life meant that, when I eventually left for university, staying away from home was not a big deal.

Appendix 5:

Junior Comprehensive Schools, 1972

The idea of two P1-S2 comprehensive schools at Lionel and Shawbost was that of the Ross and Cromarty Director of Education, Robert Inglis, with five out of eight parental meetings allegedly approving them, albeit not always with formal voting. Later another three schools (Back, Leurbost and Bayble) joined the scheme. In 1973, the then Rector of The Nicolson Institute, as we have seen in Chapter 12, described this development with some approval.

The church was a factor in approval. At some consultative meetings with parents, only the local minister spoke.

Was potential pressure on N.I. accommodation, especially with the prospect of raising of the school leaving age in 1973-74, a factor? This was a special worry for Nicolson staff and management, and then the Ross & Cromarty Education Committee. Unlike today, the then Scottish Education Dept (SED) controlled capital expenditure on building expansion.

In early 1972, Iain Smith surveyed all the West Side parents with a child in P7 asking:

What are your priorities in terms of what your children might get out of secondary education?

The resulting parental educational priorities were: 1) moral training; 2) education for advancement in life; and 3) education geared to the local environment. This third priority was limited.

Parents were also asked: which of the following would you prefer for your child?

1. To go to Shawbost/Lionel for all secondary schooling?
2. To go to Shawbost/Lionel for two years and then to The Nicolson Institute?
3. To go to The Nicolson Institute for all secondary schooling?

Analysed village by village, this was the picture.

Village	Option 1	Option 2	Option 3
Lionel	6	5	0
Cross	1	2	0
Galson	1	2	1
Airidhantuim	3	5	1
Barvas	0	1	8
Bragar	1	2	4
Shawbost	1	4	1
Carloway	0	4	6
TOTALS	13	25	21

Notes:

Three villages, Carloway, Bragar (narrowly) and Barvas favoured centralisation of secondary education at The Nicolson Institute. Barvas was a rather special case in the sense that it was the only Western Lewis village where all S1 pupils already (in 1971-2) went at 12+ to the N.I. From 1972-3 onwards, Option 2 became the default.

Ness parents favoured more than 2 years of local secondary education in Lionel *(and was the only Lewis community with some tradition of refusal of post-'qualifying exam' offers of an academic place in The Nicolson Institute)*.

Appendix 6:

The Original Pupils of The Nicolson Institute, 27ᵗʰ February 1873

Name	Parent or Guardian	Address
James Macdonald	Donald	Newton
Angus Macdonald	Donald	Newton
Christina Macdonald	Donald	Newton
Jessie Macdonald	Donald	Newton
Roderick Mackenzie	Mrs. Mackenzie	Kenneth Street
William Stewart	John	Keith Street
Murdo Maclean	Roderick	Keith Street
John Maclean	Roderick	Keith Street
William Clarke	Donald	Cromwell Street
Gavin Fowlie	Gavin	Manor Farm
John Fowlie	Gavin	Manor Farm
Donald Fowlie	Gavin	Manor Farm
Peter Fowlie	Gavin	Manor Farm
Donald Chisholm	John	Cromwell Street
Ronald Macleod	Roderick	North Beach Street
John Macleod	Roderick	North Beach Street
Christina Macleod	Roderick	North Beach Street
Donald Macdonald	Donald	Church Street
Mary Macdonald	Donald	Church Street
John Mackenzie	Donald	Bayhead Street
Donald Macinnes	Donald	Keith Street
Alexander Mackenzie	William	Keith Street
John Mackenzie	William	Keith Street
David Smith	John	Castle Gardens
John Maclennan	John	Bayhead Street
Alexander Maclennan	John	Bayhead Street
Duncan Maciver	Norman	Bayhead Street
Daniel Mackenzie	Mackenzie	South Beach Street
Donald Macleod	William	Keith Street
John Macleod	William	Keith Street
Daniel Macrae	Macrae	Keith Street
John Macrae	Macrae	Keith Street
Murdo Mackenzie	Donald	Keith Street
Colin Macdonald	Macdonald	Bayhead Street
Aulay Macdonald	Macdonald	Bayhead Street
John Morrison	Donald	Kenneth Street
John Macleod	William	Bayhead Street
William Macleod	William	Bayhead Street

Malcolm Kerr	Donald	Keith Street
Frank Watt	George	Moss End
Jane Watt	George	Moss End
Peter Watt	George	Moss End
Donald Ferguson	William	Point Street
Daniel Macdonald	Murdo	Cromwell Street
Edward Macdonald	Murdo	Cromwell Street
Kenneth Macdonald	Murdo	Cromwell Street
Murdo Macdonald	Murdo	Cromwell Street
Duncan Macdonald	Murdo	Cromwell Street
Roderick Macleod	Murdo	New Street
Donald Macleod	Murdo	New Street
Andrew Rose	Walter	North Beach Street
David Rose	Walter	North Beach Street
John Murray	William	Point Street
Norman Macleod	Mrs. Macleod	Keith Street
William Chapman	Donald	Bayhead Street
Robert Russell	Mathew	Point Street
Georgina Russell	Mathew	Point Street
Mary A. Russell	Mathew	Point Street
William Henderson	Donald	Bayhead Street
Isabella Henderson	Donald	Bayhead Street
George Young	George	Sandwick
Helen Young	George	Sandwick
Maggie Young	George	Sandwick
John Craig	William	Temperance Hotel
Alexander Mackenzie	Murdo	Bayhead Street
James Maclean	Donald	Keith Street
Alexander Maclean	Donald	Keith Street
Marjory Campbell	Mrs. Campbell	Point Street
Isabella Campbell	Mrs. Campbell	Point Street
Mary Robertson	William	Kenneth Street
Cath J. Macgilvray	John	Cromwell Street
Isabella Macgilvray	John	Cromwell Street
Elizabeth Macgilvray	John	Cromwell Street
Neil Munro	William	Cromwell Street
William Hughes	Hughes	Keith Street
Donald Macleod	Mrs. Macleod	Keith Street
James Macritchie	Peter	Keith Street
Alexander Robertson	Mrs. Robertson	Francis Street
Malvina Robertson	Mrs. Robertson	Francis Street
Maggie Robertson	Mrs. Robertson	Francis Street
Robert Mackenzie	George	Church Street
James D. Mackenzie	George	Church Street

George Hunter	John	Coll
William Hunter	John	Coll
John Macrae	Murdo	Point Street
Catherine McNeill	MacNeill	Newton
Mary McNeill	MacNeill	Newton
Evan Macleod	Mrs. Macleod	Keith Street
Houston Mackenzie	Mrs. Mackenzie	Kenneth Street
William Mackenzie	Mrs. Mackenzie	Kenneth Street
Murdo Macaulay	Donald	Point Street
Donald Matheson	Donald	Bayhead Street
Murdo Maclean	John	Keith Street
John Matheson	Donald	Bayhead Street
Donald Macleod	Donald	Keith Street
Jane Campbell	Roderick	Bayhead Street
Alexander E. Campbell	Roderick	Bayhead Street
John A. Macaskill	Donald	Bayhead Street
Donald Macaskill	Donald	Bayhead Street
William Mackenzie	Mackenzie	Bayhead Street
Donald Macdonald	Colin	Bayhead Street
Kenneth Jones	Jones	Francis Street
Duncan Maciver	Norman	Bayhead Street
Hugh B. Murray	Allan	Newton Street
Donald Macpherson	Donald	Bayhead Street

Appendix 7:

Vignettes

A collection of pen pictures of some notable alumni is available online as a companion piece to this book:

https://www.outerhebridesheritage.org.uk/discover/the-nicolson-institute-vignettes/

It would be impossible to include every former pupil of The Nicolson Institute who has gone on to contribute to the wider world or to have an impact on the school itself. The list is not an exhaustive one and can be seen as a work in progress, giving a flavour of the undoubted impact that the alumni of this island school have had, and continue to have, far beyond their native shores, and in many diverse fields.

Religion and Theology

Alexander Macdonald of Swordale: missionary in Zambia; married to the granddaughter of David Livingstone; one of the earliest secondary pupils and graduates; possibly supported by the Carnegie Trust; *attended The Nicolson Institute from 1892-93;*

Professor Donald MacKenzie of Aird: Professor of Biblical Theology at Princeton University and benefactor to the school; student in the Universities of Aberdeen, Halle and Berlin; ordained in 1910; army chaplain in the First World War; *School Dux in 1900;*

Professor John MacLeod of Aird: Church of Scotland minister and theologian in Toronto, Nova Scotia and Aberdeen University; graduated from University of Glasgow in 1914; studied for the ministry and was ordained; *attended The Nicolson Institute from 1907-1910.*

Politics

Roderick Smith of Stornoway: pharmacist and local politician; twice Provost of Stornoway; fought to ensure The Nicolson Bequests remained true to their original purposes; granted Freedom of the Burgh in 1961; *left The Nicolson Institute in 1886;*

Donald J. Stewart MP PC of Stornoway: local and national politician; Stornoway Town Councillor and Provost; elected to Westminster as sole SNP MP in 1970; awarded Freedom of the Western Isles; *attended The Nicolson Institute from 1931-1936;*

Sandy Matheson CVO, OBE, JP of Stornoway: pharmacist and local politician; last Provost of Stornoway and Convener of the Western Isles Islands Council from 1982-1990; Lord Lieutenant of the Western Isles; made a Freeman of the Western Isles in 2023; *attended The Nicolson Institute from 1952-58.*

Academia

Professor Robert M. Maciver of Stornoway: sociologist and author; lecturer in Aberdeen, Toronto and Columbia Universities; President of the American Sociological Association; one of first two pupils to gain direct entry to university from the school; *School Dux in 1897;*

Professor Norman Grassie FRSE of Aberdeen and Stornoway: internationally renowned polymer scientist and writer; Professor of Macromolecular Chemistry at Glasgow University; Fellow of the Royal Society of Edinburgh; *completed his secondary education at The Nicolson Institute; School Dux in 1941;*

Alasdair Smith of Ness: mathematician and economist; lecturer at Oxford University, the London School of Economics and Sussex University; Vice-Chancellor of the University of Sussex; Chair of the Armed Forces Pay Review Body and Vice Chair of the Competition Commission; *member of the Scottish Fiscal Commission; School Dux in 1965;*

Professor Tom Strachan FRSE of Stornoway: pioneering geneticist and writer; co-author of influential publications in human molecular genetics research; played a key role in establishing the Institute of Human Genetics at Newcastle University; *Joint Dux of the school in 1969.*

Education

Hector Maciver of Shawbost: teacher, writer, broadcaster and critic; Head of English at the Royal High School, Edinburgh; member of literary circle; *attended The Nicolson Institute from 1922-28;*

Professor Matthew M. Maciver CBE FEIS of Portnaguran: eminent Gael and educationalist; Rector of Fortrose Academy and the Royal High School of Edinburgh; Chief Executive of the General Teaching Council for Scotland; Chair of the Gaelic Broadcasting Committee; Chair of the Board of the UHI; *attended The Nicolson Institute from 1958-64;*

Angus Nicolson of Borve and Stornoway: Geography teacher and chronicler of The Nicolson Institute centenary; Royal Navy coder in World War 2; semi-professional footballer; *attended The Nicolson Institute in the 1920s.*

Literature

John Munro of Aignish: poet in English and Gaelic; winner of Mr. Gibson's inaugural school poetry competition; killed in action in France on 16th April 1918; *attended The Nicolson Institute from 1908-11; School Dux in 1911;*

Professor Derick Thomson of Bayble: scholar, publisher, editor and major Scottish poet; lecturer in Edinburgh, Glasgow and Aberdeen Universities; Professor of Celtic at the University of Glasgow; Founder of Gairm; Fellow of the Royal Society of Edinburgh and the British Academy; *School Dux in 1939;*

Iain Crichton Smith of Bayble: acclaimed poet in both English and Gaelic, novelist and essayist; English teacher in Oban High School until 1977 when he became a full-time writer; Consider the Lilies was published in 1968; created OBE in 1980 for services to literature; *attended The Nicolson Institute in the 1940s, described evocatively in* The Last Summer.

Art

Donald Smith of Newvalley, Balmedie and Bragar: artist and teacher; a graduate of Gray's School of Art, Aberdeen, following National Service; teacher in Aberdeen Grammar School, Summerhill School, and rural Lewis schools; painter of landscape and portrait, in watercolour, ink and oils; paintings feature in public and private collections; *attended The Nicolson Institute during the Second World War.*

Performing Arts

Duncan M. Morison MBE of Stornoway and Ness: pianist, composer and Freeman of the Western Isles; composer of Island Moon and arranger of traditional airs; concert pianist who enjoyed the patronage of members of the aristocracy; visiting Music and singing teacher in Lewis schools until his retirement; *attended The Nicolson Institute from 1917.*

Dolina Maclennann of Marvig: singer, actress and storyteller; Gaelic singer who pioneered its inclusion in the mainstream folk revival; performer of poetry and in television, for which she also wrote; played significant role in 7:84's ground-breaking production The Cheviot, the Stag and the Black, Black Oil; *attended The Nicolson Institute from 1950, staying in lodgings and in the Louise Carnegie Hostel for Girls.*

Sport

Alasdair Morrison of Lochs: goalkeeper in outstanding school football team which won the senior league title on two occasions, when the school competed against men's teams; represented the Scottish Amateur League against Wales and Ireland and played against future 'Lisbon Lions' on a number of occasions; a professional player for Morton and Ross County; Principal Teacher of PE at Fortrose Academy; *attended The Nicolson Institute from 1951-57.*

Merchant Navy

Donald Maclean of Stornoway: Commodore of the Cunard Fleet; as a schoolboy, joined the Stornoway Sea Cadets led by Canon Meaden; began an apprenticeship with Cunard in 1917; Senior Second Officer of the Queen Mary; senior Royal Naval Reserve officer during World War Two; Chief Officer of the Queen Elizabeth; awarded Freedom of the Burgh of Stornoway; *attended The Nicolson Institute in the second decade of the 20th century.*

Journalism and Broadcasting

William, Joanna and James Shaw Grant of Stornoway: founders, editors and proprietors of The Stornoway Gazette; William Grant and his wife Johanna were founders and proprietors of the paper; both taught in The Nicolson Institute at different times; their younger son, James, became editor on his father's death in 1932, shortly after graduating from the University of Glasgow; Chair of the Crofters Commission; Chair of the Harris Tweed Association; Joanna Morrison attended The Nicolson Institute in the mid-1890s and was the first pupil of the school to take the Leaving Certificate in English at the honours grade; *James Shaw Grant was the School Dux in 1928;*

Angus Macleod of Plasterfield: award-winning journalist; Scottish political correspondent with The Sunday Mail; political editor with The Scottish Daily Express and The Scottish edition of The Times; Scottish editor of The Times; known for his distinctive radio voice as a newspaper reviewer and political commentator; *attended The Nicolson Institute from 1963-69;*

Cathy Macdonald of Bernera: broadcaster, especially in Gaelic TV; presenter of Royal National Mod coverage; radio presenter; fronted BBC Reporting Scotland; established own production company; Chairperson of Pròiseact nan Ealan; *attended The Nicolson Institute in the 1970s;*

Maggie Cunningham of Scalpay: broadcaster and Head of Radio Scotland; first pupil from Scalpay to attend The Nicolson Institute; teacher in Tiree; founding member of Radio nan Gaidheal in 1979; Editor of Radio nan Gaidheal and Manager of BBC Highland; Corporate Secretary of BBC Scotland; Head of Radio Scotland; Joint Head of Programmes and Services, BBC Scotland (with Donalda MacKinnon); founding member of Sistema Scotland; President, An Comunn Gaidhealeach; *attended The Nicolson Institute from August 1971.*

Endnotes

Chapter 1: How It All Began
i   From a retrieved manuscript written by the late Angus Nicolson. Courtesy of his son Professor Malcolm Nicolson.
ii   See p151 MacDonald, D. (1978). *Lewis: A History of the Island*. Gordon Wright Publishing. Edinburgh
iii   *Back in the Day*. March 2019 pp18-19
iv   For a somewhat less benign view of this, see pp321-322 Devine, T. (2018). *The Scottish Clearances: A History of the Dispossessed*. Allen Lane. And p199 Hunter, J. (2019). *Insurrection: Scotland's Famine Winter*. Birlinn

Chapter 2: The Nicolson Family Legacy
i   Another remarkable example of a 19th century boy from a prosperous mercantile background achieving further elevation in life. See pp169-170, Smith, I. with Forrest, J. (2017). *Saints and Sinners: Tales of Lewis Lives*. Acair

Chapter 3: The Nicolson Institution
i   Chapter 6. Hunt, T. (2014). *10 Cities that Made an Empire*. London
ii   p149-161 Rosie, G. (2004). *Curious Scotland: Tales from a Hidden History*. London
iii   p226 Hunt, T. (2014). *10 cities that made an Empire*. London. A view of Matheson by Brian Wilson in *The Scotsman* of 13 June 2020 is not favourable.
iv   pp236-238 Bunting, M. (2016). *Love of Country*. Edinburgh
v   pp260-267 Bone, T.R. (1968). *School Inspection in Scotland 1840-1966*. Edinburgh
vi   Bone, T.R. (1968). *School Inspection in Scotland 1840-1966*. Edinburgh
vii   For similar stories in a contemporary island elementary school see pp82-87 Riley, A.K. (2020). *Canna Schooldays*. Stornoway
viii   This, in the 1973 school magazine, is an edited extract from p18 Maciver, R.M. (1968). *As a Tale that is Told*. Chicago

Chapter 4: Developing Secondary Education
i   p211 Anderson, R.D. in Bryce, T.G.K. and Humes, W.M. (Eds) (2008). *Scottish Education* (3rd ed.). Edinburgh
ii   An excellent, if very dense, discussion of these issues can be found in the definitive Anderson, R.D. (1983). *Education and Opportunity in Victorian Scotland: Schools and Universities*. Oxford. Clarendon Press
iii   p123 Bone, T.R. (1968). *School Inspection in Scotland 1840-1966*. Edinburgh. Indeed, Professor Bone points to a third category i.e. 14 pre-existing higher/endowed schools (e.g. the High School of Glasgow and Paisley Grammar School) had come under school board control in 1872.
iv   *Back in the Day* July 2018
v   See Roxburgh, J.M. (1971). *The School Board of Glasgow 1873-1919*. London
vi   (SSB) = Minutes of Stornoway School Board
vii   Minutes of Board (SSB)
viii   Log of Nicolson Institute (LNI)
ix   p164 Dobie T. in Bone, T.R. (Ed) (1967). *Studies in Scottish Education 1872-1939*. Edinburgh
x   SSB

xi	p124 Bone, T.R. (1968). *School Inspection in Scotland 1840-1966*. Edinburgh
xii	The first Secretary of the newly created Scotch Education Department i.e. its top civil servant. (1885-1904) and an alumnus of the High School of Glasgow. See p120 Lockhart, B.R.W. (2010). *The Town School: A History of the High School of Glasgow*. Edinburgh

Chapter 5: Under the Guidance of W.J. Gibson

i	pp17-18 Maciver, R.M. (1968). *As a Tale That Is Told*. Chicago
ii	p19 Maciver, R.M. (1968). *As a Tale That Is Told*. Chicago
iii	pp157-8 Macdonald, D. (1978). *Lewis: A History of the Island*. Edinburgh
iv	Probably by J.L. Robertson
v	See also p8 Secondary Department 1897-98. Nicolson Public School
vi	LNI
vii	LNI
viii	LNI
ix	LNI
x	See also p8 Secondary Department 1897-98. Nicolson Public School
xi	1897 Nicolson Public School Log
xii	p156 Dobie, T. in Bone, T.R. (Ed.) (1967). *Studies in Scottish Education 1872-1939*. Edinburgh
xiii	see SSB minute of 10 December 1894
xiv	1897-1898 Nicolson Public School Report
xv	p13 The Nicolson Institute Annual No 22. 1944
xvi	MacIver, R.M. (1968). *As a Tale that is Told: The Autobiography of R.M. MacIver*. Chicago and London
xvii	pp6-7 1973. The Nicolson Institute Centenary School Magazine. Stornoway
xviii	The Glasgow Exhibition albums are part of The Nicolson Institute archives at Tasglann nan Eilean. (Ref No GB3002 RC4/38/4)

Chapter 6: Into the 20th Century

i	Logbook of The Nicolson Institute
ii	http://www.gov.scot/Resource/Doc/82254/0115599.pdf
iii	https://www.carnegie-trust.org/about-us/our-history/
iv	p288 Anderson, R.D. (1983). *Education & Opportunity in Victorian Scotland*. Edinburgh
v	p132 Anderson, R.D. et al. (2003). *The University of Edinburgh: An illustrated history*. Edinburgh
vi	p6 1999. The Nicolson Institute 125th Anniversary Magazine. Stornoway
vii	"The efforts of the well qualified teacher at Carloway.... were directed towards securing bursaries so that his pupils could attend the secondary school at Stornoway." Paterson, K.N. in *Stornoway Gazette* 23 Sept 1972
viii	p3 1973 The Nicolson Institute Centenary School Magazine. Stornoway
ix	p46 Smith, C. (2001). *Around the Peat-Fire*. Edinburgh
x	Subsequently reproduced in *Stornoway Gazette*. Jan 17 2019
xi	p138 Cruickshank, M. (1970). *History of the Training of Teachers in Scotland*. Edinburgh
xii	http://www.stornowayhistoricalsociety.org.uk/the-nicolson-institute.html
xiii	Information courtesy of Iain Gordon Macdonald and of Ruairidh Maciver; also, p6 The Nicolson Institute Annual 1930; p24 The Nicolson Institute Annual No 23 1945; and p25 The Nicolson Institute Annual 1963
xiv	The primary data from here on are from annual Nicolson Institute school reports or (the somewhat intermittently published) Nicolson Institute school magazines, rather than from Parish Board minutes or the school log.

xv	There are photographs in the Gibson Collection (held by Tasglann nan Eilean) of pupils doing activities including bee keeping.
xvi	Comment in 1973 The Nicolson Institute Centenary School Magazine, Stornoway
xvii	A copy of the booklet is in the Gibson archives of the Tasglann nan Eilean. It is dedicated to "The critic on the hearth" i.e., Mrs Gibson. The literary allusion is interesting if, in the 21st century, a little obscure.
xviii	See Campbell, J. (2020). *Haldane: The Forgotten Statesman who Shaped Modern Britain* London
xix	On-line Hansard. House of Lords 1916

Chapter 7: The Great War Years

i	Letter excerpts from the William John Gibson collection held by Tasglann nan Eilean (1992.50). Transcripts by Ceitidh Chalmers, Dawn MacDonald, Vivienne Parish, Barry Shelby, Lorraine Shewan, Margaret Smith and Hazel Tocock; excerpts selected, and footnotes annotated by Iain Smith; proofreading by Seonaid McDonald and Ken Galloway; sub-editing by Joan Forrest. Additional material by Ken Galloway.
ii	p12 The Nicolson Institute Annual No 5 1917 (Ref No GB3002 RC4/38/9)
iii	The archived letters are part of the W.J. Gibson Collection. (1992.50.70 (1)-(47)
iv	Comment in *Sgàthan* 1973 Centenary school magazine. (Ref No GB3002 RC4/38/9)
v	p1 The Nicolson Institute Annual No 4 1916 (Ref No GB3002 RC4/38/9)
vi	http://www.adb422006.com/ROH/index.html
vii	The *Loyal Lewis Roll of Honour* provides a detailed list of the Armed Forces and the range of Battalions/Companies. They include: The Royal Navy; Royal Navy Reserve; Seaforth Highlanders; Gordon Highlanders; Cameron Highlanders; Ross Mountain Battery; Also those from Lewis who served from Canada and elsewhere.
viii	Bank of England inflation calculator

Chapter 8: The Final Gibson Years

i	The definitive work on this for many years was accepted as Nicolson, N. (1960). *Lord of the Isles*. Stornoway (op cit). Today it is Hutchinson, R. (2003). *The Soap Man*. Edinburgh. A good summary of it is found in pp238-242 Bunting, M. (2016). *Love of Country*. Edinburgh. Of some historic interest is a book by Lord Leverhulme's niece E. Macdonald, *20 Years of Hebridean Memories*.
ii	An issue that exercised Lord Leverhulme. See pp121,130-131, Hutchinson, R. (2003). *The Soap Man*. Edinburgh
iii	As reported in *Sgàthan*, the Nicolson Institute Centenary school magazine
iv	Tasglann nan Eilean GB3002 RC7 Dr J.L. Robertson Bequest
v	*Loyal Lewis Roll of Honour*. See https://digital.nls.uk/rolls-of-honour/archive/100229276
vi	*Loyal Lewis Roll of Honour*. See http://digital.nls.uk/rolls-of-honour/archive/100231628
vii	Information from a variety of sources, including Iain G. Macdonald and Donnie Macdonald.
viii	As Mrs Gibson informed her daughter.
ix	K.N. Paterson, reported in *Stornoway Gazette* January 17th 2019
x	Archives of the UK Carnegie Trust
xi	The Year of Homecoming took place in 2023 to commemorate the centenary of the departure of the emigrant ships of 1923. *Sy Gone By*. Summer/Autumn 2022. Stornoway Historical Society Journal.
xii	Hebridean Connections website records: on Saturday 21 April 1923, The *Metagama* sailed from Stornoway with 300 young Lewis emigrants on board, all but 20 of them young men, with an average age of 22.

xiii	See also pp228-235 Bunting, M. (2016). *Love of Country*. Edinburgh
xiv	About this time, Leverhulme's plans were getting into serious difficulties, notably with some people from the district of Back. See p153 Hutchinson, R. (2003). *The Soap Man*. Edinburgh
xv	See p173 and preceding pages in Hutchinson, R. (2003). *The Soap Man*. Edinburgh
xvi	'The demand for and the price of fish was plummeting' p155 Hutchinson, R. (2003). *The Soap Man*. Edinburgh
xvii	Probably father of Professor R.M. Maciver; and founder in the previous decade of Maciver's Garage which traded in Ford cars. See p70 MacIver, R.M. (1968). *As a Tale that is Told*: The Autobiography of R.M. MacIver. Chicago
xviii	pp16-17 *Sgàthan* 1973 Nicolson Institute Centenary school magazine
xix	Gibson, W.J. (1925). *A Record of the School*. From W.J. Gibson Collection. 1992.50.6. Tasglann nan Eilean
xx	Edited from a manuscript by the late Angus Nicolson working with a team of N.I. school student researchers; and featured in *Sgàthan,* the 1973 Centenary School magazine

Chapter 9: Into the 1930s

i	This section on Macrae, adapted from the 1973 Centenary School Magazine, originally written by Angus Nicolson
ii	p51 The Nicolson Institute Annual No 24 1946
iii	p10 The Nicolson Institute Annual No 28 1954
iv	The Hebridean Connections website records, 'TB Macaulay was born in Canada, 8th in line from Domhnall Cam, the chief of the Macaulays in Uig' https://www.hebrideanconnections.com/people
v	Wrote Angus Nicolson in the 1970s. A slight misquotation.
vi	p3 The Nicolson Institute Annual No 8 1930
vii	Mackenzie, W.C. (1932). *The Western Isles: Their History, Traditions and Place-Names*. Paisley
viii	A claim often made; but quite hard to prove. The losses were undoubtably grievous. See p64 Hutchinson, R. (2003). *The Soap Man*. Edinburgh
ix	Note courtesy of Kate Adams.
x	In the early 1970s.
xi	p22 The Nicolson Institute Annual No 15 1937

Chapter 10: The Nicolson, World War II and its Aftermath

i	Replaced, in 1962, by the Scottish Certificate of Education. The 'group' requirement for a minimum number of passes had been abolished in 1950
ii	pp1-3 The Nicolson Institute Annual No 22 1944
iii	pp3-4 The Nicolson Institute Annual No 22 1944

Chapter 11: Post-War Nicolson, 1945-1968

i	p5 The Nicolson Institute Annual No 25 1947
ii	p29 Wilson, W.M. Winter/Spring (2019) in *Stornoway Historical Society Journal,* Stornoway
iii	Note by Alasdair Morrison.
iv	For a very much less sanguine view, see pp14-16, Maclean, N. Winter/Spring (2019) in *Stornoway Historical Society Journal,* Stornoway
v	p16 Maclean, N. Winter/Spring (2019) in *Stornoway Historical Society Journal,* Stornoway
vi	Annie Macsween
vii	p40 The Nicolson Institute Annual No 25 1947
viii	Catriona Dunn

ix	Ken Galloway
x	p14 Maclean, N. Winter/Spring (2019) in *Stornoway Historical Society Journal*. Stornoway
xi	Alasdair Smith
xii	Malcolm Smith
xiii	p16 Maclean, N. Winter/Spring (2019) in *Stornoway Historical Society Journal*. Stornoway
xiv	p29 Wilson, W.M. Winter/Spring (2019) in *Stornoway Historical Society Journal*. Stornoway

Chapter 12: Into the 1970s and the School's Centenary

i   Former Rector of The Nicolson Institute, Dr Frances Murray, recalls her youth.
ii   Iain Smith
iii   https://www.bbc.co.uk/news/uk-scotland-39044445
iv   With thanks to Ken Galloway.
v   Catriona Dunn

Chapter 14: Into the 21st Century

i   A 2021 international report concluded that, at least from the perspective of teachers, this was a heavily bureaucratised process. See https://www.gov.scot/publications/oecd-independent-review-curriculum-excellence-2020-2021-initial-evidence-pack/

Appendix 4: A History of the Hostels

i   The Nicolson Institute Annual No 5 1917 (Ref No GB3002 RC4/38/9)
ii   Named after the wife of Andrew Carnegie. See Chapter 9
iii   K.N. Paterson, reported in *Stornoway Gazette* January 17th, 2019
iv   Named after the sister of Viscount Haldane: she had been a formidable champion of hostels for Highland schools and possessed a great intellect. See first set of photoplates in Campbell, J. (2020). *Haldane: the Forgotten Statesman who Shaped Modern Britain*. Largely home-educated, she wrote a *'Life of Descartes'* about 1905 for which the University of St Andrews awarded her an honorary LLD. She was also a Companion of Honour and the first woman JP in Scotland.
v   Archives of the UK Carnegie Trust

 Riaghladair Carthannais na h-Alba
Carthannas Clàraichte/
Registered Charity SC047866

First published in 2023 by Acair
An Tosgan, Seaforth Road, Stornoway, Isle of Lewis, Scotland HS1 2SD

www.acairbooks.com
info@acairbooks.com

All rights reserved.

Text © the authors (see Acknowledgements)

Photographs: see Acknowledgements

The right of Iain Smith and Joan Forrest to be identified as the authors of the work has been asserted by them in accordance with the Copyright, Designs and Patent Act 1988.

No part of this publication may be reproduced, stored in a retrieval system nor reproduced or transmitted by any means, electronic, mechanical, photocopying or otherwise, without the prior permission of the publisher.

Typeset and designed by Joan Macrae-Smith on behalf of Acair

A CIP catalogue record for this title is available from the British Library

Printed by Gomer Press, Llandysul, Wales

ISBN 978-1-78907-150-4